will it make a theatre

will it make a theatre

a guide to finding, renovating, financing, bringing up-to-Code, the non-traditional performance space

Compiled and written by Eldon Elder; associate writers Marsha Imhof and Sharon Lee Ryder; with drawings by Eldon Elder.

This book is made possible with public funds from the New York State Council on the Arts—Theatre Program; National Endowment for the Arts, Architecture, Planning and Design Program—Cultural Facilities Research and Design; Department of Cultural Affairs, City of New York.

This book is also made possible with funds from the Chase Manhattan Bank, The Dramatists Guild Fund, The Ford Foundation, League of New York Theatres and Producers, Morgan Guaranty Trust Company, New York Community Trust, Robert Sterling Clark Foundation, and Shubert Foundation.

Book editor: Judy Sagarin

Book design: Robert Fitzpatrick

Additional illustrations:

23, 24, 72–73: Robert Cabrera, Architect

26–27: Redrawn from a design by Peter Blake and Brian Smith, Architects

74, 75: Redrawn from a design by Christopher Hacker

76–77, 78–79: Office of John Chimera, Architect

85 (platform module models): Design conceived by Michael Fischetti and John Chimera

96: Redrawn from a design by T. Miles

97: Robert Taylor, design and draft

Copyright © 1979 by OOBA

First edition
Second printing

All rights reserved. For information address OOBA (Off Off Broadway Alliance), 162 West 56th Street, Room 206, New York, N.Y. 10019

Distributed by Drama Book Specialists (Publishers) 150 West 52nd Street, 4th Floor, New York, N.Y. 10019

ISBN: 0-933750-00-5

Library of Congress Catalog Card Number: 79-84365

about the publisher

The Off Off Broadway Alliance (OOBA) was founded in 1972 by the Off Off Broadway theatrical constituency as a central service office. The original purposes were to serve as a forum for discussion among the theatres, to help solve mutual problems of credibility and accessibility, and to serve as a public information source. The core mandate for the office was to perform those functions which would make it easier for the member theatres to achieve their artistic goals.

OOBA is now a league of not-for-profit professional developmental theatres in New York City and is dedicated to nurturing the conditions and processes which encourage the theatre artist to thrive.

Primary Activities: representation of the Off Off Broadway arena with the press, City departments, agencies, other professional theatre arenas; labor/management representation; Off Off Broadway data tracking and analysis; training in administrative and technical areas; advocacy; consultation with Off Off Broadway theatre constituents; audience development; serving as information source (including publication development).

OOBA is publishing this handbook in response to the chronic need for more effective, centralized guidance in the search for space and in bringing that space "up to Code."

—Ellen B. Rudolph, Executive Director

contents

introduction

This book addresses itself to the particular needs and problems of the small, not-for-profit theatre and other performing arts companies looking for a permanent space to turn into a theatre. Although it contains information of value to the established company planning to remodel or relocate in a new space, it is especially aimed at aiding the new company looking for a non-traditional space in which to create its first theatre.

This book will tell you where to look; what to look for; what kinds of spaces to avoid; what types of lease arrangements to negotiate; how some other groups have found and converted non-traditional performing arts spaces. It will help you assess your needs. It will not be your lawyer, architect, or consultant; but it will help you understand what is involved and how to make the best decisions. It will introduce you to agencies, City people, neighborhoods, and non-traditional buildings where innovative possibilities exist. It will help interpret the Codes for you.

Survival for the small, not-for-profit theatre depends on getting more for less—if possible for free—and it is the intention of this book to provide as many recommendations and answers to this perpetual problem as possible.

We hope it will be a humanistic handbook—practical, down-to-earth, drawing on experience of many, but tempered with the awareness that not all guidelines recommended in this book are applicable to every group's requirements, and that not all can be satisfied in the beginning.

It is intended to be a survey; and, as such, some chapters will be more informative than others to readers with different areas and levels of expertise. Once you have read the book go back and use applicable sections as a manual while planning your theatre.

While the book chooses New York City agencies and theatre organizations for its primary examples, its principles and methods for implementation apply to creating a theatre space for any small not-for-profit performance group in any city.

part one
the search for a space

1

developing guidelines

Probably no theatre has ever been created according to a set of rules, perhaps none ever will be; but there can be no doubt but that it is worth the effort to develop a set of guidelines that presents a clear image of what you are looking for in a theatre before you begin the search for space. To do this you need to first develop a sense of who you are, how you are unique, what you want to accomplish and how you intend to do it—in short, a purpose and a program.

There are many questions to ask yourself and the others who will be involved in your company. Question your purpose as it relates to space. The most unique quality that an Off Off Broadway theatre, or other small not-for-profit group, offers its audience is its commitment to a particular artistic point of view. Without defining this point of view or purpose, and translating it into space requirements, you cannot intelligently choose a space.

Define your goals: both short-term goals and long-range objectives. It is difficult, when starting out, to think beyond the immediate goal—producing a play or a season of plays—but making some projections with regard to future goals can save you from irreparable mistakes in the choice and conversion of space now.

The search for space must be constantly related to the money, materials and manpower that you have. Keep firmly in mind at all times an assessment of your potential resources. While pinpointing your artistic space needs, there must always be a parallel, hard-nosed consideration of how to pay for what you will get. For the small, not-for-profit theatre there are three types of potential resources: money, materials and sweat. You will need to assess your potential in all three areas. More imaginative solutions are possible when all three resources are combined.

In all this beginning planning and deliberation it is good to know that theatre people love to talk about what they are doing and what they have done. They are generous with help, advice, tips on dos and don'ts, and can provide a compatriot's comfort when you most need it. Off Off Broadway producers, artistic directors, designers, and technicians are exceedingly accessible to anyone who is serious; so talk to them.

• Commence by articulating an artistic purpose. This should be a clearly focused statement of what you are about. This artistic purpose, once stated—as a manifesto if you like—is the heart of your program.

• Follow the statement of purpose with a summary of your goals. Ask yourself: What kind of plays do you want to present? What kind of audience do you hope to present them to? Where do you hope to be in three years time? What do you expect to have accomplished? What future goals have you set for yourself?

• Make an assessment of your space needs. In order to do this, the first, most obvious, question is what kinds of theatre you intend to present. Will you do staged readings, workshops, or full productions? Spectacles with music and dance, or intimate drama? Narrow this list by a reexamination of your purpose and goals. Ask yourself if you want to do classics, which usually means large casts; or revivals, which were originally conceived for presentation in conventional proscenium form; or experimental and new playwrights' works, which require space with the greatest possible flexibility and versatility in size and configuration.

At the same time keep in mind desirable secondary functions, none of which should be allowed to dictate any weakening of the theatre's capacity to serve its primary function; such as dance, poetry, cabaret, children's theatre, classes, and/or musical events.

• Consider how these needs will affect the size and shape of your stage and auditorium.

• Determine how large or small an audience you will want. Allow for expansion in the future. How will you want the audience to relate to what you are doing? Do you want intimacy or distance, contact or separation? Over 74 persons creates added Building Code problems; over 100 may alter Actors' Equity Association (AEA) requirements.

Force yourself to make a hard-nosed decision about what audience you want to reach. Consider how that will affect the size and shape of the auditorium. What type of building will this dictate? Where should you locate your theatre in order to attract your desired audience?

• Next consider the question of your production requirements. Will there be minimal amounts of scenery or a great deal? Will you build your own scenery; if you do, where will you build it? On stage, in the lobby, or in a shop? Will the shop be on or off the premises? Will your productions be heavy on lights and sound? Will your productions have large casts or small? What dressing room and costume handling facilities will you need? Will you build costumes? Where?

• Since someone will have to do the planning, publicity and paper work, consider the office spaces that will be needed. Support spaces and administrative spaces are as important as the performance spaces. Anticipate the number of persons involved in administration, not only in the beginning but also in the future.

• Consider your public relations space needs. Will there be staff? Will there be volunteer workers?

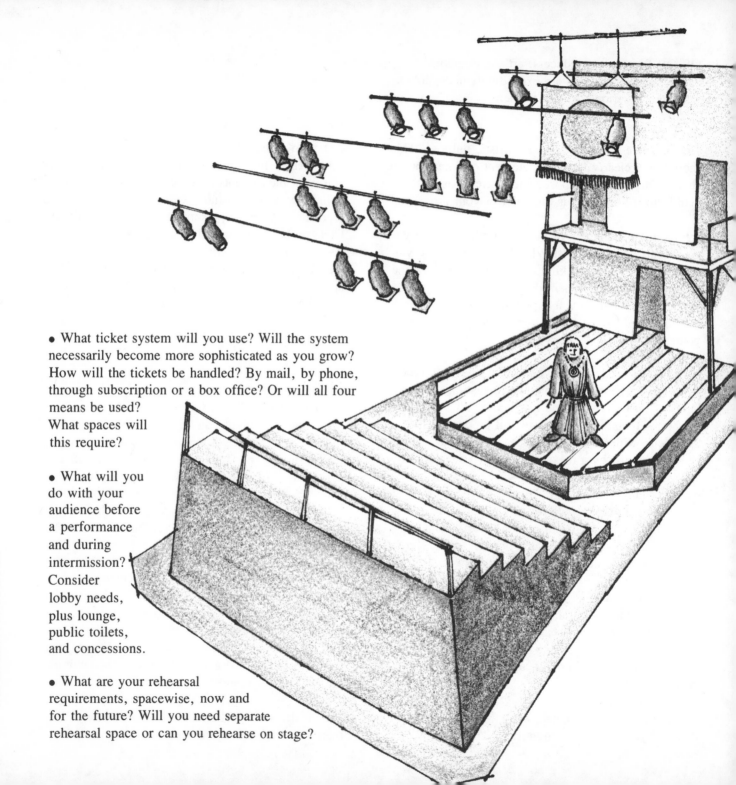

• What ticket system will you use? Will the system necessarily become more sophisticated as you grow? How will the tickets be handled? By mail, by phone, through subscription or a box office? Or will all four means be used? What spaces will this require?

• What will you do with your audience before a performance and during intermission? Consider lobby needs, plus lounge, public toilets, and concessions.

• What are your rehearsal requirements, spacewise, now and for the future? Will you need separate rehearsal space or can you rehearse on stage?

• Will you need storage for scenery and for props you plan to reuse? What equipment and materials will you store?

• Consider scheduling and how it will impact on the amount and kinds of space you will need. If, for instance, you plan to schedule productions in rotating repertory, you will have to have more rehearsal space as well as adequate storage to handle scenery and costumes for one or more productions while another is on stage. The amount of storage space will affect how much time will be needed to strike one set and mount another.

• Can you schedule rehearsal times for new productions that will allow you to use your own theatre for rehearsals while another production is playing? How would sharing space affect your programming and scheduling?

• Go back through your list of activities and the spaces they will require. Look for ways of consolidating them. Ask yourself if all your projected activities are essential at the beginning or if some of these can be put off for later. If necessary, consider a program of phasing, a plan that allows you to grow over a period of time.

Ask yourself: What is important now? What can wait till later? It may be nice to do workshops, readings, and full productions, but until you can accommodate them all, some activities can wait until you have established yourself and can consider expanding.

• Ask yourself: How much money do you have? How much money can you raise? How much do you need? What is the difference?

The gap between the money you have and the money you need can be at least partially closed by material and labor resources. Check within your company to determine what people are skilled in designing, building, or electrical and plumbing work. What friends do you have who might contribute professional advice you could not otherwise afford? Again there are city, state and federal agencies that offer assistance to stretch your manpower resources. These are listed in Chapter 7.

Estimate the resources you have for donated materials and for suppliers from whom you can get materials inexpensively. Obviously, the more you can get in donated labor and materials the further what money you do have will stretch.

This list of self-examining questions seems extremely simplistic and therefore, perhaps, unnecessary. However, the truth is that many beginning producers and artistic directors organize a company and commit themselves to a space without asking and answering these questions, and as a result find themselves making some expensive, avoidable mistakes. Once you make a commitment to a space, it will be difficult to make adjustments and you will be forced to select your plays and to schedule around its limitations.

You will not be able to rigidly and dogmatically stick to every detail of your program. Don't expect to. Circumstances will force you to modify it. But, if clearly expressed, it will remain as a guide and a measuring stick throughout the life span of your theatre.

2

shape and size

Since you will make your theatre by converting and renovating an existing space, it is unlikely that you will ever have the exact shape and size you dream of having. It's just not in the cards, and you will settle for some compromises. Still, it is essential before looking for space to examine all the possible theatre forms in order to determine the configuration and size that are right for you.

Almost everyone wants an ''all-purpose'' space in the beginning; a space where they will be able to present *any* kind of theatre. But as the search for the all-purpose space goes on and on it becomes clear that such a space is either not available or not affordable, and it becomes necessary to push yourself to say exactly what you most want in a theatre, nailing down what kinds of theatre you actually will do.

basic theatre configurations

This survey of configurations will assist you in making a choice of exactly what kind of theatre you want.

Proscenium Stage. The Proscenium arch encloses the performance area and the audience faces the performance from one side only. Useful if scenic effects are part of your plan. More than any other configuration the Proscenium creates actual and esthetic distance. Not practical in the small, low-ceilinged spaces most frequently available.

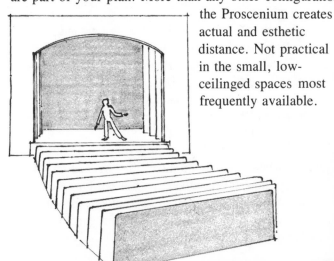

End Stage. Again the audience faces the performance area from one side only; but without a Proscenium arch, the End Stage can provide more intimacy and contact. This is probably the type of stage most often found Off Off Broadway. Can work in a long, narrow space. Height is desirable, but not absolutely essential. Actor access needed from one end of space only.

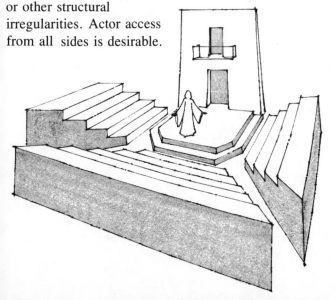

Open or Thrust Stage—Three-sided Arena. A stage extends into the center of the audience with seating around three sides, which can provide intimacy. Requires a wide building. Can be useful where there are lower ceilings or for working around structural columns or other structural irregularities. Actor access from all sides is desirable.

Theatre-in-the-Round—Four-sided Arena. The audience completely surrounds the performance. Not good for large scale scenery. Can be useful for working around columns. Provides intimacy. Actor access from four sides. A squarish space is needed.

Center Stage—Two-sided Arena. The audience faces the performance area from two opposite sides. Not good for large scale scenery. Can provide intimacy. Audience and actor access from both ends is desirable. Works for a rectangular space.

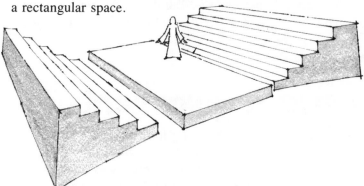

flexible and multiform theatre

The ambitious artistic director frequently begins wanting "total flexibility"—a multiform space that can convert to any configuration. This is difficult, if not impossible, to achieve. However, some forms and spaces convert more easily than others: an End Stage into Center Stage; Open Stage (Thrust) into Theatre-in-the-Round. It should be noted that change-overs are not only time consuming, but also expensive. They require a great deal of careful planning. The flexible space requires more storage and support space.

It is true that the "all-purpose theatre" is frequently the "no-purpose theatre," but virtually all theatres are multipurpose in that they are sometimes used for events and performances other than their primary function. Most theatre configurations can serve more than one type of performance.

Without compromising your vision or concept of theatre, it would be practical and worthwhile to consider what secondary purposes your theatre space can serve. This should be assessed in the frame of full utilization of the space and possible sources of income through rental.

Before you decide on one particular form conduct an investigation of a cross section of small theatres in converted spaces. Study them under performance and non-performance conditions to see how they function. Take notes on each space based on considerations discussed in this chapter. Talk to the artistic forces who chose these forms. Deciding which configuration suits your needs and vision best will guide you in finding the right space.

size requirements

Small theatres are known for their ingenious use of small spaces, but there are limitations as to how small a space can be and still function properly as a theatre. This section will deal with the minimum amounts of square footage you will need in the various areas of your theatre. These square footage figures are derived from the Building Code's minimum requirements and from the minimum standards used by consultants and architects. The resulting dimensions are, practically speaking, the absolute minimum amount of space needed for an area to function properly in its intended use.

The areas discussed are broken down into two categories: *necessary* and *optional*. The necessary areas are those which are considered to be absolutely essential to the running of a theatre, no matter what its size. They include: the acting area, backstage area, seating and aisles, dressing rooms, technical control area, lobby, box office, and rest rooms.

In some small theatres even these necessary areas are not affordable and spaces must serve multiple functions. Anyone who has worked Off Off Broadway can relate tales of the leading lady dressing in the public rest room, or a technician jostling the actors to get to the scenery. But the functions of these spaces are necessary to the performance, even if spaces may have to serve double or triple duty.

The optional areas are considered desirable to facilitate the operation of a theatre and include: rehearsal space, offices, workshops (scenic and costume), lounge area, and storage areas.

NECESSARY AREAS

the acting area

Consider the size of the stage with relation to the type of productions you envisage within this space. A minimum stage can be as small as 240 sq. ft.: 20' × 12' or 15' × 16', for example.

Below is a sampling of the sizes of a few small stages:

theatre	stage size	sq. ft.
Theatre Off Park	17' × 19'	323
Amas Repertory Theatre	16' × 22'	352
Drama Committee	16' × 16'	256
Meat and Potatoes Co.	16' × 19½'	312

However, some productions have been successfully mounted on even less space, for example, *Ain't Misbehavin'* at Manhattan Theatre Club: MTC Cabaret, 6' × 14' stage, 84 sq. ft.

An average sized stage is generally considered to be in the vicinity of 525 sq. ft.: 25′ × 21′ or 35′ × 15′; the Impossible Ragtime Theatre's Stage I is 625 sq. ft.: 25′ × 25′. Take into consideration that scenery and props will decrease the actual amount of free space an actor will have. If dancing and musicals are part of your plan, you will need a larger stage to accommodate the movement. 300 sq. ft. may be comfortable for a solo dancer, but for a company it will be a tight squeeze.

A reasonable maximum stage size for a small theatre can be considered around 1,000 sq. ft.: 40′ × 25′. The Hudson Guild has a 28′ × 38′ stage, 1,064 sq. ft.

off-stage spaces

Although a 4′ × 6′ room may be lovingly referred to as "off-stage space" by many a small theatre, cramming actors, scenery, and technicians into an oversized closet is not an ideal approach to figuring off-stage space.

The amount of square footage needed for off-stage is generally considered to be a minimum of 50% of the stage space. Therefore, if your stage is 240 sq. ft., 120 sq. ft. will be a rough estimate of the off-stage space needed. Depending on your theatre's configuration, this space may be broken up into smaller areas, or may be contained in one space.

Consider the amount of space you will need for the following with relation to the productions you will present:

- the amount of scenery or props to be stored off-stage
- the number of actors waiting for entrances
- space needed for cross-overs
- the stage manager (if not in the control booth)
- the technicians waiting for a scene change

All of these should be considered in estimating the total off-stage space your theatre will require.

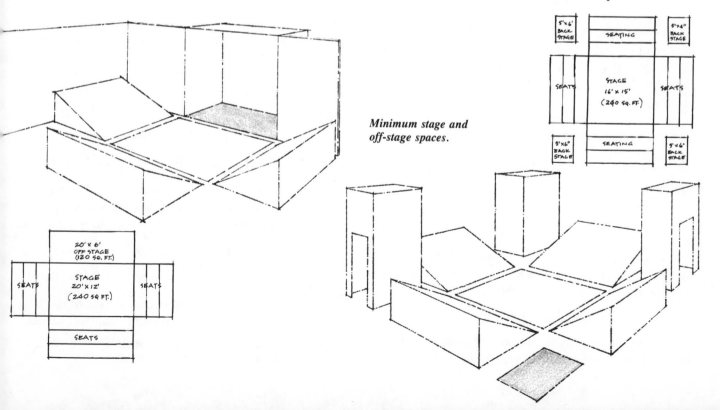

Minimum stage and off-stage spaces.

seating area

This area is comprised of two parts: the seats, and the aisles which lead to the seats.

Seats. An 18″ wide seat with a back-to-back measurement of 30″ will comply with the new Building Code requirements, but the resulting seat plan is so tight that it should not even be considered.

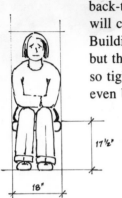

PERSON SQUEEZED INTO 18″ WIDE SEAT

A more realistic and comfortable figure can be obtained by using 21″ as the minimum seat width and 34″ as the minimum back-to-back measurement. The result is 4.9 sq. ft. minimum per seat (for ''rule of thumb'' estimates: 5 sq. ft. per seat).

You can compute your square footage requirements as follows:

74 seats × 5 sq. ft. = 370 sq. ft.

A more generous seating arrangement may be figured by using a 22″ seat width and a 36″ back-to-back measurement, 5.5 sq. ft. per seat:

100 seats × 5.5 sq. ft. = 550 sq. ft.

Consider carefully the number of seats you plan. The Building Code has many specifications for 74

occupants or less and 75 occupants or more (see Chapter 15). The Actors' Equity agreement governing the Off Off Broadway participation of union actors limits most theatres to 100 seats.

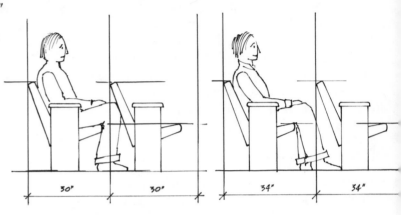

30″ BACK-TO-BACK—MINIMUM BUILDING CODE REQUIREMENT

34″ BACK-TO-BACK—MINIMUM ALLOWANCE FOR COMFORT

Aisles. The minimum Building Code requirement for width of an aisle is 36″ in most situations. To figure a rough estimate of minimum aisle space needed, you can use 23% of the total seating square footage. Using the examples of seating square footage given above, you can compute as follows:

23% of 370 sq. ft. (74 seats) = 85 sq. ft.

23% of 550 sq. ft. (100 seats) = 126.5 sq. ft.

Obviously, to gain an estimate of total square footage needed within the seating area, you simply add the seating square footage and the aisle square footage:

370 + 85 = 455 sq. ft. needed for 74 seats*

550 + 126.5 = 676.5 sq. ft. needed for 100 seats**

Bear in mind that these figures are for rough estimates only, and are the absolute minimum needed.

*Based on 21″w × 34″ back-to-back seating
**Based on 22″w × 36″ back-to-back seating

public rest rooms

The Building Code, in some situations, requires 1 toilet and 1 urinal for every 100 persons and 1 sink for every 200 persons. Although it is possible to comply with this requirement by providing only one facility, two should be considered the minimum capable of handling men and women separately. You will need to allow a minimum of 24 sq. ft. per facility, so allow at least 48 sq. ft. total.

dressing and lavatory space

The Meat and Potatoes Co.—aptly named—has a live-in producer for economy reasons whose living space must, on occasion, double as dressing room space.

Although one step above changing costumes in the public lavatory, it can hardly be considered a viable solution to the dressing room requirement.

The minimum amount of dressing space needed should be computed at 16 sq. ft. per person. For example, for 6 persons you will need 96 sq. ft. The type of shows you plan to produce should serve as a guide to the amount of space required for dressing rooms.

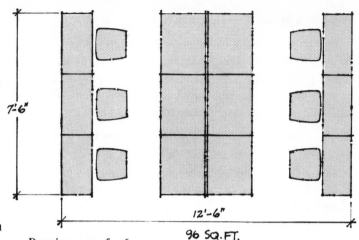

Dressing space for 6 persons.

of space needed to accommodate these facilities and this figure requires plumbing to be on two sides of the wall. Therefore:

24 sq. ft. (lavatory space)
+ 96 sq. ft. (dressing space) = 120 sq. ft.,

the minimum space needed to accommodate 6 actors with minimum comfort.

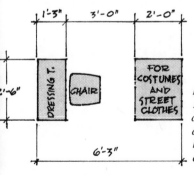

Minimum dressing space for 1 person allows for 2' 6" × 1' 3" dressing table, 1 chair, and 2' × 2' 6" for hanging costumes and street clothes.

It should be noted that Actors' Equity suggests 1 washbasin for every 4 persons, and 1 toilet for men and 1 toilet for women for every 6 persons, and requires a minimum of 1 toilet and 1 washbasin to be made available to the actors. 24 sq. ft. is the barest minimum

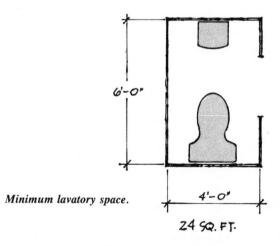

Minimum lavatory space.

And don't forget to make provision somewhere in your theatre for the required Equity cot.

SHAPE AND SIZE

11

technical control space

Consider the number of technicians who will use this space at one time: lighting technician, sound technician, and stage manager. Depending on the amount and size of your equipment, this square footage will vary. The minimum space needed is approximately 66 sq. ft.

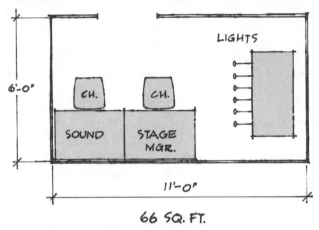

66 SQ. FT.

Technical control space allows 3 persons to share space: 1 sound technician, 1 stage manager, and 1 lighting technician.

lobby

The minimum amount of space needed for 1 standing person is considered to be 1 sq. ft., so for a minimal lobby space:

1 sq. ft. × *# of seats*

will give you an estimate of the square footage needed. This minimal figure assumes that not all the members of an audience will use the lobby at the same time. 2 sq. ft. per person will give you a lobby of a more generous size.

In many situations the Building Code requires a *safe area* (see Chapter 15) to be located within the theatre space, and the required minimum is also 2 sq. ft. per person. It is possible that the lobby could double as the safe area.

Bear in mind that these square footage estimates are based upon free floor space, so if you plan to add furnishings within this area—chairs, tables, lamps, plants—you will need to increase the total square footage proportionately.

box office

There are two basic approaches to creating a box office space: open and enclosed. If your box office is open—a table or counter set up within the lobby area—you will need to add at least 25 sq. ft. to your lobby square footage total to accommodate this addition.

An enclosed box office will require a minimum of 30 sq. ft. to accommodate 1 person comfortably.

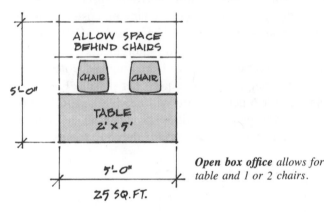

Open box office allows for table and 1 or 2 chairs.

Enclosed box office allows for 1 person seated or 2 persons standing with 1' 3" counter space on two sides.

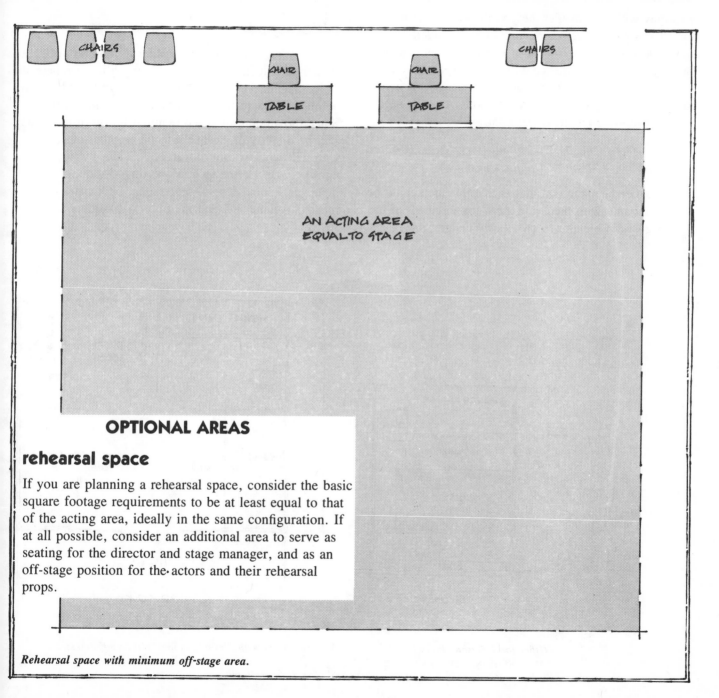

CHAIRS

CHAIRS

CHAIR

CHAIR

TABLE

TABLE

AN ACTING AREA
EQUAL TO STAGE

OPTIONAL AREAS

rehearsal space

If you are planning a rehearsal space, consider the basic square footage requirements to be at least equal to that of the acting area, ideally in the same configuration. If at all possible, consider an additional area to serve as seating for the director and stage manager, and as an off-stage position for the actors and their rehearsal props.

Rehearsal space with minimum off-stage area.

lounge/bar

You may wish to consider the possibility of a lounge or bar area. 4 sq. ft. per person should be considered to allow for a minimum amount of comfort, assuming that the majority of the audience will use the space at one time. If you wish to consider adding a bar or concession counter (see open box office illustration) you will need to add at least 25 sq. ft. to the total:

74 seats × 4 sq. ft. = 296 sq. ft. + 25 sq. ft. = 321 sq. ft. (total lounge).

Another factor to consider is that this area could be used to comply with the "safe area" requirement of the Building Code, mentioned previously under *lobby*.

office space

For an office, you should consider a minimum of 36 sq. ft. per person. If you plan on having filing cabinets and office machinery within this area you will need to add additional square footage to your total office space. Since the amount of space required for an office area will be directly proportional to the number of people who will work within this area, consider the total number who use the area at one time—administrators, managers, bookkeepers, secretaries, publicists, fund raisers, volunteers—and multiply that number by 36 sq. ft.

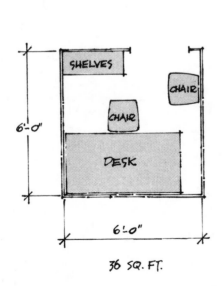

36 SQ. FT.

Office for 1 person allows 1 60" × 30" desk, 2 chairs and 1 shelf unit.

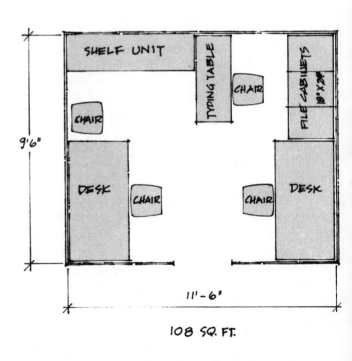

108 SQ. FT.

3 person office with files allows for 2 60" × 30" desks, 1 typing table, 4 chairs, 3 standard file cabinets, and 1 5' 6" × 1' 6" shelf unit.

THE SEARCH FOR A SPACE

14

workshop spaces

Scenery construction shop. There are two approaches to figuring your square footage requirements for scenic construction space.

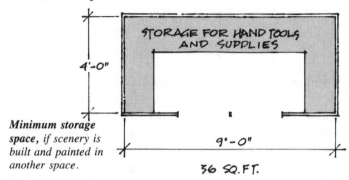

Minimum storage space, if scenery is built and painted in another space.

36 SQ. FT.

If you plan to build and paint scenery in one of the other spaces already mentioned—stage, lobby, lounge area, or in another space entirely, then you will only need an area in which to store your tools, hardware, and painting supplies. 36 sq. ft. should be considered the bare minimum needed.

If you plan to build and paint scenery in a separate shop area, you will need additional space: 196 sq. ft. will give you a minimal shop area.

Two other considerations within this space are a slop sink for cleaning up brushes and paints, and a fireproof paint locker or vault. Allow another 12 sq. ft. for each facility, which brings your total estimate to 220 sq. ft.

STORAGE AREA FOR TOOLS

ALLOWS FOR LAYOUT OF TWO 4 X 8 SHEETS OF PLY

14'-0'

196 SQ. FT.

Minimum construction space assumes additional storage shelves and cabinets above head height.

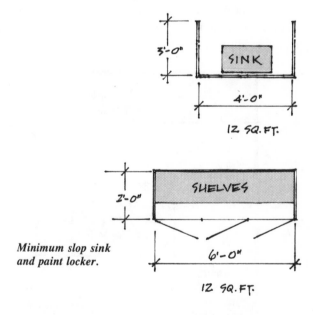

SINK

3'-0"

4'-0"

12 SQ. FT.

SHELVES

2'-0"

6'-0"

Minimum slop sink and paint locker.

12 SQ. FT.

Costume shop. The same two approaches hold true for the costume shop as for the scene shop. If you plan to construct costumes in another space, your only requirements will be a storage area for your supplies. 60 sq. ft. should be considered the minimum amount of space you will need to store supplies.

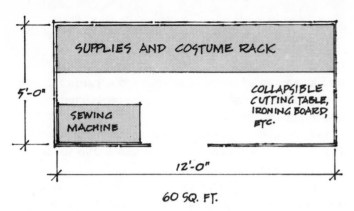

60 SQ. FT.

Minimum storage space assumes costumes are built in another space and that actual costume storage will be elsewhere.

If you wish to construct costumes, you will need to plan on at least 144 sq. ft., 12' × 12', as a minimal costume shop.

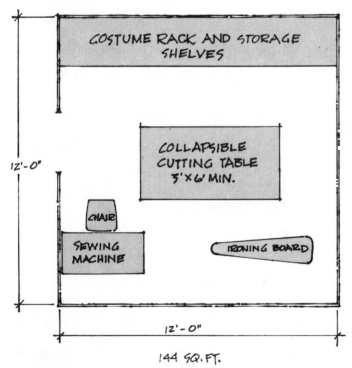

144 SQ. FT.

Minimum costume shop assumes actual costume storage will be elsewhere.

storage

Storage spaces are always at a premium. It is hard to determine a minimum square footage estimate in this area since it will depend on the amount and size of the items you will wish to store. Take into consideration all the possible storage spaces you may need: costumes (including hats, shoes, accessories, pocketbooks, costume props); scenery (platforms, step units, flats, draperies, screens, construction supplies); properties (hand props, furniture props, set dressing); painting and supplies (brushes, buckets, paint cans, ladders); lighting (instruments, cables, spare lamps, replacement parts); also, office supplies, janitorial supplies, scripts, programs, flyers, those wonderful finds on the street that you know will come in handy "one of these days." The list is seemingly endless.

The important point is that you are aware of all the possible types of storage your particular theatre will need and take into consideration exactly how much storage space is right for you with relation to the type of theatre company you are. For example, repertory companies need space to store full sets of scenery, costumes, and props, whereas companies doing only one show at a time may not need to store as much, since scenery is dismantled and most costumes and props are returned. One final point—to which all small companies will attest—there is never enough storage space, no matter how much you have. (See Chapter 10 for storage details and dimensions.)

estimating total square footage

A rough square footage total can be obtained by adding all the individual areas together.

Theatre A and Theatre B in the chart are representative of two small theatres with different space requirements based on the square footage estimates used in this chapter. Theatre A is a 74 seat theatre with only the very basic minimums. Theatre B is a 100 seat theatre with more ample facilities.

	Theatre A		Theatre B	
stage	240 sq. ft.	(15′ × 16′)	525 sq. ft.	(25′ × 21′)
backstage	120	(50% stage min.)	300	(generous)
seating	370	(74′ × 5′ min.)	550	(100′ × 5.5′)
aisles (23% seating)	85		126.5	
public rest rooms	48	(men and women)	48	(men and women)
dressing room	96	(6 person)	160	(10 person)
actors' rest rooms	—		48	(male and female)
technical control	60	(3 person)	140	(6 person)
lobby	74	(not "safe area")	200	("safe area")
box office	25	(open box off.)	30	(enclosed box off.)
lounge	—		321	(w/counter)
rehearsal space	—		783	(includes off-stage)
office	36	(1 person)	108	(3 person)
scene shop	36	(storage only; build on stage)	220	(building space w/ slop sink + paint vault)
costume shop	60	(storage only; sew in lobby)	144	(sewing space)
storage	—		100	(small storage area)
totals	1,250 sq. ft. *		3,803.5 sq. ft.*	

*Please note: Square footage figures do not include an allowance for corridor or mechanical spaces (such as boiler room or air conditioning space). It is very difficult to accurately estimate these spaces as sizes will depend largely upon the actual layout of the theatre.

As you can deduce from comparing the two examples, Theatre A is very small and not well equipped for any considerable amount of scenery building and painting or costume construction. The square footage of Theatre A is probably comparable to a very small Off Off Broadway house used for readings and minimal setting productions, therefore it includes no storage spaces. As there is no additional rehearsal space, the scheduling of productions and performances cannot be too tight unless additional space is rented elsewhere for rehearsal purposes.

Theatre B is somewhat better equipped to do full scale productions, since there are small scenic and costume shops, a larger stage, and rehearsal space.

Please note that both examples are used only for illustration purposes and that your square footage requirements may vary greatly.

3

what to look for

You have been through the process of assessing your needs and have an idea of how your theatre space will have to function. You also have an idea of how you want your theatre to look, the size and shape space you need and the configuration you wish to fit into it. These assessments will guide you in looking for a space that meets your unique requirements.

Since you are seeking a non-traditional theatre space, one originally intended for another use, it is important to recognize what types of spaces are suitable for conversion. The guidelines given here are not intended to hamper an imaginative and flexible approach to the search for a space. Having a clear idea of what to look for will aid greatly in the narrowing down and weeding out process and could, in the long run, save a great deal of time and expense.

general characteristics of the potential space

height

You will need height. Not only does a high ceiling enable you to rake your seating for adequate sightlines, it also gives you greater flexibility in handling scenic pieces and stage lighting. It allows you height over the stage, the chance to create a small balcony for some of the audience or to install the control booth above the seating. Also, height creates an illusion of space that can help make up for a small space, or a narrow one.

Height can help solve the problem of not being able to afford all of the square footage that you really need. With sufficient headroom you can double-deck many activities: put your office space over the box office, stack costume storage over the dressing room and toilets. Don't overlook the thickness of the loft beams and flooring in your calculations.

If you have a space that is 25′ × 100′, a total of 2,500 sq. ft., you might gain an extra 1,250 sq. ft. of

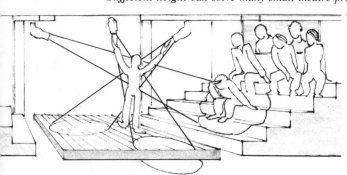

space by double-decking everything except the theatre space. That's a lot of extra space for no extra rent. This approach to the problem of space requires materials and possibly paid labor, so such an arrangement is not entirely without cost to you. However, if you amortize the expense over the years you expect to occupy the space, the cost will be negligible compared to rent for an equal amount of square footage.

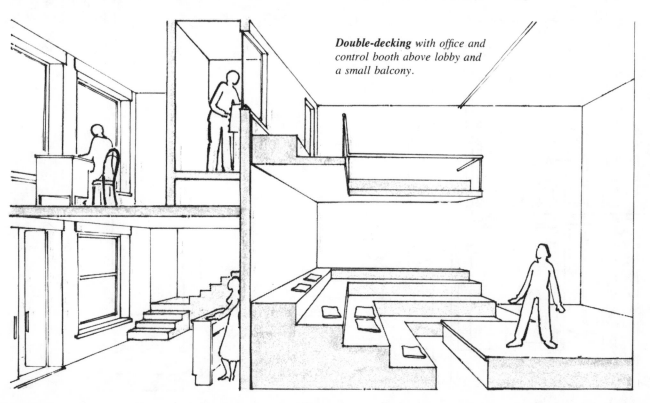

Double-decking with office and control booth above lobby and a small balcony.

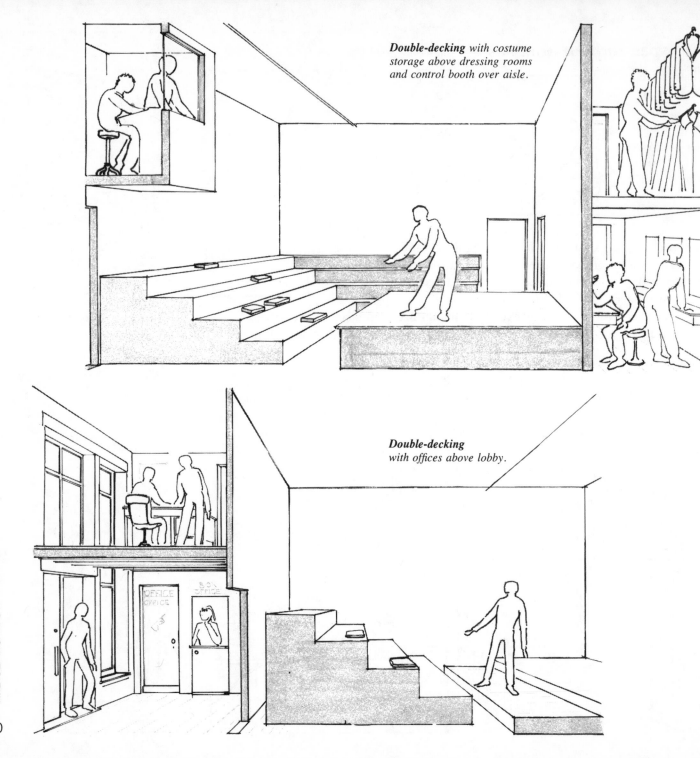

Double-decking with costume storage above dressing rooms and control booth over aisle.

Double-decking with offices above lobby.

free-span without columns

Clear space without columns is very important. The arrangement of your theatre space will be much easier if you don't have to work around columns. If columns do exist in a space you are considering, don't assume you can remove them. Measure the distance between the columns as well as the width of the room to determine how these columns will limit your seating and staging

A row of load-bearing columns down the center of a loft or store space is very common. If the span between columns is 25' or more, it may be possible to design the theatre around them without too much compromise; but if the span is much less, they may impose insurmountable problems.

configurations. (The evaluation checklist in Chapter 5 includes an entry for these measurements.)

If you want a "flexible theatre," in which you can change the arrangement from production to production, you will definitely want a space that has free-span without columns. Columns put a severe handicap on using the space in more than one way.

Before you settle on a space with columns, think carefully.

width and depth

A too-narrow room, as in small town houses or brownstones, will force you to have all the seats very close to the acting space if you position them along the length, or else, if you place all the seats in short rows across the width, some members of the audience may be too far away.

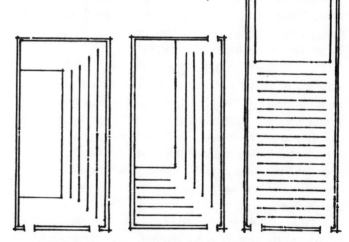

Remember, when looking at a space, that you are looking at the whole space, which will then have to be subdivided. It may be difficult to imagine the proportions of your theatre while standing in a raw space. So, before making a commitment, take the dimensions of the space being considered and plot what has to go into it.

location within the building

Advantages of a ground floor space. Renting a ground floor space is a wise space strategy. For one thing, you will gain visibility on the street, which can be worth a lot in terms of publicity.

For another, ground floor space will almost certainly be easier to bring up to Code. If you plan on an audience of 74 people or less per performance, there is a definite advantage in a ground floor space. For 74 or less you are required to have only one means of egress; but this one egress must open directly onto the street and not onto a public hallway, which is clearly impossible above the ground floor. (See Building Code sections on *egress*, in Chapter 15.)

Ground floor space will also provide greater ease in loading in the materials for building your theatre and the sets for your productions, as well as for loading costumes, props, and furniture.

Often the basement will be included with the ground floor, since it is of little benefit to anyone else in the building if access to it is through the ground floor space. This adds terrific space at probably a nominal increase in rent per square foot.

Renting on two adjacent floors. Another strategy to consider is renting on two adjacent floors instead of all on one floor. This provides a more compact arrangement and might be less expensive. With access stairs, two floors will provide you with a ready made cross-over for actors and crew. Basement and/or second floor space are usable for almost all support space functions.

Intar Theatre, part of the 42nd Street Theatre Row Development, has broken through the ground floor to the basement to achieve an unusually steep rake to the seating and to give a two story height over the stage space.

The Lion Theatre, also part of the 42nd Street Theatre Row, broke through to the second floor to give additional height over the playing area.

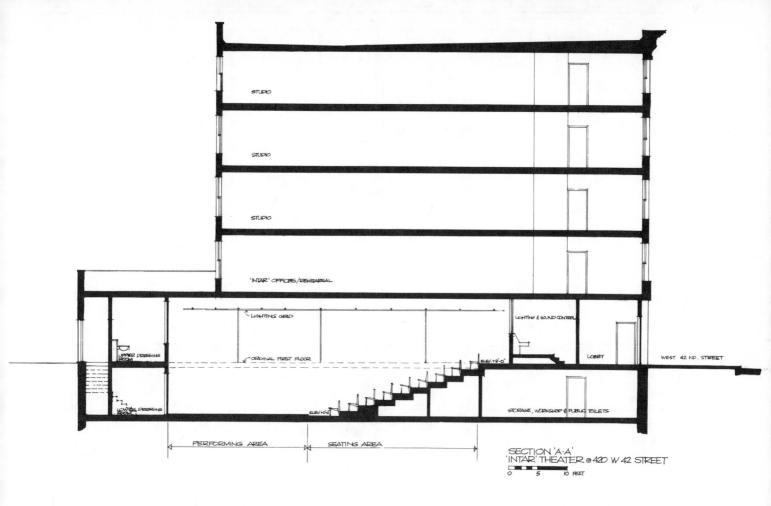

STUDIO

STUDIO

STUDIO

'INTAR' OFFICES/REHEARSAL

LIGHTING GRID

LIGHTING & SOUND CONTROL

ORIGINAL FIRST FLOOR

ELEV. +9'-0"

LOBBY

WEST 42 ND. STREET

UPPER DRESSING ROOM

LOWER DRESSING ROOM

ELEV. +0'-0"

STORAGE, WORKSHOP & PUBLIC TOILETS

PERFORMING AREA

SEATING AREA

SECTION 'A·A'
'INTAR' THEATER @ 420 W 42 STREET

0   5   10 FEET

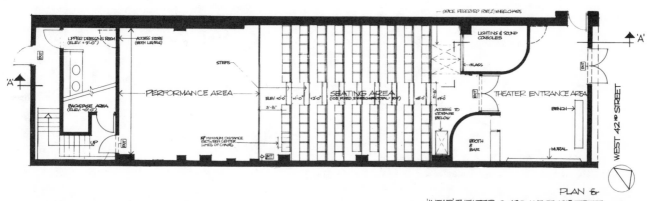

SPACE RESERVED FOR (3) WHEELCHAIRS

UPPER DRESSING ROOM
(ELEV. +9'-0")

ACCESS DOORS
(BOTH LEVELS)

LIGHTING & SOUND
CONSOLES

'A'

STEPS

GLASS

'A'

PERFORMANCE AREA

ELEV. +0'-0"

+1'-0"   +2'-0"

SEATING AREA
(105 FIXED, 3 WHEELCHAIR SPECIAL - 109)

+8'-6"

THEATER ENTRANCE AREA

WEST 42 ND STREET

BACKSTAGE AREA
(ELEV. +0'-0")

3'-8"

ACCESS TO
STORAGE
BELOW

BENCH

UP

18" MINIMUM DISTANCE
BETWEEN CENTER
LINES OF CHAIRS

BOOTH
& BAR

MURAL

PLAN &
'INTAR' THEATER @ 420 WEST 42 ND STREET

0   5   10 FEET

ROBERT CABRERA-ARCHITECT
305 EAST 63 ST. NEW YORK N.Y.

WHAT TO LOOK FOR

23

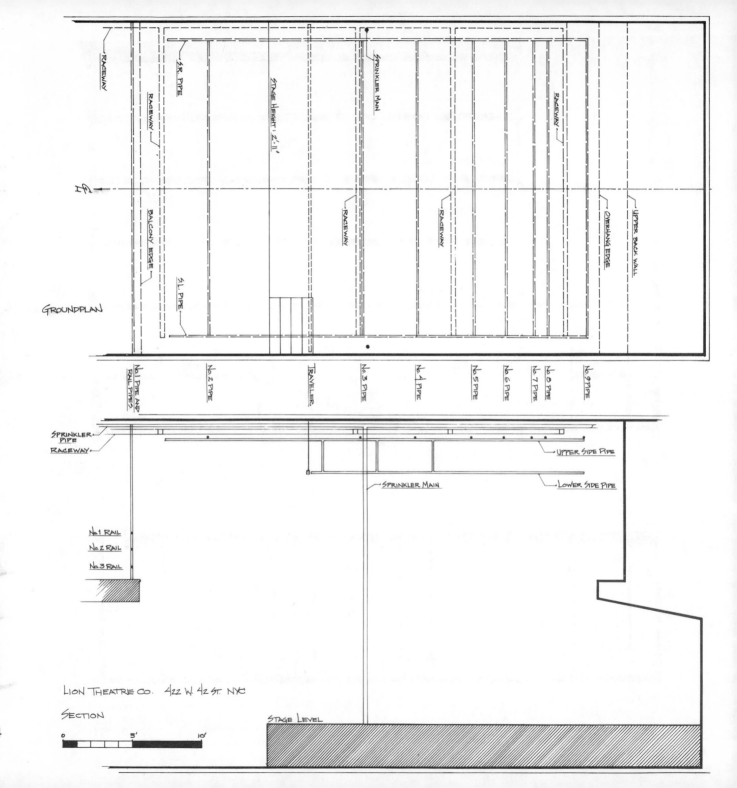

GROUNDPLAN

RACEWAY

S.R. PIPE

STAGE HEIGHT: 2'-11"

SPRINKLER MAIN

RACEWAY

RACEWAY

RACEWAY

RACEWAY

RACEWAY

BALCONY EDGE

S.L. PIPE

OVERHANG EDGE

UPPER BACK WALL

No.1 PIPE AND RAIL PIPE 2

No.2 PIPE

TRAVELER

No.3 PIPE

No.4 PIPE

No.5 PIPE

No.6 PIPE

No.7 PIPE

No.8 PIPE

No.9 PIPE

SPRINKLER PIPE

RACEWAY

UPPER SIDE PIPE

SPRINKLER MAIN

LOWER SIDE PIPE

No.1 RAIL

No.2 RAIL

No.3 RAIL

LION THEATRE CO.   422 W. 42 ST. NYC

SECTION

0   5'   10'

STAGE LEVEL

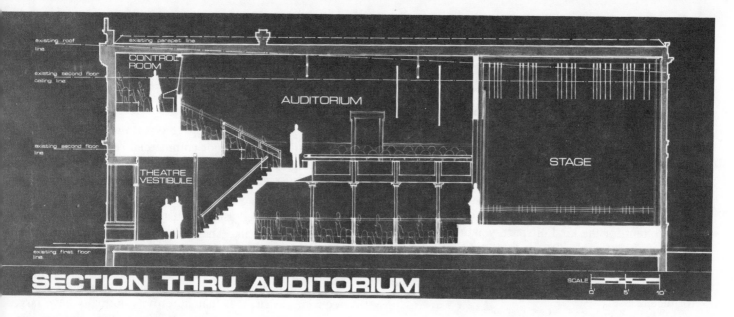

SECTION THRU AUDITORIUM

existing roof line

existing parapet line

CONTROL ROOM

existing second floor ceiling line

AUDITORIUM

existing second floor line

THEATRE VESTIBULE

STAGE

existing first floor line

SCALE
0   5'   10'

Klondike Fever Theatre, Skagway, Alaska. *The White Pass and Yukon Railway Station and office built in 1900, a historic landmark, has been planned for adaptive reuse as the Skagway Performing Arts Center. One half of the 2 story structure will be gutted to accommodate a 300 seat theatre with orchestra seating and an old-fashioned music hall type gallery.*

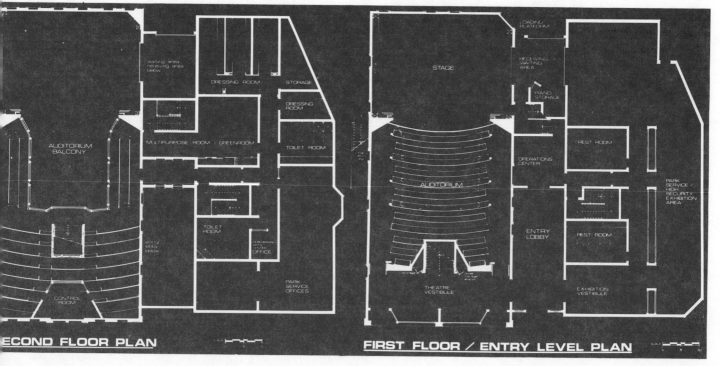

AUDITORIUM BALCONY

waiting area receiving area below

DRESSING ROOM

STORAGE

DRESSING ROOM

MULTIPURPOSE ROOM / GREENROOM

TOILET ROOM

entry lobby below

TOILET ROOM

PERFORMING ARTS OFFICE

CONTROL ROOM

PARK SERVICE OFFICES

ECOND FLOOR PLAN

STAGE

LOADING PLATFORM

RECEIVING WAITING AREA

PIANO STORAGE

OPERATIONS CENTER

AUDITORIUM

REST ROOM

ENTRY LOBBY

REST ROOM

PARK SERVICE / HIGH SECURITY EXHIBITION AREA

THEATRE VESTIBULE

EXHIBITION VESTIBULE

FIRST FLOOR / ENTRY LEVEL PLAN

types of buildings

Most cities will have the building types described in this section. Certain of these types—such as loft or light manufacturing buildings, or store fronts—will lend themselves more easily to conversion for small theatre use than others. Fortunately these are plentiful in most cities and their rents are on the lower end of the scale. $2.00–2.50 per square foot is usually considered a good average rent for the kind of space you are looking for.

Some of the types of spaces listed here have the advantage of having been planned as a place of assembly and are therefore easier to bring up to Code for theatre use.

loft buildings, warehouses, and manufacturing buildings

Loft buildings, warehouses, or manufacturing buildings offer some good bets. These will vary in size from a small, dumpy three story building with a brick facade, to a large heavy masonry building or a cast iron structure. These buildings are tough. They were built to house manufacturing concerns using heavy machinery. They can and have taken a lot of abuse, and the structure is very solid.

As more and more of these small manufacturing and wholesale concerns are moving to areas outside of the center city, these spaces are becoming available for other uses. Landlords are also finding out that other uses will bring them increased rentals and higher rents. They generally seem amenable to renting to theatre groups.

Many of these buildings are going co-op and being turned into living lofts, but generally the ground floors are not used for this purpose. If you contact such a co-op group (they are listed in neighborhood papers such as *The Village Voice*) you might make an attractive deal on the rent in exchange for improving the ground floor space.

storefronts

Storefronts are another space type to consider. Generally, ground floor commercial spaces were built with high ceilings. This, as well as the fact that many of these spaces were also built without columns, makes them very suitable.

Spaces used as stores usually have direct access from the sidewalk. They generally include basement storage as well. Two more reasons to consider this type of space.

The potential drawback, which you might not consider as such, is that storefronts normally have large glass windows for display. You may find some imaginative use for them; if not, be prepared to spend some money to replace the glass with a masonry wall. There should be no structural problem in doing this.

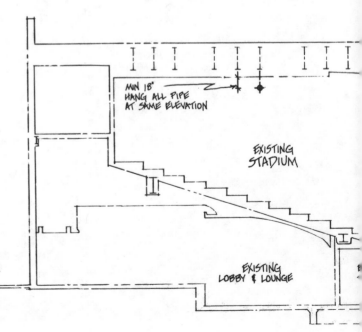

MIN 18" HANG ALL PIPE AT SAME ELEVATION

EXISTING STADIUM

EXISTING LOBBY & LOUNGE

OTHER BUILDING TYPES THAT WORK

banks

Some small theatres are housed in buildings that were formerly banks; for example, The Bouwerie Lane Theatre. Banks are traditionally built to last. They will handle heavy live loads (see Building Code requirements, Chapter 15), and most are fireproof construction. Banks usually have good ceiling height, plus a wider than usual free-span between columns.

If you are fortunate enough to find a bank space still intact, you will have quite a find. However, the cost of dismantling the heavy marble counters or removing the vault could be substantial, and is not a job you could do yourself.

movie theatres

Old movie theatres are an obvious building type to consider. A movie house may already have a box office, a lobby, a lounge, offices, rest rooms, and a control booth; in short, almost all the optional spaces in addition to the necessary ones for a theatre. It might even have seats. Don't count on a ready-made stage, however. This will probably have to be added by carving out space from the audience; but since there will doubtless be too many seats for Equity requirements, turning seating space into stage space will serve a dual purpose. There will not be dressing room spaces either. Movie houses are classified as places of assembly.

Unfortunately there are not many small movie houses on the market in most cities, and the grand, large ones from the glorious twenties are white elephants. They are much too big and too costly to renovate for a single tenant, but a group of theatres could joint venture, perhaps through a developer, to remodel a large movie theatre into several smaller theatre spaces.

The Roundabout Theatre's Stage I is an interesting conversion of a movie theatre: 350 seats, and a stage 90' deep and 60' wide. The mezzanine was retained for seating, and the stage was built over the entire orchestra seating section of the movie theatre. Dressing rooms, toilets, prop and scenery storage are all below the stage.

Roundabout Theatre section.

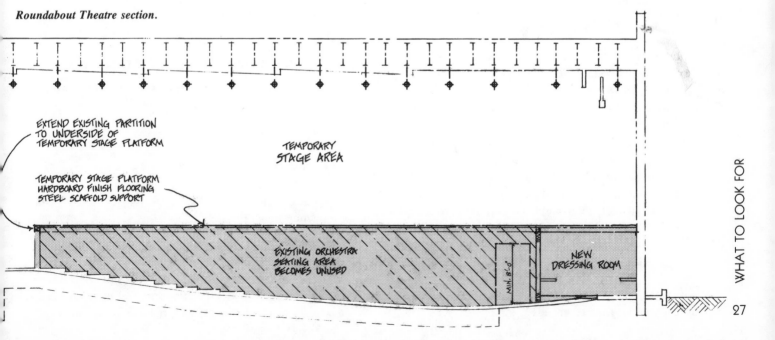

EXTEND EXISTING PARTITION TO UNDERSIDE OF TEMPORARY STAGE PLATFORM

TEMPORARY STAGE PLATFORM HARDBOARD FINISH FLOORING STEEL SCAFFOLD SUPPORT

TEMPORARY STAGE AREA

EXISTING ORCHESTRA SEATING AREA BECOMES UNUSED

Min. 8'-0"

NEW DRESSING ROOM

churches

Churches are another type of property becoming more and more available. While you may not be able to afford to rent a whole church property, most were built with large halls for suppers or Sunday School meetings, and some congregations, feeling the economic pinch of dwindling membership, rent out the parish hall in a variety of temporary or permanent arrangements.

The Counterpoint Theatre has such an arrangement with the Church of the Good Shepherd on West 65th Street just around the corner from Lincoln Center. The Joseph Jefferson Theatre Co. performs in the sanctuary of the Little Church Around the Corner and Theatre of the Riverside Church has two spaces in the labyrinth of buildings surrounding the church, one for dance and one for drama. At Riverside, the church is the producer. Judson Memorial has long been used as a theatre space. Church spaces are classified as places of assembly and will have a Certificate of Occupancy.

(See Chapter 4 for information on locating available church spaces.)

housing developments

Another place to look for space is in the housing developments constructed, owned, and operated by city governments. Many of these large housing projects include a community facility building which houses various activities, among them a community meeting room. For example, the Hudson Guild Theatre operates in a theatre that is part of a large housing project in Manhattan's west 20s. The theatre group is part of the social services program offered to the local community, although, in fact, their audience is drawn from a much larger area.

OFFBEAT SPACES TO CONSIDER

All of the following spaces and building types have been used by small theatre groups.

supermarkets

Former supermarkets offer large open spaces with better than average ceiling height. They are usually in residential areas. Like other stores they usually include basement space. The Dume Spanish Theatre is located in a former supermarket in Sunnyside, Queens, N.Y.; the Roundabout Theatre's Stage II is in the storage space beneath a supermarket.

nightclubs

Nightclubs are also classified as places of assembly. These spaces are often fireproof and have the required secondary exits, as well as ample air conditioning. These are some of the reasons why Seattle Repertory chose to renovate a supperclub to house their 2nd Stage.

pubs, bars, restaurants, ballrooms, and art galleries

Pubs, ballrooms, and galleries are particularly adaptable to cabaret theatre. Interart Theatre converts, by means of movable panels, from a gallery, to a theatre, to a gallery. These spaces are classified as places of assembly.

city and federal surplus properties

Every city has surplus property for sale. Here are just a few of the available types from which to choose:

- firehouses
- police stations
- military/National Guard armories
- schools
- courthouses
- wharves and warehouses

This list is further supplemented by all the buildings taken over for tax default.

City surplus buildings usually have major flaws—they have been neglected for years, so the roof leaks, a wall is cracked, the heating plant is deficient, or a section of the floor is going. Still, if you find the right building at the right price, and have the resources and manpower to put it into shape, it could be worth it.

(See Chapter 4 for details on locating surplus buildings and Chapter 6 for help with financing.)

landmark buildings

Landmark designated buildings are another, if rare, source of potential theatre space.

There are restrictions placed on what can be done to a building once it has been designated as a landmark; on the other hand there could be benefits in tax relief or funding for rehabilitation. The New York Shakespeare Festival got $125,000 in 1967 for renovations of their building from the New York State Preservation Trust.

It would be important that the landmark designation allow ''adaptive reuse,'' which is the kind of preservation that allows alterations to the interior as long as the exterior of the building is not changed.

(See Chapter 4 for information on finding landmark buildings.)

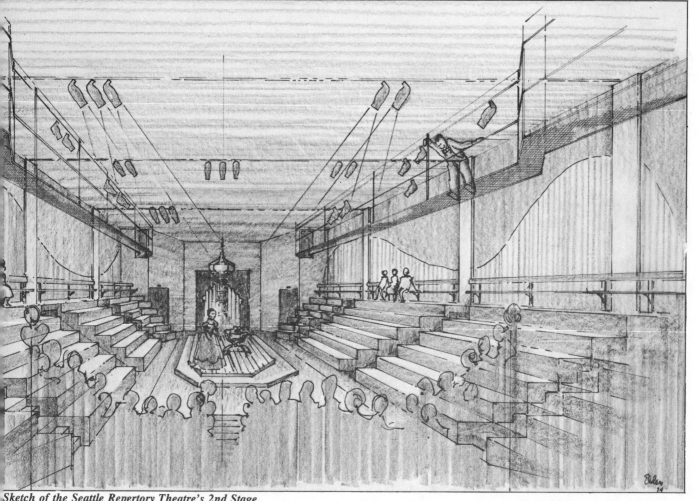

Sketch of the Seattle Repertory Theatre's 2nd Stage.

4

how to find it

The search for the right space is not an easy task. It will require a lot of time, patience, and perseverance on your part. The channels of communication are not centralized, so anyone hunting for space must use a variety of methods. Before you start looking, there are some general strategies you should consider and a lot of information you should have.

Such factors as zoning, Equity requirements, Urban Renewal, property values, and rent levels make some areas of a city more suitable or less expensive for theatre use than others. Although some of the following discussion pinpoints specific areas or neighborhoods in New York City, the general principles hold true for all cities.

This chapter discusses the neighborhood characteristics of potential locations and then reviews the means and strategies for finding available space. It examines the use of classified ad sections, real estate agents, and some agencies and organizations involved with specific types of spaces.

where to look

It is important, when seeking the non-traditional theatre space, to know something about the areas of the city in which you'll be looking. While it is good to keep an open mind about neighborhoods, it is wise to be aware of problems that could arise from locating in an area with possible built-in problems, one that is not zoned for theatre use, for instance, or one that is slated for redevelopment.

The factors listed below should be taken into account as you look for available space.

zoning districts

Zoning is a basic and very important fact of life in any city. Zoning shapes the city. Zoning was developed to encourage certain types of activities in certain areas and to prevent incompatible activities, or uses, from intruding on each other. However compatible or unobtrusive you feel your theatre to be, the person living next door may not share your enthusiasm. For this reason, the zoning laws were adopted as a very dispassionate and objective document for determining what activities can locate where.

Under the New York City zoning laws, certain activities that go on in the city are grouped into categories called Use Groups. Theatre is a Use Group 8 activity and, as such, is permitted by right only in certain zoning districts. Whenever possible locate in the proper zoning district. Should you wish to locate in a district not zoned for theatre use, a variance will be required. (See Chapter 14 for specifics on zoning districts and zoning variances.)

So, before setting out to look for a space, familiarize yourself with the zoning regulations outlined in this book and consult zoning maps (available at the Department of City Planning; see Appendix) to find out specifically where theatre use is allowed. And before signing a lease, check it all again. Don't rely on landlords or rental agents to give you correct zoning information. They are interested in renting, but you are responsible for seeing that your ''use'' conforms to the zoning laws.

Urban Renewal and redevelopment areas

Locating in an Urban Renewal area slated for heavy redevelopment could affect you in two ways. First, you could find yourself having to move in two or three years' time if a building you occupy is to be demolished. Some landlords will not tell you this ahead of time, since they are interested in renting the space. Second, because of the redevelopment, the rents in the area are likely to rise.

If you want to know if a space you are considering is in an Urban Renewal area, or want to check on the likelihood of demolition or redevelopment, check with the Community Board for the district. They will have the information. (See Chapter 6 for Community Board districts and phone numbers.)

property values and rents

Central locations, such as midtown Manhattan, are expensive because they are desirable and more in demand than other areas of the city. Prices only go up in this area.

Then there are areas that once had low-rental spaces, but have also become desirable and expensive. SoHo is one of these areas.

However, there are still good potential theatre areas that have not met with such increased popularity. NoHo, the area north of Houston but south of the Village, is one. The area around Second and Third Avenues between 1st and 14th Streets is another, as is the area bounded by 14th and 34th Streets, from Park Avenue to Ninth Avenue. Lower Manhattan, with the beginnings of a residential population and excellent transportation from all parts of the city, may be ripe for theatre location.

Downtown Brooklyn, Atlantic Avenue from the East River to the Brooklyn Academy of Music (BAM), is another low-rent area of loft-type and commercial buildings that is ripe for theatre development. As in the Clinton Urban Renewal district, there are large residential areas nearby from which to draw an audience.

Once you start your search, you will discover the areas where the rents are lower than in prime midtown locations.

areas with Equity contract restrictions

In New York City, the area bounded by Fifth and Ninth Avenues between 34th and 56th Streets, as well as the area between Fifth Avenue and the Hudson River from 56th Street to 72nd Street, carries certain restrictions on contracts issued by the Actors' Equity Association (AEA).

Actors' Equity contracts prohibit the use of the Off Broadway Contract within this area unless explicit permission is granted by Equity. (AEA has given permission under certain circumstances.) This means that it might be difficult, should you begin to be able to pay full Off Broadway salaries, to grow into such a contract in this area of the city.

These restrictions will pose no problem to you if you do not envisage yourself growing beyond an Off Off Broadway Developmental Theatre Contract.

Contact OOBA for more information.

how to find it

Armed with all the general parameters of the problem, the next question is how to find what is available. Basically it requires being very resourceful.

The following sources of information should help.

newspapers

City newspapers. The classified ads in city newspapers are all basically alike. Examine the organization of *The New York Times* Sunday classified section as an example.

Look for the heading "LOFTS—MANHATTAN." Most of these listings are commercial spaces, not living lofts. Usually the square footage of the space is given; sometimes the rent is quoted; and often there is a brief description which will have to be deciphered.

23 ST, 50W CHELSEA LOFT
App. 7900 sq ft suitable for whse/distr/lgt mfg, studio. Off st. Full bsmt. SS elev + Hvy Frt Elev. Hvy Power. Spklrd, frprf bldg. Prin. only. Call John Doe 866-3247

Decoded, this ad would read: *Approximately 7900 sq. ft. suitable for wholesale, distribution, light manufacturing, or studio. Off the street loading. Full basement. Self-service elevator and a heavy freight elevator. Heavy electrical power. Sprinkler system and a fireproof building. Principals only may call (no brokers).*

These listings are arranged numerically beginning with 1st Street, followed by named streets arranged alphabetically, so you can quickly scan the column to find the particular area which interests you. Often spaces are listed by area—SoHo, TriBeCa, etc.—and these will be found among the alphabetical listings.

Next check "STORES—MANHATTAN," which usually follows "LOFTS." Most stores will be ground floor locations, usually with an entrance directly off the street. As explained in Chapter 3, a ground floor could have distinct advantages. It is worth checking.

One last category to check is "BUSINESS PLACES—MISC.," which appears just before the apartment listings, and occasionally advertises usable space.

Neighborhood papers and other weeklies. The smaller newspapers often list good spaces. *The Village Voice* classified section is one good example. Study its listings in this order: "LOFTS FOR RENT" (a large section with many offerings), "LOFTS FOR SALE," "COMMERCIAL SPACE," "STORES FOR RENT." One other category in the *Voice* to be aware of is "REHEARSAL STUDIOS." It is the best listing of such space in any New York paper.

Trade papers to check for space listings include *Backstage* and *Show Business*.

Like other cities New York has many weekly papers which are neighborhood oriented, like the *Westsider,* the *SoHo Weekly* and the *Chelsea News.* Their classified sections are very small but are not necessarily limited to just their neighborhood. They are worth checking out because they often carry listings not placed in the larger papers. Some of these papers are available at newsstands, others are only distributed, free, in local banks, stores, and apartment buildings.

real estate agents

Newspapers are certainly the place to start looking, but they only contain a partial listing of what's really available. The majority of spaces are rented by managing agents who may advertise one space but really have ten more like it.

Except for the very large management companies that manage properties all over the city, the smaller agents usually deal with a certain geographic area of the city or with a certain type of commercial space. The best way to discover the renting agents for specific areas is to respond to classified ads. If you call in answer to a specific ad and the space has already been rented, ask the agent what similar spaces might be available. Be as specific as you can about what you are looking for—the area in which you are interested, the size of the space needed, the amount of rent you are willing to pay, any features you prefer, like ground floor, private entrance, or high ceilings.

Take the time to look at spaces that may not exactly fit your requirements, because you won't know until you get there how accurately the agent has described the space.

Commissions and fees. There is often a commission involved when a space is rented.

Some buildings are managed and maintained by the actual landlord. Others are run by a management company hired by the landlord to do the same thing. If you are dealing directly with a landlord, there should never be a fee. If you are dealing directly with a management company hired by a landlord, there also should be no fee required from you.

If, however, you are dealing with a real estate agent whom the management company has hired to rent the space, there may be a fee. Usually, this is paid by the landlord for commercial space (unlike residential spaces where the tenant pays the fee).

Be sure to check with any agent, before using his services, as to whether or not you will be charged a fee. The fees involved are sometimes 10% of a year's rent. It is wise to know first.

If you are dealing with a sublease situation, or have answered an ad placed by the tenant himself, be cautious. The previous tenant may want a "fixture fee" for the improvements made to the space. Unless the space has been used as a theatre, you will probably not want to pay for the improvements. It is not legal for a tenant to demand a fixture fee, but it is a practice that goes on. If the space is so fantastic that you must have it, look on the building facade or in the lobby for a sign that designates the managing agent. Try calling the managing agent and saying that you have heard that the space might become available and that you are interested. If they know the tenant is trying to get a fixture fee, the management will probably cooperate with the tenant and you will get nowhere. But, if not, you may have a chance to get the space without the fixture fee.

walk the streets

Another way to find space is simply to walk the streets of the area in which you want to locate. Often spaces for rent are not listed in any paper or with any agent. Instead, signs are hung out or placed in windows with a number to call. While you may spend a lot of time walking around, you need only call to see the ones that interest you. Most theatre groups, when asked how they went about looking for space, said that at one point along the way they simply got out and either walked or

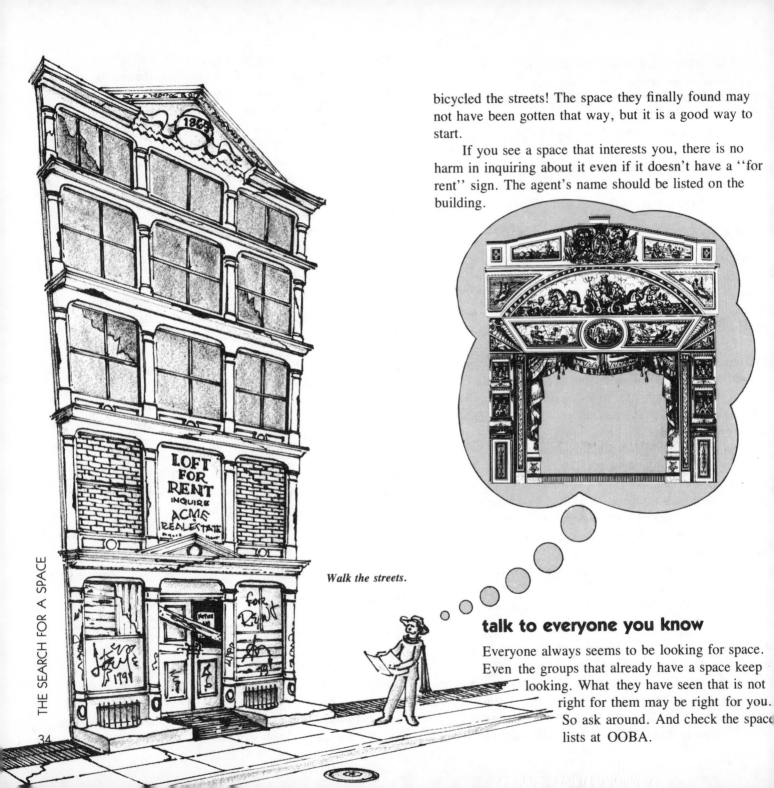

bicycled the streets! The space they finally found may not have been gotten that way, but it is a good way to start.

If you see a space that interests you, there is no harm in inquiring about it even if it doesn't have a ''for rent'' sign. The agent's name should be listed on the building.

Walk the streets.

talk to everyone you know

Everyone always seems to be looking for space. Even the groups that already have a space keep looking. What they have seen that is not right for them may be right for you. So ask around. And check the space lists at OOBA.

locating specific types of spaces

Some specific types of spaces can be located through special interest organizations or government agencies.

churches

The Council of Churches. To assist theatre, dance, music, and other groups looking for space in a church, the Council of Churches, through its Department of Church Planning and Research, maintains a list of available churches and church spaces as one of its services. A talk with the Council office is the first step. They will want to know as much about your needs as possible. Here are some of the things to determine before contacting the Council:

- The area of the city in which you would like to locate.
- How much space you are asking for.
- How much time you need. And what times?
- Maximum and minimum seating you can live with.
- How much electricity you need. How many lights?
- Whether you need storage space. Office space? Rehearsal space?
- How much you can afford. In rent? For purchase?
- Whether you are interested in sharing church space.

The Council of Churches represents 17 denominations and 5 other agencies, such as the YMCA and YWCA.

In New York, the Council of Churches is located at:

475 Riverside Drive
Room 456
New York, N. Y. 10027   (212) 749-1214

The Reverend Leland Gartrell is Divisional Director of the Department of Church Planning and Research.

Scouting church locations. Walk the neighborhood that interests you and knock on church doors. Go where your group has contacts.

In New York there are many interesting church spaces in all five boroughs; for example, downtown Brooklyn is an especially interesting church space place. Since most theatre groups want the Manhattan exposure, an innovative plan might be worked out to rehearse and administer the theatre in a church outside of Manhattan—giving perhaps two performances for the Parish, then moving to a Manhattan location for the rest of the run.

Negotiating the space. Once you have talked to the Council and gotten their list of available spaces, you should be prepared to negotiate with the individual churches.

According to Mr. Gartrell of the Council, "With most churches, the theatre group will have to do the work; they will have to go to the church and present themselves—sell themselves. Churches are traditionally conservative.

"The church will want to know who is in charge of the group, with whom they can negotiate. Though they may need income, though their spaces may be underutilized, many churches refuse groups because they sense a lack of central leadership.

"The question of incorporation must be clearly defined. It is very important to the church in terms of insurance. Insurance companies are urging that churches take only incorporated groups."

housing developments

Whether or not there are active community programs going on in housing development facilities will determine their availability for rental to groups from outside the development.

In some cases, you might convince the authorities to make you a part of their program, as in the case of the Hudson Guild Theatre. (See Chapter 3.)

For information on available space in New York City housing developments, contact:

> New York City Housing Authority
> 5 Park Place
> New York, N.Y. 10007   (212) 233-8878

surplus buildings

Don't expect to find many surplus properties in fashionable or recently revitalized areas like SoHo, or NoHo, or even TriBeCa. Most are in marginal neighborhoods spread throughout all five boroughs, including interesting areas ripe for theatre development such as downtown Brooklyn. This will be true of surplus buildings in all major cities.

City surplus buildings are on the auction lists available from the City's Bureau of Sales, Division of Real Property, but they can also be rented or purchased through a negotiated sale from the City's Department of Real Estate. This is the name in New York, but every city has its surplus property sales.

For information on public auctions of buildings in all boroughs and for *Auction Sale* booklet, which lists all surplus properties up for sale, contact:

> Department of General Services
> Bureau of Sales
> Division of Real Property
> 2 Lafayette Street   Room 1903
> New York, N.Y. 10007   (212) 566-7550

To apply for rental of City-owned buildings or for aid in purchase, contact:

> Department of Real Estate
> 2 Lafayette Street   18th Floor
> New York, N.Y. 10007   (212) 566-7633

> Supervising Real Estate Manager
>   for Manhattan   (212) 566-7650

Federal surplus properties can be checked through the General Services Administration in Washington, D.C., but most cities will have a local federal office.

For information on federal surplus property in the New York City area contact:

> U.S. General Services Administration
> Business Service Center
> 26 Federal Plaza
> New York, N.Y.   (212) 264-1234

landmark buildings

It is the concern of the New York Landmarks Conservancy to promote landmark quality buildings, help save endangered landmark buildings, and assist in recycling buildings of architectural importance. It is an advocacy organization. It is a not-for-profit corporation. Most major cities have equivalent private organizations addressing themselves to the same problems.

It is New York City Landmarks Preservation Commission, the City agency, that is empowered to make landmark designations. A designated landmark may be altered only with the approval of the Landmarks Preservation Commission.

A group interested in a building recommended for recycling for artists can check with the Commission for information. It is even possible to rally forces to get an important building declared a Landmarks Building, as in the case of the Astor Library/Public Theater.

For information about landmark buildings contact:

> New York Landmarks Conservancy
> 17 Battery Place
> New York, N.Y. 10004   (212) 425-4085

> New York City Landmarks Preservation Commissio
> 305 Broadway
> New York, N.Y. 10007   (212) 566-7577

> The National Trust for Historic Preservation*
> 740–748 Jackson Place, N.W.
> Washington, D.C. 20006   (202) 638-5200

*There are six regional and field offices throughout the United States. The mid-Atlantic field office, also at national headquarters, serves New York and the mid-Atlantic states. The National Trust can give locations and addresses of offices serving other geographic areas upon request.

5

evaluating
a space

Renting or buying a space is a major commitment. Take all the time necessary to make certain it is the right space for you. You will need to know what to look for when inspecting the space, in the building exterior as well as the interior, and what to look for in the surrounding neighborhood.

Cost will be among the deciding factors and one to keep in mind while evaluating the specifics. In addition to the initial cost of renting or buying the space, what will be the cost of desired renovations and necessary repairs? What expenses will be involved in bringing the space up to Code?

You need to be aware of potential problems that might not be readily apparent—heat in the winter (if you happen to be looking at the space in the summer), intrusive noises in the evening (if you are checking the space in the daytime). Find out who your neighbors are and if their use of the building might interfere with your own. Who shares exits and entrances and for what? Spend some time in the space, during the day and at night.

In addition, if a special arrangement is in question—perhaps the rent is low but you will have to share the space with time limitations imposed—you will have to carefully weigh the sacrifices against the advantages.

The guidelines below, and the checklist at the end of the chapter, should lead you through a knowledgeable evaluation to the right decision.

the neighborhood

Make notes of your first impressions of a building and the surrounding area.

Does the building appear to be in good condition, or is it in a state of deterioration? Take a good look at the other buildings on the street. What condition are they in? If renovations are being done on some of them, it's a good indication that the neighborhood is on the upswing. If, on the other hand, there are any deserted buildings, signs of recent fire or neglect, be warned.

What else about the street is of note? Is the garbage collected regularly? Are the street lights functioning and is the street well lit at night?

What about the surrounding neighborhood? Take a moment to consider your audience and your actors walking through these same streets, from the bus stop or train station. Are there any trees along the way? Any restaurants or pubs nearby? Are there any galleries or shops to browse in?

It could be of benefit if the area is already populated by several theatres—an area already identified by an audience. For example, since the Public Theater established itself on Lafayette, this street has become more and more populated by Off Off Broadway theatres. As a result, other amenities, like restaurants, have grown up to fill a need.

Take into account the safety of the area. Visit it at night. Do you feel safe walking through the streets? Are there adequate street lights? Is there some activity on the street?

Take everything into account. Your initial impressions of the neighborhood are likely to be shared by your audience.

transportation and accessibility

Another important consideration when looking for space is that of public transportation. How easy will it be for your audience to reach the theatre? Make certain the area is well serviced by public transportation.

Check the parking situation. Is there a parking lot nearby? Is on-the-street parking permitted during performance hours in the immediate area? Check the posted signs to determine parking limitations. Even though, in some areas, only a small proportion of your audience may come by car, parking is still an important consideration. Make it as easy as possible for people to come to your theatre. Your company may have vehicles to park as well.

noise

One critical problem is noise; either noise from adjacent tenants or ambient external noise.

Inside, noise transmission most often occurs between floors. Find out what the use is upstairs. Is there likely to be intrusive noise during performance hours? If the space upstairs is lived in by someone who plays a stereo very loudly, you may have a problem; particularly if the only thing that separates the two of you is a wooden floor and a tin ceiling.

Soho Rep has this problem. They estimate the cost of soundproofing the ceiling might run as much as $5,000–6,000. Clearly situations like this are best avoided.

Bond Street Coalition shares space with The Ladies Fort Jazz Club, which is located in the basement. It was free space for the cost of renovation! But their performance time is limited to the hour-and-a-half before the club opens—unless, of course, they can work jazz into the script!

If there are other tenants on a floor, check the partitions that separate the spaces. Go into the neighboring space and make noise while someone listens on your side of the wall. Knocking on the walls will also give you some indication of their relative solidity. Remember also that while you may not hear adjacent tenants who make very little noise, they may very well hear you. Can you build, hammer, and saw during all-night tech sessions, or rehearse with loud voices and loud music?

External noise factors are harder to judge; at the same time they are not quite so troublesome. If there is a subway line nearby, there may be rumblings and vibrations transmitted by the trains, as at the Public Theater. Often, heavy truck traffic will transmit vibrations as well as a low level of noise. These intrusions are more on the level of a nuisance.

However, a bar or disco next door or across the street can create havoc with a performance. Check it out. And don't locate next door to a firehouse!

Street noise may be a greater problem during the summer months when, if there is no air conditioning, you open your windows. Consider this if you locate on a street with a lot of activity during the evening. When the windows are open, the noise level will rise considerably. Soundproofing may be difficult. (See Chapter 9.)

One OOB producer recommends taking a sleeping bag and "living" in a space around the clock for a couple of days to check out the noise, before signing a lease.

inspection of the building

Initial reactions are notoriously deceptive and nowhere is this truer than when looking at old buildings. They are romantic, intriguing, full of "possibilities." The imagination commences to work overtime to weave fantasies. Your emotional response on first encounter with a building is important, but ultimately the condition behind the facade will be more important. So take a closer look at the condition of any building in which you are seriously interested and check it for what signifies trouble. Much of this will be applied common sense. Later, before you reach a final decision, an expert should be consulted.

The building conditions discussed below will be even more important to consider if you are buying your space, but should not be overlooked if your plan is to rent. Use the checklist provided at the end of this section while inspecting the building.

what to look for in the building exterior

Settling. First see if the building is *plumb*—both horizontally and vertically. It should be at right angles to itself and to the ground. Older buildings have a tendency to settle and become slightly out of line—it is the degree to which they have settled that you should check. Look at the rows of windows and the lintels above the doors and windows; they will give a good indication of just how much the building is out of plumb.

Masonry. Examine the masonry for signs of cracking and opening up. Also look for loose stones and sagging corners.

Cornices. The condition of cornices is best ascertained from the roof. Note any cracks, crumbling or missing pieces.

Roof. In addition to examining the cornices, it is very important to check the roof itself for damage. Walk around. Take note of the condition of any skylights, vents, chimneys, or water tower. Look for signs of leakage. It is also a good idea to look at the ceiling directly under the roof for any signs of *spawling* (crumbling, rotten plaster) due to leakage, especially around the ceiling, electrical fixtures, molding, or chimneys.

Fire escapes. If there are any fire escapes, a good way to check their condition is to simply walk on them. Take note of any rusting corrosion, any weak or missing sections.

Stoops, entrances, and doors. Check the alignment of the doors with the door frame for sagging. Exterior doors should conform to the Building Code, and they should open out. Will it be easy to load in or out through the doors in their current size and location? Check the condition of any steps leading to the doors, and the stoop for signs of crumbling or missing sections.

Back-of-building. In cities, it is sometimes difficult to see the back of a building. But, if at all possible, it is important to check it for the same problems or flaws listed above. There may be a window, courtyard, fire escape, or adjacent building from which you can get a good look.

what to look for in the interior

Floors. Check for any slanting, sagging, or warping of wooden floors; look for unevenness and cracking in concrete ones. Find out what materials are used in the construction of the floor and, if possible, get a look at the beam supports underneath to check for dry rot or sagging.

Take note of the *live load* of the floor. In a commercial building this information should be posted on a wall; if it is not, ask the owner for the previous Certificate of Occupancy or check at the Plan Room in the Department of Buildings. (See Appendix for address.)

Stairs and corridors. Take a good look at the stairs and corridors. Are they open or enclosed? What materials are used in their construction, wood or steel? Check for signs of wear—for loose or broken steps, for sagging sections. Are the railings and their supports intact? Any *winders* (stairs that make turns)? Check the width of the stairs and corridors—3'8" is a Code requirement for *means of egress*. Also, if used as a means of egress, there are *fire rating* requirements. (See Chapter 15 for definitions.) So check the construction of the walls surrounding these stairs and corridors.

How difficult will it be to load in and out on the stairs and through the corridor?

Elevators. If there are elevators, ask to see them in operation and try operating them yourself. Check the load capacity, usually posted inside the elevator. Will the size accommodate scenery and materials? If shared, are there any restrictions on its use—a limit on hours in operation?

Walls and ceilings. Take note of the materials used in wall and ceiling construction. Check for signs of dampness and leakage. If there are indications of leaking, try to determine the origin—through the roof or through exterior masonry, or is it localized around plumbing, windows, or vents?

Columns and load-bearing walls. If possible, discover which walls and columns are load-bearing and essential to the structural support. Load-bearing walls and columns cannot be removed without the substitution of costly support beams.

Windows and sashes. Check for alignment. Check for rotten frames and broken window panes that must be replaced. Try opening and closing all the windows.

Basement. Look for a water level line—a "ring around the bathtub" could indicate basement flooding. See if the boiler leaks.

If the type of building construction is not clear, the basement is a good place to see the construction since basements are often unfinished. If it is finished, the owner will probably allow you to pull down a small piece of basement plaster for a good look at the construction. With relation to the fireproofness of a building, wood construction is the type that should cause the most concern, exposed steel is better, and steel enclosed in masonry is the best.

Heating, air conditioning, ventilation systems. If possible, ask for each of the systems to be "fired up"—turned on—so that you may check the operational efficiency, including the noise level. Make a note of the type of heating and air conditioning systems being used. If the building is occupied, check with current tenants regarding the efficiency of these systems.

Electrical power. It is important that you make note of the type (AC or DC) and the amount of current (amperage) and the voltage supplied to the space in which you are interested. Usually each floor will have a fuse box or circuit breaker panel with the amperage marked. If not, take a look in the basement near the main service box for the building. 4-wire, 3-phase, 200-amp, 120-volt AC service should be considered as the minimum a small theatre will need for stage lighting; anything less will severely limit your stage lighting ability.

Consideration must also be given to the additional power necessary to service the rest of the theatre. These requirements will vary.

If the amount of current available is not adequate, Con Edison will run any additional amount of current needed in from the street free of charge, but a licensed electrician will have to install the proper fuse boxes and cable necessary to handle this additional load.

While you are at the box or panel, note the age and condition of the wiring—old cloth-covered or cracking rubber-covered, or newly rewired. Also check to see if the space has its own meter or if the meter is shared with another space. Ask if the building is grounded (new Electrical Code requirement). Note the general condition of outlets and sockets and take note of any exposed wires.

Plumbing. It is very difficult initially to tell if all the plumbing works. Commence by turning on all the faucets and flushing all the toilets. Check for plumbing leaks by examining the surrounding plaster. Make a note of the number and location of sinks, hot and cold taps, toilets, and drains.

In some buildings there may be an interior roof drain which runs on the inside of an interior wall, so if there are signs of leakage this could also be the cause.

Fire prevention and emergency systems. Check out the means employed for fire prevention within the space, such as a sprinkler system. Make note of the location and condition of the system and ask when it was last inspected. If there are fire extinguishers around, take a look at the date on the tags—this will be a good indication of the last time the space was inspected. Inquire about a fire alarm system and how it works.

Ask about an emergency light system and how it works. Ask to see it tested. Make a note of the location of the lights hooked into this system.

Security. It is wise to check all the possible means of entry which may be used by unauthorized persons. While on the roof take note of any doors, skylights, or trap doors and the means of locking them. If there are fire escapes note the accessibility of the windows to them. How many exits are there in the space and where do they lead? Are there any shared corridors? If the theatre will occupy the ground floor, are there separate entrance-ways for the floors above? Note the location of the windows with relation to the sidewalks, passageways, and courtyards. Any means of locking these windows? Any exterior entrances to the basement? In general, how easy will it be to secure this space from unauthorized entry?

can it be brought up to Code?

Generally, a potential space will not meet all Code requirements. (this chapter provides specific checklists that will help to determine the possibilities of bringing a potential theatre space up to Code.)

A good strategy to follow in estimating Code repairs is to carefully check out each potential space to determine what would be required to bring it up to Code for 100 seats. Here's where the architect or contractor friend on your Board can help. If possible do not settle on a space which cannot be brought up to Code—a space with an egress violation that is structurally impossible to correct; or a space on the tenth floor of a loft building; or a space which, because of the nature of the industry above it, requires installation of a 2 hour fire-rated ceiling at $5,000-8,000. All of these are real problems existing in OOB theatres now in operation.

It is quite possible to convert, renovate, and open your theatre in a space that is not up to Code. But sooner or later as your visibility rises, established OOB producers all agree, you may be forced by fire inspectors and building inspectors to eliminate the violations on the space or shut down. Therefore be sure you choose a space that can be brought up to Code; and, if it is necessary for you to ''phase'' the repairs you make, be sure you do the ones to insure public safety first.

Read the chapters on Codes to determine what conditions will call for only minimal changes or additions to meet the requirements. Any space that calls for major structural, electrical, or plumbing repairs, egress construction, or major interior repair work, should be avoided, no matter how cheap the rent. Not only are the costs prohibitively high for these changes, but often one thing leads to another and costs have a way of doing the same.

phasing

As far as the Building Code is concerned, you have to do everything that is required at the start in order to get a Certificate of Occupancy. Phasing should be considered if your budget won't allow you to bring a space up to all the Code requirements.

A suggested phasing strategy is to rent a ground floor space and plan initially to bring it up to Code for no more than 74 seats. You are required, in this situation, to have only one means of egress from your space, which the ground floor location will provide. If the space is in good condition otherwise, there should be little that you will have to do to the building.

Once you are established you will be in a position to increase the number of seats to more than 75, which means putting in a second means of egress. This can be done by building a 2 hour fire-rated exit passageway leading to a new exit door that will have to be put in an exterior masonry wall. Compare the plans shown for under 74 and for 100 seats (see the Old Code section of Chapter 15) and the concept will be clearer.

Planning to increase your capacity by 25 seats will require, perhaps, that you rent a little more space initially than you might have otherwise. Your space will be perfectly legal with one means of egress for 74 seats or less and perfectly legal with two means of egress for 100 seats.

It will be necessary, when expanding to 100 seats, to file for a Place of Assembly Permit. You will have to draw up another set of plans showing the new seating arrangement as described under the procedures for filing.

This same strategy will not work if you rent space above the ground floor. There, regardless of the number of people, you must have two means of egress from the start.

Other possibilities for phasing include subleasing space that you could not use immediately, to offset rent, or getting an option to take over adjoining space.

is it worth the rent?

dollar-per-square-foot value

One way to assess just how much you will be getting for the rent being asked is to compute and compare the dollar-per-square-foot costs of different spaces.

Measure the dimensions (length and width) of the space and multiply to determine the square footage. Then divide the total yearly rent by the total number of square feet; this will give you a dollar-per-square-foot value.

$$L. \times W. = sq.\ ft.$$
$$Annual\ rent \div total\ sq.\ ft. = \$/sq.\ ft.$$

For example: a small loft is approximately 25' x 100', giving a total of 2500 sq. ft. per floor.

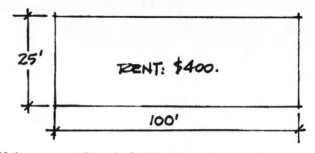

If the rent per floor is $400 per month, then the annual rent is $4,800 so:

$$4800 \div 2500 = \$1.92/sq.\ ft.$$

and you realize you have a very good price. ($2.00–2.50/sq. ft. is a good average rent.)

The table below provides a sampling of the dollar-per-square-foot costs for representative small theatre spaces.

table of cost in dollars-per-square-foot—1978

company & theatre	rent/month	annual rent	total sq. ft.	$/sq. ft.
* Joseph Jefferson Theatre	$100.	$1,200.	4,788	$ .25
† The Interart Theatre	1,200.	14,400.	28,000	.51
† Ensemble Studio Theatre	337.	4,044.	5,200	.78
New York Stage Works	620.	7,440.	4,800	1.55
** Playwrights Horizons	2,000.	24,000.	15,000	1.60
** Lion Theatre Co.	1,000.	12,000.	6,250	1.92
Colonnades Theatre Lab	725.	8,700.	4,000	2.18
†† Shelter West	917.	11,004.	4,830	2.28
Soho Repertory	692.50	8,310.	3,600	2.31
Jean Cocteau Rep.	1,750.	21,000.	6,750	3.11
Circle Repertory	4,294.	51,528.	5,000	10.31

* Space is located in a church
** Four wall lease arrangement (see Chapter 6 on *commercial leases*)

† Condemned building under Clinton Urban Renewal
†† Same space is rented to film group under separate lease (shared)

trade-offs

Using the dollar-per-square-foot formula you can easily compare the value of several spaces to see which is the better buy, everything else being equal. But nothing ever is equal. Finding a space will be a matter of "trade-offs." A good location and a higher rent versus a not-quite-so-good location and a cheaper rent. It's rarely that simple, however. You will find a not-quite-right space in good condition; it will be in an excellent location at a rent which is a little cheaper than an almost perfect, but very run-down space, in a not-so-bad location. These are most likely the kinds of decisions with which you will be faced, which is why it is so important to determine at the start what your needs and resources are. The trade-offs you make in selecting a space could affect your original goals, and to some extent dictate the kinds of productions you present.

There are many trade-off factors accounting for the wide spread in rents, such as location in a church or housing development, the type of lease offered, a sharing space arrangement. All of these possibilities should be considered when you are looking. The deals made by some existing OOB companies are worth considering for the trade-off factors involved.

Hudson Guild Theatre. The Hudson Guild Theatre is located in a housing development. They pay $1.00 a year rent and have many services furnished by the Housing Authority, such as maintenance, heat/AC, electricity, janitor services, and security. The principal drawbacks of this seemingly perfect deal are running an artistic organization on the bureaucratic level of social service agencies, and sharing the space and the staff with the many other activities of the housing development. As a department of Hudson Guild they have a responsibility to teach classes—16 hours per week—in theatre and dance related activities. The theatre staff spends one third of its time in community activities. And there are kids under foot everywhere—400 of them!

There are also drawbacks to the space itself—no off-stage space, not enough office space, no storage.

Being a part of the Hudson Guild has also proved to be an obstacle to the theatre in getting funding. The Guild regards the theatre as a non-essential program, and therefore requires that the theatre be self-supporting. But the Guild will not permit the theatre to seek funding from any agency or corporation that already gives to the Guild's other programs. This eliminates most of the potential donors in New York City, including those who give to the Guild through the Greater New York Fund.

Interart Theatre and Ensemble Studio Theatre. The Interart Theatre and the Ensemble Studio Theatre are both located in a condemned building in the Clinton Urban Renewal area, which is City-owned. The rent is very low (see preceding table), but they are on a month to month—30 day notice—basis and the rent can and has been raised without notice. An uneasy feeling and a gamble. Also public transportation is inadequate. Not enough electricity. No repairs. No services. The boiler keeps breaking down. They make their own improvements.

New York Shakespeare Festival (NYSF). The New York Shakespeare Festival leases the entire Public Theater building from the City of New York for one dollar a year rent. The building includes the seven performance spaces, the lobbies, box office, rehearsal spaces, and administration offices for the Festival.

The Public Theater is an "adaptive use" conversion of the famous old Astor Library, designated Federal Historic Building and New York City Landmark. The adaptive use landmark category permits the NYSF to alter the interior if necessary, but forbids them from changing the exterior of the building except with approval of the New York City Landmarks Preservation Commission.

The NYSF purchased the Astor Library building in 1966, shortly after the Landmarks designation cooled the interest of a developer who had plans for buying and demolishing it to put up a high-rise. The purchase price was $575,000. In addition the NYSF spent $2,000,000 on restoration and improvements between 1966 and 1971. These monies were essentially private donations.

By 1971 the NYSF was a million dollars in debt. In December of 1971 the City purchased the building from the NYSF for $2,600,000 with the lease-back agreement to NYSF at a dollar a year, thus wiping out the debt and repaying NYSF for their improvements. It is essentially a net lease arrangement. Although the City retains the responsibility for any major structural repairs, the NYSF is obligated to maintain the building. So, for a dollar a year and a commitment to "continue to use the building in the public interest," the NYSF seems to have it made. However, since 1971, the Festival has spent another $500,000 in general improvements and the annual maintenance cost is a hefty $240,000 a year at current prices.

The Performing Garage. The Performing Garage, the original space of Richard Schechner's Performance Group, is part of an artists' residential cooperative in SoHo. The initial lease in 1967 was for ten years at $1,000 per month with no increases and it included the theatre's share of the maintenance as well as an option to buy at the 1967 price, which the group has opted to do. The drawbacks include a shared entrance, which reduces security, and noise problems—a baby's bed next to their wall in the adjoining space. Also they must provide their own utilities including heat.

In The Performance Group's recently acquired second space, The Envelope, an 1869 Landmark loft building, the rent is low—*9500 sq. ft.* (including a basement for storage) @ *$7,200 annual rent = $.76/sq. ft./yr.*—on the agreement that the group will make a "legal" theatre in the space. Recent discoveries since moving into the space indicate this will be very costly if not impossible to do. They admit there might have been second thoughts, if the problems had been identified beforehand. They have a ten year lease on the space.

Joseph Jefferson Theatre Company. Churches can provide good space plus many advantages. The Joseph Jefferson Theatre Company, located in the Little Church Around the Corner, pays only $100 a month ($1,200 annually) toward their expenses—heat, electricity, janitorial and maintenance costs. The church already has its Place of Assembly Permit and the theatre is protected from fire and electrical inspections, and certainly from any harrassment.

However, since they perform in a working church, they must strike part of their stage every Saturday night, clear out dressing rooms and prop room which are shared with the church choir; and there are certain times during the year, such as Lent, when they must dismantle the entire stage and all their equipment, and move out. During these periods, they must either suspend performances or set up temporarily in space nearby. The labor involved is enormous.

costs of renovation and conversion

The realities of the cost of renovation and conversion must be faced early, before a final decision on space is made. Costs of renovation are difficult to determine. Nonetheless, an estimate needs to be made before commencing work and a construction budget determined. There are two methods for figuring costs and arriving at a budget.

per square foot estimate

Renovation costs are traditionally determined on a square foot basis. This is the method most frequently employed by architects and engineers. It is the method used for estimating a complete job—new plumbing, electrical wiring, heating, ventilating, and new interior finishes. In this case, estimates could range from a low of $10 per square foot to a high of $60 per square foot, with the average at $20 to $30 per square foot; a 2,500 sq. ft. space could cost as little as $25,000 (primarily cosmetic) or as much as $150,000, depending on the design and the quality of the materials and labor involved. When using this method to estimate the cost of a theatre, a separate budget is made for special stage equipment. These budget figures would be developed by the theatre consultant.

materials/equipment/labor estimate

Since in all probability you will be doing much of the work yourself, you can save a great deal in labor costs. Labor can amount to 50% or more of the estimated costs. Therefore a better method to employ for figuring costs for the small, not-for-profit theatre is a do-it-yourself method of estimating where you ask yourself what has to be done to a particular space to convert it to the theatre you want; then you prepare an estimate for materials, equipment, and labor costs.

Compare your checklist of what the space has—or does not have—with a list of what you want. Make a complete list of everything that will have to be done. Next make a list of all the materials and equipment that will be necessary. Then make a list of all labor that must be paid for. This do-it-yourself budget breaks down into three major items: (1) materials, (2) equipment, and (3) paid labor and fees.

Materials. Start getting comparative prices over the phone for the materials you will need. Some lumber yards can be 50% higher than others.

You can do some of the groundwork in estimating the cost of materials even before you find a space. If, for instance, you want to use risers for seating, figure out how much lumber it will take to build them according to the number of seats. Whether or not the risers are built as originally conceived, the amount of lumber needed and the cost won't vary substantially.

Also, estimate the cost of a running wall. Walls are made up of 4' x 8' sheetrock and 2" x 4" lumber. Estimate the cost of a wall 8' high and 16' long; use this figure as a measuring stick for walls.

Paint is another item that can be estimated if you know the approximate square footage you intend to rent.

The cost items which will remain unknown are those involving the renovation of the actual space you select. Admittedly these costs can vary widely, so careful consideration of the estimated renovation cost for each potential space is crucial. Expert assistance should be sought in developing these estimates.

Equipment. Make a budget for stage and auditorium equipment: list what will be needed. Repeat the process of comparative pricing.

For example, if you plan on traditional fixed theatre seats or a type of movable seat, begin investigating what they cost. Look for sources of used seats. Get some idea of what 74 or 100 seats are likely to cost—new or used.

Now make a list of other equipment that will be necessary in the other areas of the theatre such as the offices, rehearsal room, lobby, box office, shops and dressing rooms. Start pricing this equipment.

Professional assistance and labor. Make a budget of anticipated professional fees and paid labor. For instance, architects', consultants', and general contractors' fees may vary widely. Comparative pricing can be done in this area prior to finding your space. It is also important to check the capabilities of these professionals, possibly by contacting other theatres that have used their services.

If you plan to act as your own general contractor, which should save a substantial amount of money, you will need to check comparative fees and reputations of electricians, plumbers, riggers, carpenters, and any other specialized laborers that may be required.

The budget. It is important to make up a complete budget even if some of the equipment items are not purchased immediately or if some of the services are rendered by your own staff or by volunteer labor. This will give you a complete picture.

After studying the chapters on the Codes, and after a lot of looking, you will become familiar with the kinds of spaces to look for that will require minimal alterations or additions. Plumbing, electrical work, heating/cooling systems, and structural changes are all costly. Don't go into a renovation where extensive work in these areas is necessary without first getting careful estimates.

Heeding the advice of those who have been through the process, you can count on the truth of one unhappy axiom—everything costs more than anticipated.

sample budget
The Performance Group

MEMO 12/25/77

to: Richard Schechner, executive director
from: Bruce Rayvid, technical director
re: renovation costs, 35 Wooster Street

FIRST FLOOR INTERIOR

item	renovation	materials	cost	hours
floors	lay new floor, 4000 sq. ft.	150 sheets particle board	$1,500	140
	finish floor	16 gallons	200	18
walls and ceilings	scrape and paint 6000 sq. ft.	40 gallons	600	110
insulation	install and seal doors, windows, skylights	4 doors 2 windows	700	120
		insulation drapes	300	
heating	clean steam heaters (7)	gas and electric	500	55
	install thermostat and timer system	lines and accessories		

item	renovation	materials	cost	hours
plumbing	repair toilets (3)	sump cleaner	200	
	repair sinks (2)	toilet fixtures		
	replace old lines	copper pipe	300	
	install hot water heater	50 gallon tank	250	
	install shower	stall type	300	
	test sprinkler system			120
electrical	re-circuit for dimmer capacity	riser and lines	300	
		dimmer board	1,500	
	improve existing conduit and receptacles	E.M.T. and wire fixtures	500	
	install work lights and switching system	overhead fixtures	700	
	install exit and emergency lighting	patch board		
		to code	500	120
passageway to "Performing Garage"	remove wall section	bricks, mortar	400	
	install double doors	2 sets doors	700	
	soundproof and insulate	soundstop board	200	
	phones and intercom		600	120
			$10,250.00	803

labor costs: 803 hours at $7.50 per hour*   + 6,022.50

COSTS, FIRST FLOOR INTERIOR $16,272.50

BASEMENT INTERIOR

item	renovation	materials	cost	hours
office	construct office	sheet rock, 2x4	700	140
		sound stop		
		furniture	500	40
		doors	100	15
floors	new floor for office and rehearsal areas	100 sheets particle board	1,000	90
	finish	12 gallons	150	15
walls and ceilings	scrape and paint	40 gallons	600	100
heating and ventilation	install gas heater and vented fans in office and rehearsal area	2 5,000 btu heaters vents to code 2 fans	900	80
plumbing	install toilet and sink	toilet and sink fixtures	400	100
	repair gas and water leaks in boiler	waste and water lines	400	
electrical	install office and rehearsal lights	E.M.T. and wire	700	60
	install conduit and receptacles	lighting fixtures		
office entrance	construct separate entrance and stairway to office	door and hallway	800	130
		staircase	400	
	bell and buzzer		200	15
trap door and stairway	construct trap door for storage of large scenery in basement	2 x 4, hinges	200	30
		particle bd.		
		staircase	200	30
			$7,250.00	845

labor costs: 845 hours at $7.50 per hour   +6,337.50

THEATRE EXTERIOR

		materials	cost	hours
facade	scrape and paint restore where possible	20 gallons	400	100
signs/flags	construct hanging apparatus for signs and/or banners	steel, pulleys, cleats	500	40
overhead rolling door	install garage door for night security	16 x 45 rolling door, locks, motor drive	1,500	100
lighting	install outdoor sign and safety illumination	8 P.A.R. 150w lamps conduit, fixtures	400	40
stairway	install easy access stairs and rails for audience to code	metal stairs and rails	800	80
			$3,600	360
		labor costs: 360 hours at $7.50 per hour	+2,700.	
		COSTS, THEATRE EXTERIOR	$6,300.00	

MISC. FEES

Lawyer		2,000
Architect		2,000
Licensing		1,000
		$5,000

TOTAL COSTS: RENOVATION 35 Wooster Street

first floor interior	16,272.50
basement interior	13,587.50
theatre exterior	6,300.00
misc. fees and licensing	5,000.00
	$41,160.00

*The $7.50 per hour for labor costs is an estimated average hourly wage; obviously professional licensed plumbers and electricians cost much more, but this increase is offset by an estimated amount of volunteer labor and also by labor performed by the permanent staff.

EVALUATING A SPACE

evaluation

Once you have examined several buildings with a critical eye for structural defects and shortcomings, you can sit down with the notes you have made and begin to compare, putting them in order of desirability.

Keep in mind the limitations of your money and manpower resources with relation to what each building will require. The chapters in this book on the Building, Electrical, and Fire Prevention Codes will help you to evaluate your findings in terms of Code requirements. Make notes on each building with relation to what needs to be done—rewiring, plastering, new floor, new plumbing, additional doors, knocking out walls. Note the expenses involved and your resources for advice, inexpensive labor, and materials.

The main point is to be aware of all the problems of a space before making a commitment. Walk into a new space with your eyes wide open.

The Evaluation Checklist can be reproduced on standard 8½ × 14 xerox sheets for use on the site. Fill out and keep a checklist for each space under consideration. Make rough floor plans on the reverse side of the checklist.

50

evaluation checklist

specifics

Date of visit: _____

Weather: sunny rainy hot cold damp dry snowy

Building address: _____

Building orientation: N S E W NE NW SE SW

Contact: _____

owner agent other   **Phone:** _____

Rent per month: _____   **Annual rent:** _____

Total square footage: _____   **Cost per sq. ft.:** _____

Dimensions: height   width   depth   total sq. ft.

1st fl.			
2nd fl.			
3rd fl.			

Neighborhood: residential commercial manufacturing

Building type: brownstone storefront loft
other _____

Building age: _____

Previous use: _____

Neighbors: business residence occupied vacant

right _____

left _____

above _____

below _____

Building's zoning designation: _____

exterior conditions

Facing: board brick brownstone clapboard other _____
general condition: _____

Steps: stone wood concrete other _____
general condition: _____

Doors: wood steel metal glass other _____
frames: wood steel   dimensions: _____
general condition: _____

Backyard: dirt concrete other _____
dimensions: _____

neighborhood

Nearest subway stops: _____

Nearest bus stops: _____

On-the-street parking: _____
restrictions: _____

Nearest parking lot: _____
hours: _____   fee: _____

Street and sidewalks: potholes cracks crumbling irregular
good

Street lights: well-lit adequate poor

Roof access: ladder stairs trap door

Roof: new old holes leaks cracks bubbles
general condition: _____
Roof parapet: wood molding gutter drainpipe other _____
general condition: _____
Fire escapes: yes no
general condition: _____
Repairs needed: _____
General impression: _____

Nearest restaurants and pubs: _____
hours: _____
Nearby shops, hardware stores, etc. : _____

Special factors: Urban Renewal landmark building
Equity contract restrictions _____
city-owned federal-owned other: _____
General impression: _____

---

mechanical systems

Heating: steam hot water forced air unit ventilating
oil electricity
age: _____ general condition: _____
Air conditioning: throughout roof units none
general condition: _____
Electrical: A/C D/C
service: to floor: _____ phase _____ wire _____ amps _____ volts
to buildings: _____ phase _____ wire _____ amps _____ volts
circuit breaker panel fuse box location: _____
number and location of outlets: _____

additional service required: yes no
general condition of wiring: _____
Plumbing: clear patched broken
number and location of bathrooms: _____
number and location of sinks: _____
hot water heater: adequate inadequate inoperable
capacity: _____ gallons
general condition: _____
Security: doors: locks gates bars
windows: locks gates bars
number of exits: _____ alarm system: yes no
Emergency systems: sprinkled extinguishers fire alarm
emergency lighting

Repairs needed: _____
General impression: _____

---

interior conditions

Floors: wood concrete linoleum tile other _____
live weight load: _____ lbs. per sq. ft.
general condition: _____
Stairs: wood marble concrete metal stone
open enclosed width: _____
general condition: _____
Corridors: wall construction: _____
width: _____ general condition: _____
Elevators: yes no passenger freight manual automatic
dimensions: _____ capacity _____ lbs.
Walls and ceilings: brick plaster sheet rock concrete block
drywall other _____

general condition: _____
Columns: yes no measurements between: _____
Windows: number: _____ dimensions: _____
frames: wood steel aluminum
glass: broken cracked missing panes
general condition: _____
Basement: finished unfinished material: _____
beams: wood steel concrete & steel
floor: dirt wood tile linoleum other _____
general condition: dry damp water marked
repairs needed: _____
general impression: _____

Rough layout:

part two
how to get it

negotiating for a space

buying or renting

Most small theatres starting out find it easier to rent a space than to buy one. However, some small theatres have found it to their advantage to own their space—renting out the top floors as rehearsal space, commercial space, or, if it is lawful, as living space, to help defray the costs of maintaining the building.

In owning a building, however, a theatre group must be prepared to deal with the very real responsibilities that are inherent in paying the costs of ownership: maintenance of exterior and interior—both operational and architectural expenses; meeting the cost of fuel, gas, water, electricity; collecting rent; making mortgage payments. Some producers feel that the time consumed in owning and maintaining a building takes too much time away from creative work.

Renting may diminish many of the responsibilities associated with owning a space. Just how much responsibility is transferred to the theatre company is a matter to be negotiated in the lease. In a net lease situation, a great deal of the responsibility for the building is assumed by the tenant.

real estate taxes

Although a not-for-profit theatre has tax exempt status under the federal laws, it is not exempt from paying local real estate taxes. If a theatre is renting only a portion of the building, its share of real estate taxes will be passed on to it by the landlord as part of the rent, naturally. In New York City these taxes are usually 15–23% of a building's total rent revenues.

Even if a landlord has tax exempt status (which is usually limited to religious, charitable, or educational organizations), a theatre as a tenant is not exempt from real estate taxes. The church, for example, must pay real estate taxes on the part of its building rented by the theatre, unless the church can establish that the theatre's use is reasonably incidental to the purposes of the church, or that the theatre is an extension of the church.

Tax advantages to a theatre company that owns its space are possible, but are by no means automatic or even easy to negotiate or obtain. In New York City, for example, restrictions on exemptions have recently been tightened. A theatre that uses part of its space for teaching might apply for real estate tax exemption for that part of the space only. If teaching is part of your plan, it would be well to state in your incorporation that one of your purposes is educational.

commercial leases

Commercial leases have no guidelines established by law, so all points of the lease are up for negotiation. As in any bartering situation each party will try to get the best possible deal. It will be a matter of give and take.

Any lease should clearly spell out which party is responsible for what. If either you or the landlord make concessions, promises of repairs, or changes in the lease, make sure they are in writing. Verbal agreements or ''gentleman's handshakes'' will probably not hold up in a court of law should any misunderstanding arise in the future.

background information

Before entering into lease negotiations, both parties need to do some background checking. As a prospective tenant, you may be asked to provide the landlord with financial statements and character references. It is unfortunate, but small theatres are not thought of as good tenant risks: non-payments, violations, and lack of responsibility are all cited as reasons. You may need to ''prove yourself.'' Consider bringing in your lawyer, perhaps an architect and theatre consultant, to meet with the landlord prior to lease negotiations. If you can favorably impress the landlord, lease negotiations may go a lot smoother.

Just as a landlord checks potential tenants, you should be checking out your prospective landlord. The information you glean may help you at the bargaining table. The following is a list of items to check:

Zoning. Check with the Department of Buildings to be sure you are in the correct zone for a theatre. If not, a zoning variance will be needed and many landlords are not willing to go through this costly and lengthy procedure. (See Chapter 14.)

Square footage. Accurately measure the space and compute the dollar-per-square-foot value (see Chapter 5). Often the square footage figures quoted by agents or brokers are rough estimates. Know exactly how much space you will be getting.

Incidentally, when a broker states the number of square feet, he is calculating it from the outside of the walls. His estimate does not make any deduction for columns, stairways, lavatories or other unusable areas within the space. The difference will generally be a loss of about 20% of the space.

Unpaid taxes. If the building's taxes are in arrears, this will affect you as a tenant. If the City takes over a building, you will not be evicted. If the building is sold at Public Auction, however, the new owner is not obligated to retain the theatre as a tenant. Ask the owner to give you proof; specifically, the receipted bill for the payment of real estate taxes, or consult the "in rem" listing at the Department of Tax Collection to see if a court notice has been issued for non-payment of taxes. You will need to have the block and lot number of the property in order to look up this information.

Unpaid mortgage payments. If the landlord is behind in his mortgage payments and loses the building, there is no guarantee that the mortgage company will allow you to remain. Ask to see financial statements on the building to check on status of mortgage payments. If you are renting a large part of the building, tell the landlord to get from the mortgager a letter saying the mortgage is current and that the mortgager has not sent a notice of default to the owner.

Outstanding violations. Check with the Department of Buildings to determine if there are any violations on the building which have not been corrected. If there are, this will hold up your Certificate of Occupancy application (see Chapter 18). Therefore, violations should be considered during lease negotiations.

Repairs and improvements. Make a note of all repairs and improvements that will be necessary to convert the space into a theatre. Get estimates on the costs involved. It will be easier to negotiate for repairs and improvements if you and the landlord each have a clear idea of the dollar costs.

Previous utility bills. Find out how much was spent in the past twelve months on heating and electricity, and any other utilities that you may be paying. This will give you a rough estimate of the costs involved above and beyond the rent.

Extended vacancy. If the space has been empty for a long time, the landlord will probably be anxious to rent and may be receptive to concessions in the lease, so it is worth investigating.

Other tenants. A good way to find out what kind of landlord you will be dealing with is to talk to other tenants in the building or to the previous occupant.

lease negotiations

There are points of negotiation which are common to all commercial lease arrangements; in addition, there are special clauses which must be negotiated by theatres because of the nature of the business.

The following apply to standard commercial lease negotiations:

Length of lease. A long lease will allow time to recoup any investments made on improvements. Each time the lease expires, the landlord has the right to raise the rent; there are no legal restrictions on the amount of this increase as in some residential leases. Consider no less than a 5 year lease.

Renewal options. The right to renew your lease, after the initial lease term, should be negotiated at the outset. Establish the amount of rent that you will pay during the renewal period, if you exercise the renewal option.

Amount of rent. The final rent figure should reflect any expenses or improvements which have been negotiated—going up or down depending on which party is paying for what.

Escalation charges. The landlord may request a clause to cover any increase in his operating costs which may occur during the term of the lease. This "escalation" will be in addition to the base rent. Escalation for real estate tax increases over the starting year is very common. The percentage of an increase in real estate taxes charged to you is usually based on the percentage of the building you rent. In this case, find out what your percentage of the building is and make sure the negotiated allowance for tax increases is fair.

Another way the landlord may figure the escalation charge is to base it on the "cost of living index." Try to avoid this. You are better off basing escalation rent on his real operating costs: fuel, taxes, insurance. Try to establish a maximum amount, beyond which you will not be required to pay.

Improvements. Renovations and improvements needed to convert the space into a theatre will have to be negotiated. A landlord may be willing to pay for structural changes—strengthening the floor or ceiling, repairing the stairways, adding toilets and sinks, or running additional power to the space. If you must pay for all improvements, try to get a concession in the rent for the first six months to a year, to offset part of these "front end" expenditures.

Operational costs. Heating, electricity, air conditioning, any costs involved with the actual operations of the building and your space, will need to be negotiated. Also consider the times of day and night that you will need heat and air conditioning. Many commercial buildings shut down operations at the end of a working day, so there may be extra costs involved to receive these services at night and on weekends.

Net or four wall leases. One way to get a lower rent is to rent on a *net,* or *four wall,* lease. A net lease will also give you the freedom to make any necessary improvements. However, expect to be responsible for all of the interior repairs and most of the operational costs. Be sure you are aware of all the costs involved. You will need to negotiate the responsibility for the structural systems: internal wiring, heating, and air conditioning, the plumbing and the boiler.

If you are negotiating for a net lease, you should insist that the landlord obtain a *nondisturbance agreement* from the mortgager. This is a written guarantee that, in the event of a foreclosure on the property, you will be permitted to remain in the space for the duration of the lease, if you are current in your rent payments and are meeting your other lease obligations.

Assignment and subleasing. *Assignment* gives the tenant the right to turn over the entire lease and premises to another party, in the event that he may be unable to finish out his lease. *Subleasing* is a short term renting of the space by the tenant, who will remain responsible for the space.

A landlord will resist these clauses and the best you may get is his agreement that "consent will not be unreasonably denied." The landlord may also ask for the right to examine all sublet agements prior to giving his approval. Because of the special nature of theatre, try to arrange a subleasing agreement without approval. This will give you the flexibility to handle the unexpected opportunity, such as another company needing rehearsal space or a hit show in need of a home.
Note: if there is any profit from a sublease, the landlord may demand all or part of it. This will have to be negotiated.

Violations. If there are outstanding violations on the building, you should make it the owner's obligation to cure any existing violations at his own expense. Also, add in a clause for any non-tenant created violations which may occur in the future.

Insurance. Most landlords will require liability insurance from their tenants. Ask about the fire insurance on the building to determine if the contents are insured. Many landlords will only have structural fire insurance and each tenant will have to be responsible for getting personal property and fixtures insured.

Option to buy. Consider negotiating an option to buy with an eye to possible future development.

The following points apply specifically to theatrical leases:

Definition of uses. Theatrical *use* implies use of a space for shows, rehearsals, and all that goes with setting up a show; if the space is to accommodate other uses, offices for instance, it will be necessary to specify this in the lease. Consider holding classes and lectures and showing films to gain extra revenue. Consider all possible uses for the future; negotiate for the unexpected.

The right to advertise. An agreement must be made concerning exterior signs used for advertising and their location on the building or the street. Again, plan for the future.

Other tenants. Negotiate a clause with the landlord stating that he may not rent adjacent spaces—above, below, or to either side of you—to any prospective tenant whose use of the space would in any way interfere with the operation of your theatre—because of noise from machinery, for example, or evening use. In addition, include any future tenants whose use of a space within the building would cause the operation of the theatre to become illegal, such as a high hazard occupancy group. For example, the Building Code prohibits a Place of Assembly from being located within 250 feet of any business that uses explosives.

Warranty of production content. The landlord may request protection or indemnification against any productions that violate the law in any way.

Necessary permits. The landlord may require that all permits necessary for the creation and maintenance of a theatre be obtained, and that proof of such be given.

innovative ways to use government resources

There are many innovative legalistically and politically sophisticated city, state, and federal real estate packages that can be put together for the benefit of the not-for-profit theatre sector. No two packages are ever exactly the same. Considerable legal assistance will be needed to make it all happen if you take this funding route. But, conversely, there are great financial possibilities and rewards.

The following should suggest strategies for getting property, capitalizing on discounts, making use of government programs for redevelopment, and the like.

tax abatement

For New York City, there are, under the Office of Economic Development (OED), two channels that can as a not-for-profit theatre or aggregate of theatres through t abatement. They are the Business Investment Incentive Program (BIIP) and the Industrial Commercial Incentives Board (ICIB). BIIP and ICIB can function separately or they can work in concert to accomplish abatement of (1) existing taxes on a property, and (2) taxes on improvements.

Business Investment Incentive Program (BIIP). This program has the authority to remove existing taxes on a property if doing this will serve to stimulate jobs and economic development. An aggregate of small theatres would find it easier to get this assistance. Theatre Row on 42nd Street took advantage of this program.

The program, which was developed to find an indirect way of giving tax abatement to industry, works through the City Public Development Corporation (PDC) or the State Urban Development Corporation (UDC), which are both quasi-public corporations.

Under BIIP the title to the property could pass directly to PDC or UDC. Also under BIIP, the City might take title to a property under certain circumstances. For example, if the property had substantial tax arrears, the City would take title in order to deal with this problem. It could, in turn, negotiate a lease-back arrangement with the theatre group, as was the case with the Theatre Row properties and the 42nd Street Redevelopment Corporation. It is important to note that under BIIP, title and improvements are passed on to the City.

There would be an "in lieu of tax" payment to the City. The lease-back payment would be negotiable. It would be substantially less than the real estate taxes on the property were it privately owned. For instance, it might be an amount that is based on a percentage of the organization's profits. However, this is subject to negotiation with each organization and varies with every project.

Under such an arrangement, the lease is long-term; 30 years, plus two 10 year options, for a 50 year total is a typical example.

Any organization that has title to a property is eligible. However, there are two obvious areas of difficulty for the small theatre company: first, financing the purchase and thus acquiring title; second, financing the rehabilitation. This is one reason why a group under an umbrella organization has a better chance. A small individual theatre probably would not qualify.

Even though small groups might not qualify for BIIP, they are encouraged to contact OED for advice and assistance. For instance, OED has information about and listings of property in their "Space Bank."

Business Investment Incentive Program
Office of Economic Development
225 Broadway
New York, N.Y. 10007   (212) 566-3812

Industrial and Commercial Incentives Board (ICIB).
ICIB gives direct abatements of increases in real estate taxes due to improvements. This does not remove existing taxes—it only affects increases. Title to the property would be passed on to PDC or UDC. Unlike BIIP, title to the improvements need not be passed on to the City.

Taxes are abated under a specified formula: for instance, the abatement might be gradually reduced over a 10 year period. This is to help the recipient project's cash flow during the first years.

Tax benefits may be obtained in either of two ways. For reconstruction, rehabilitation, or modernization of an existing structure: 95% of the *increased assessed value* will be exempted from real property taxes upon completion of the project, decreasing by 5% a year for the next 19 years.

For new construction: 50% of the assessed value of new construction will be exempted from real property taxes, upon completion of the project, decreasing by 5% a year over a 10 year period.

If a developer retains title to improvements, the developer can apply for *direct* tax abatement for those improvements.

Industrial and Commercial Incentives Board
Office of Economic Development
225 Broadway
New York, N. Y. 10007   (212) 566-0207

J51. J51 legislation is a New York City incentive plan. Its purpose is to encourage improvement of unused or underutilized property by giving a tax abatement or tax deferral to the owner for renovation.

Under J51 existing taxes can be abated depending on reasonable allowable costs of improvement, and it also provides exemption from reassessment for the amount of the improvements for a certain agreed upon number of years. If your improvements to a building result in a Class A, multiple dwelling Certificate of Occupancy, then you are eligible, automatically, for J51.

Although it applies only to housing, the City recently expanded the law to include formerly non-residential buildings that are converted to housing, such as lofts. There is some agitation to further modify the J51 law to apply to cultural facilities in renovated buildings.

If a theatre group structured a building conversion package to include living spaces as a part of the renovation it might be eligible for J51. Remember, however, that a Certificate of Occupancy is a prerequisite to getting J51 benefits, which means the renovation must bring the building up to Code.

> Housing Preservation and Development
> Department of Development
> J51 Unit, Room 9166
> 100 Gold Street
> New York, N. Y. 10038   (212) 566-0621/2

not-for-profit corporations

Various types of not-for-profit corporate structures, which have been created through legislation, serve as means for acquiring public monies or benefits—such as Community Development (CD) Funds, tax abatements, mortgage money—and/or as a mechanism for the lease or purchase of surplus properties. The first type, a Local Development Corporation (LDC), would be set up under the New York State Not-For-Profit Corporation Law. The second type, the Public Development Corporation (PDC) and the Urban Development Corporation (UDC), are quasi-public corporations established through State legislation primarily to implement the disposition of property.

These represent two different approaches that a developer or a theatre group interested in acquiring surplus property might employ.

Local Development Corporation (LDC). Not a source of funds, a Local Development Corporation is a means for steering the group towards sources of public monies or benefits, such as Community Development Funds, tax abatements, mortgage money. Perhaps its principal value is that it can lease or purchase properties from the City government without going through public auction.

Eligibility for forming an LDC is based on guidelines similar to those for eligibility for CD Funds (see Chapter 7)—the group must have charitable or public purposes that will spin-off jobs and economic impact.

A not-for-profit developer representing a theatre group, or an aggregate of theatres, would file to incorporate under Section 1411 (Local Development Corporations) of the New York State Not-For-Profit Corporation Law. Any group can file for an LDC; however, it is better to do it under an umbrella organization. The 42nd Street Redevelopment Corporation is a Local Development Corporation. It is the umbrella for the group of theatres in Theatre Row. The theatre groups are sub-tenants of the Corporation, but the Corporation put the redevelopment project and the property package together.

The main advantage of this strategy for a theatre group is that the City can lease or sell land and/or a building to an LDC without taking bids; it can be done for a negotiated sale price. This eliminates the risk to the theatre of expensive preparation, feasibility studies, and the like, only to lose the property to a higher bidder at public auction.

Public Development Corporation (PDC) and Urban Development Corporation (UDC). The single theatre company wishing to acquire City surplus property might find it more advantageous to use the mechanism of the PDC which has certain powers to deal directly with one specific developer or theatre group.

PDC is a Local Development Corporation governed by a Board of Directors; it was established primarily as an implementation tool in the disposition of City-owned property. As such it could serve as a conduit for the theatre and the Office of Economic Development in the negotiations for and the acquistion of a City surplus property.

UDC acts in much the same capacity for the State. It was the Harlem Urban Development Corporation that implemented the proposal for the renovation of the Loew's Victoria on 125th Street into The Harlem Performing Arts Center, for example.

acquiring city surplus property

Theatre groups interested in buying or leasing property owned by the City (see Chapter 3 for types of buildings included on the the City surplus list and Chapter 4 for how to locate surplus property) will have to work through various City agencies to lease or purchase the property and to negotiate a payment arrangement. Although this is a long procedure, there could be financial benefits involved.

First the Department of Real Estate must be called to determine the status of the property. It could be that it is about to go on the auction sales list, in which case bids will be taken, and the theatre company may have competition.

Cities acquire property in numerous ways; most frequently by taking possession due to tax arrears. A group interested in a property that has fallen into substantial arrears can inform the City of such property and propose that it be taken over by the City. The City's acquisition procedure (*in rem*) usually takes about one year.

The interested party can approach the Department of Real Estate, or the Office of Economic Development (OED), with a proposal for the use of the property.

If OED agrees that the proposal is good and will benefit the City, they will place a "property hold"—for three months or six months with possible renewals—on the property. This allows them time to study the value of the proposal and make recommendations.

Next, the OED negotiates with the theatre group and with the City agency in charge of the property to see under what conditions the property could be made available to that group. Together they construct a proposal to promote the project to the City.

A proposal could be made for a long-term lease with "in lieu of tax payment" or purchase. The City would then agree to lease, or sell, the property to the theatre. The actual deal would probably include use of the Public Development Corporation. PDC is a quasi-public corporation that could serve as a conduit through which the City property could be leased or sold to the theatre. Local Development Corporation or Urban Development Corporation could be used for the same purpose.

The new City charter requires that the proposal go through the Uniform Land Use Review procedure. The procedure for approvals takes about six months, possibly more, possibly less. These are the steps it would involve:

- Application is submitted to the City Planning Commission.
- City Planning certifies application "complete."
- City Planning then refers proposal to local Community Board.
- Community Board must review proposal and make recommendations. It has the option to hold public hearings.
- Community Board returns its recommendations to City Planning Commission.
- City Planning Commission holds hearings on projects which require its action.
- City Planning Commission adopts or rejects proposal.
- City Planning Commission, if it approves, submits proposal to Board of Estimate for approval. Board of Estimate must also hold a public hearing.
- And, finally, the Board of Estimate passes on the project.

legal assistance

Any theatre group about to obtain a space, whether renting or buying, will want the assistance of a lawyer who can protect its interests and give advice.

Most leases are written by lawyers for the landlords. If renting a space, a lawyer will be needed to interpret the lease and aid in negotiations.

If buying a space, a lawyer will again be needed for negotiations and drawing up the necessary papers. The many good real estate deals available to not-for-profit organizations through government agencies can be quite complex and will require extensive legal advice.

Don't allow yourself to be rushed into signing a lease, or into putting down deposit monies, without consulting a lawyer.

A lawyer will also be necessary for drawing up contracts—with architects, for instance, or with theatre consultants that may be hired. If a zoning variance is required, a lawyer will again be needed.

A lawyer on your Board of Directors may be able to give aid and advice. If not, check with OOBA for lawyer referrals, or with Volunteer Lawyers for the Arts and Volunteer Urban Consulting Group (see Chapter 7).

Community Boards

It is generally good policy to make contact with the Community Board in your district as soon as you plan to occupy a new space, as you may need their support, their help, or, if a variance is required, their approval.

Community Boards are just what their name implies. Members are political appointees who are responsible for the districts they serve. The Community Boards were established to give advice to the City Planning Commission on matters of land use. Their responsibilities may include budgeting and inspection of local services such as police and sanitation, establishing land-use policy, passing on proposed new construction in the area, and reviewing zoning variances for a change of use.

There are 12 Community Boards in the Borough of Manhattan, each chaired by an individual. These chairpeople make up the Borough Board, which is directly responsible to the Borough President. Each local Community Board is comprised of approximately 50 members, each of whom has a residence or business in the district or has an interest in the district for a professional reason.

Community Districts

From the map reproduced here, you can find out into which Community District your building falls. Each Community Board has a district office and a district manager who is a full-time employee. The district numbers, addresses, and telephone numbers of the Community Boards for Manhattan are:

# 1	280 Broadway	374-1421
# 2	5 West 3rd St.	533-1617
# 3	175 West 4th St.	533-5300
# 4	326 West 42nd St.	736-4536
# 5	745 Fifth Ave.	753-2620
# 6	330 East 26th St.	679-2287
# 7	5 West 63rd St.	362-4008
# 8	316 East 88th St.	427-4840
# 9	454 West 145th St.	234-7768
#10	215 West 125th St.	222-4877
#11	307 East 116th St.	831-8924
#12	3960 Broadway	781-3802

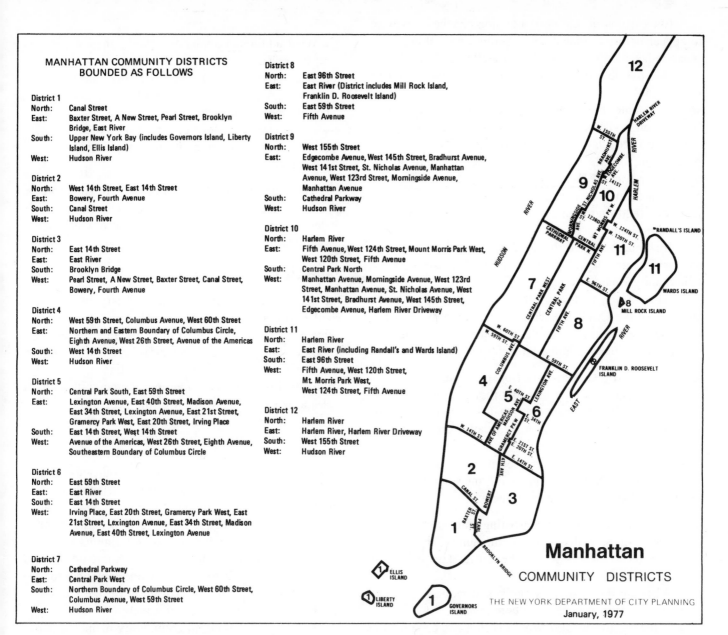

MANHATTAN COMMUNITY DISTRICTS BOUNDED AS FOLLOWS

District 1
North: Canal Street
East: Baxter Street, A New Street, Pearl Street, Brooklyn Bridge, East River
South: Upper New York Bay (includes Governors Island, Liberty Island, Ellis Island)
West: Hudson River

District 2
North: West 14th Street, East 14th Street
East: Bowery, Fourth Avenue
South: Canal Street
West: Hudson River

District 3
North: East 14th Street
East: East River
South: Brooklyn Bridge
West: Pearl Street, A New Street, Baxter Street, Canal Street, Bowery, Fourth Avenue

District 4
North: West 59th Street, Columbus Avenue, West 60th Street
East: Northern and Eastern Boundary of Columbus Circle, Eighth Avenue, West 26th Street, Avenue of the Americas
South: West 14th Street
West: Hudson River

District 5
North: Central Park South, East 59th Street
East: Lexington Avenue, East 40th Street, Madison Avenue, East 34th Street, Lexington Avenue, East 21st Street, Gramercy Park West, East 20th Street, Irving Place
South: East 14th Street, West 14th Street
West: Avenue of the Americas, West 26th Street, Eighth Avenue, Southeastern Boundary of Columbus Circle

District 6
North: East 59th Street
East: East River
South: East 14th Street
West: Irving Place, East 20th Street, Gramercy Park West, East 21st Street, Lexington Avenue, East 34th Street, Madison Avenue, East 40th Street, Lexington Avenue

District 7
North: Cathedral Parkway
East: Central Park West
South: Northern Boundary of Columbus Circle, West 60th Street, Columbus Avenue, West 59th Street
West: Hudson River

District 8
North: East 96th Street
East: East River (District includes Mill Rock Island, Franklin D. Roosevelt Island)
South: East 59th Street
West: Fifth Avenue

District 9
North: West 155th Street
East: Edgecombe Avenue, West 145th Street, Bradhurst Avenue, West 141st Street, St. Nicholas Avenue, Manhattan Avenue, West 123rd Street, Morningside Avenue, Manhattan Avenue
South: Cathedral Parkway
West: Hudson River

District 10
North: Harlem River
East: Fifth Avenue, West 124th Street, Mount Morris Park West, West 120th Street, Fifth Avenue
South: Central Park North
West: Manhattan Avenue, Morningside Avenue, West 123rd Street, Manhattan Avenue, St. Nicholas Avenue, West 141st Street, Bradhurst Avenue, West 145th Street, Edgecombe Avenue, Harlem River Driveway

District 11
North: Harlem River
East: East River (including Randall's and Wards Island)
South: East 96th Street
West: Fifth Avenue, West 120th Street, Mt. Morris Park West, West 124th Street, Fifth Avenue

District 12
North: Harlem River
East: Harlem River, Harlem River Driveway
South: West 155th Street
West: Hudson River

Manhattan
COMMUNITY DISTRICTS
THE NEW YORK DEPARTMENT OF CITY PLANNING
January, 1977

appearing before the Board

Whether or not you choose to inform the Community Board of your existence before or after you have established yourself will be partly determined by whether or not you require a zoning variance. If you do, it is best gotten before you spend time or money renovating a space, and even before you sign a lease. (See Chapter 14 for more information on getting a zoning variance.)

Even if you do not need a zoning change, it is wise to appear before the local board before undertaking your plans rather than to wait until you are in need of help.

One possible funding source to your group could be Community Development (CD) Funds, which, while not under the Community Board's immediate jurisdiction, must pass their review and gain their approval. (See Chapter 7 for a more complete description.) While it might be possible to submit an application for CD Funds without going through the local board, they do not take lightly to such avoidance and you could find yourself very low on the priority list of funding items.

It should be noted that at least one group, the Interart Theatre, found its space through the local Community Board.

Also, if you find yourself having difficulty with one or more of the City's agencies, the Community Board can often help you through the red tape involved or provide sound advice about procedure.

Concerns of the Community Boards. Community Boards are not out to get you, but they are charged with the responsiblity of seeing that what is done or proposed to be done is in the interest of the whole community which they serve.

When considering a proposed new activity, whether or not a zoning variance is involved, these are some of the things that are of concern to them:

• What will happen to the existing tenants of a space? If the business really serves a community, the Board may want to make sure that the tenant stays in the area and can easily relocate.
• What are the landlord's motives in requesting a variance? Will it benefit the community?
• Is theatre use viable? Would such a use enhance the community? Is there evidence that the theatre is financially viable?
• What would the change mean for the existing neighborhood? How does it fit in with or complement existing uses?

• What additional demands would a theatre use make on the existing services in the community (sanitation, police)? Would it generate more noise, traffic, and parking problems? What are its hours of use; do these conflict with other uses?
• In the case of a theatre, would the productions involve nudity or perversity that might not be welcomed?

These are the questions to think through before you appear at a meeting of the Board. Bring as much evidence as you can to prove your theatre will benefit the community.

gaining local support

The need for community support will largely depend on whether you are locating in an area that is very residential. These areas tend to be rougher on reviewing proposed zoning changes, because there is a residential community to protect. If you are locating in a heavily commercial or manufacturing area, community support will not be essential, as most of the people only occupy the area during the day and are not as deeply concerned about other uses after regular business hours.

It is a common mistake of many groups not to gain community support for their project. Your local board office can give you a good reading on whether you should attempt to get community support and can also give you the names of the more vocal persons in the district who are likely to voice their opinions.

Beyond seeking help from the Community Board, you should approach the problem on a neighborhood basis. If there is a Block Association for the block on which you intend to locate, start there.

One way of talking to community members is to take a walk around at a time when people are likely to be out. Introduce yourself and talk up your plans with several of your neighbors. Talk with local merchants. They know who's who in the community and they also have something at stake in the matter.

7

resources for making it happen

It is very difficult for the new theatre company with no track record to obtain any kind of funding, particularly money for bricks and mortar. However, in the hunt for funds for renovation of your theatre space, you do have one definite advantage: you can approach agencies and foundations that support city and/or neighborhood revitalization (not necessarily through the arts), if your theatre will contribute positively to an area's regeneration.

There is not much specific information that can be given as to which particular foundations to approach. The Foundation Center, listed in this chapter, can probably provide the best leads. Several ideas are suggested here as well for using available resources in innovative ways to create funds for renovation.

The main purpose of this chapter is to lead you to the variety of resources, both money and people, that provide funding, or provide services and answer needs other than funding that are equally vital to you in the acquisition and conversion of your space.

funding

There are basically two types of funding resources available for the small theatre group that needs financial help with conversion of a space: funds for feasibility studies and funds for renovation and conversion.

FUNDS FOR FEASIBILITY STUDIES

The National Endowment for the Arts and the New York State Council on the Arts provide funding in the first category. Since one emphasis of these funding programs is on architectural design and planning, the right use of such a grant could cover payments for designs and blueprints for space conversion. Some theatre groups have had success in having architectural renderings paid for in this way.

It should be noted that there are also private foundations, not listed here, that consider support for feasibility studies.

National Endowment for the Arts (NEA)

Architecture, Planning, and Design Program— Cultural Facilities Research and Design. NEA's Planning and Design Program includes a category for "Cultural Facilities Research and Design" which is described as follows:

> To assist communities in the planning and design of exemplary cultural facilities . . . The Endowment does not provide money for acquisition of real estate, construction, or repairs to buildings. Grants are available for design and planning studies, research on aspects of facility design and management, feasibility studies, preparation of information to support promotion of a facility, planning for adaptive use of old buildings for arts-related use, and technical studies related to lighting, acoustical, and similar problems.

Organizations are also encouraged to apply if they plan to improve access for the handicapped through design.

The maximum grant awarded is $30,000; but most are not that large. Be realistic in your request. Unrealistically large requests will be rejected. Funds are usually "matching."

National Endowment for the Arts
Architecture, Planning, and Design Program
2401 "E" Street, N.W.
Washington, D.C. 20506   (202) 634-4276

New York State Council on the Arts (NYSCA)

Architecture and Environmental Arts Program. NYSCA describes this program as follows:

> Support is available to determine the appropriateness of adapting existing structures for cultural use. Support is intended to assist established organizations in the early stages of planning and will be directed toward professional fees for study of use, economic and architectural feasibility.

At present this is a brand new program, without precedents for funding patterns. Support is contingent upon availability of funds. Capital construction money is not available in this program. For example, there is no money for bricks and mortar, or for architectural drawings in relation to capital construction.

When budget permits, other NYSCA programs, including its Theatre Program, give Technical Assistance Consultants' Fees. This is money for consultants whose specialities may be administrative, legal, fiscal, or design. Either the theatre can choose a consultant from an approved NYSCA list, with NYSCA paying the fees; or NYSCA will help pay for another qualified consultant of the theatre's choice. These grants are limited to three days. In this way theatres' consultants fees can be partially reimbursed.

New York State Council on the Arts
Architecture and Environmental Arts Program
80 Centre Street
New York, N.Y. 10013   (212) 588-2863

FUNDS FOR RENOVATION

One source of funds for renovation is Community Development, a federal program administered by the Department of Housing and Urban Development (HUD). With the right approach, the small not-for-profit theatre could be eligible for this type of funding.

Community Development (CD) Funds

Theatre projects are relatively new in this arena. CD Funds are available to private, not-for-profit developers; or for real estate on which it is extremely difficult to raise money for improvements. The former criteria would probably apply to an aggregate of small theatres such as Theatre Row on 42nd Street in New York City; the latter to the large, "sexy" theatres in need of rescue, such as Loew's Flatbush and Loew's 125th Street in New York City; Shea's Buffalo in Buffalo, New York; or possibly a Radio City Music Hall.

It would be misleading to imply that CD assistance is readily available for the small, individual theatre group; still getting CD Funds for small theatres is not impossible. A theatre group with an historic structure, such as a landmark designation building in need of renovation, might, for example, be eligible for CD funding.

Funds are available for either planning or development. Either an aggregate of theatres or the individual theatre may be able to get funds for all purposes: front-end planning, acquisitions, and renovation.

A project requesting CD Funds must be sponsored by a City agency and could be routed through the Mayor's Office of Economic Development—or through the New York City Department of Cultural Affairs. Projects approved for CD Funds must satisfy federal guidelines as well as City criteria. In general, the project must have a substantial impact on industry in the area, or on an improvement of the area; it must create a number of new jobs or preserve existing jobs; "lead to job development, employment, and job training"; prevent the loss of an essential physical resource; rehabilitate or preserve existing facilities; generate a high ratio of additional public or private funds. Other criteria include "projects in which citizens will contribute funds or services to sustain and improve their own environment," and "projects that enhance land use."

In New York the Community Development Fund Program is under the Office of Management and Budget (OMB), where the Office of Community Development has been set up for this purpose.

Office of Management and Budget
12th Floor, Municipal Building
New York, N.Y. 10007   (212) 566-6563

Urban Development Action Grants (UDAG)

These are federal funds from HUD that are given to economic development projects to leverage private investment. UDAG funds can be used in a number of ways, as direct grants, for instance, or as second mortgage financing. An eligible city agency must act as the sponsor for the developer, which can be either profit-making or not-for-profit.

The City of New York prefers to use UDAG to assist large projects. Though a small theatre might not be eligible to apply for and receive UDAG funds directly, it could benefit indirectly as a part of a larger development with UDAG funding.

service organizations

This survey of service organizations is limited to those which might be of help in solving a small, not-for-profit theatre group's space and renovation problems. The services available range from help with loans, to advice and technical assistance, to programs that increase box office sales. There are also organizations that provide information or publish handbooks, directories, or journals on relevant topics, such as funding, consultation resources, and the City Codes.

The Fund for the City of New York

This fund is not actually arts-oriented and it has no funds for bricks and mortar. There are, however, two areas in which it might be able to help.

The first is in providing technical assistance.

The second, and where it can probably be most helpful, is in giving short-term loans for cash flow problems; in the case, for instance, of the theatre that has an NEA or NYSCA type grant and is waiting for the actual cash. There is no interest charged; just a 1.5% service charge.

To find out exactly what you have to do to qualify for a loan, call Nancy Castleman at the Fund.

The Fund for the City of New York
419 Park Avenue South, 16th Floor
New York, N.Y. 10016   (212) 689-1240

Volunteer Urban Consulting Group (VUCG)

VUCG "provides professional management assistance to not-for-profit organizations." Any not-for-profit organization is eligible to apply. Charges, if any, are based on the ability to pay.

VUCG teams up volunteer professionals from the business world with not-for-profit organizations. Their assistance covers a wide variety of areas: finance planning and budgeting, accounting, insurance advice, internal operations, marketing, organizational structure and policies, and real estate.

In the past, they have helped such groups as these: The Puerto Rican Traveling Theatre (assisted with firehouse lease negotiations), Theatre Development Fund (advised on commercial lease for the housing of the Costume Collection), Ensemble Studio Theatre (made real estate contacts for the Ensemble in their search for new space), Stage Company (assisted in recruitment of Board members); and have aided many arts organizations with bookkeeping, budgeting, and management related problems.

Contact may be made with VUCG by either writing or calling.

The Volunteer Urban Consulting Group
300 East 42 Street
New York, N.Y. 10017   (212) 687-7420

Volunteer Lawyers for the Arts (VLA)

Legal assistance is available free of charge on arts related issues only (this includes real estate problems for performing arts groups). Services are limited to not-for-profit art organizations with annual operating budgets of under $100,000. All requests must be submitted in writing, giving a description of the group and the problem. If eligible, VLA assigns a volunteer lawyer to the group to assist in the resolution of the legal problem.

Most legal proceedings are time consuming and you can anticipate that the procedure will take time.

> Volunteer Lawyers for the Arts
> 36 West 44 Street
> New York, N.Y. 10036   (212) 575-1150

Pratt Institute Center for Community and Environmental Development

Working with not-for-profit groups, the Pratt Center gives technical assistance on feasibility studies and physical space proposals. Architecture and environmental design students work in conjunction with faculty. They do charge a fee but assist the group in obtaining funding for the services provided by the Center.

Ron Shiffman is Director; Rex Curry, Assistant Director.

> Pratt Institute Center for Community and
>   Environmental Development
> 275 Washington Avenue
> Brooklyn, N.Y. 11205   (212) 622-5026

Foundation for the Extension and Development of the American Professional Theatre (FEDAPT)

FEDAPT's primary objective is to develop the administrative and managerial capabilities of professionally oriented emerging and existing theatres. Among their services is the preparation and distribution of a packet that includes some information applicable to finding and renovating space, entitled "Investigation Guidelines for Setting Up a Not-for-Profit Tax-Exempt Regional Theatre" ($10 plus postage).

FEDAPT has assisted several Off Off Broadway theatres in management areas and is planning to expand its involvement in the area of small, not-for-profit theatres. Consultant fees are usually taken care of by FEDAPT, but this depends upon the agreement made with the individual group.

Write to FEDAPT for more information or help.
Frederic B. Vogel is Executive Director.

> FEDAPT
> 1500 Broadway
> New York, N.Y. 10036   (212) 869-9690

The Foundation Center

The Foundation Center offers a free weekly orientation to the world of foundation funding in its New York Center. Also in New York, the Foundation Center Library offers the use of all books and periodical publications relevant to foundations, who they are, and what they fund. In addition, the Center publishes the *Foundation Directory*, as well as a number of other directories and indexes which profile private foundations and their grants.

The Center also has a library in Washington, D.C., and has established a network of regional cooperating collections across the country.

Publications include:

> *The Foundation Grants Index*
> *COMSEARCH Printouts*
> *International Philanthropy*
> *The National Data Book*
> *Foundation Center Source Book Profiles*
> *Foundation Grants to Individuals*
> *About Foundations—How to Find the Facts*
>   *You Need to Get a Grant*

The Foundation Center
888 Seventh Avenue
New York, N.Y. 10019   (212) 489-7120

United States Institute for Theatre Technology (USITT)

USITT publishes a list of Theatre Consultants, which can be purchased from them for $20. A copy is also available in the OOBA office for reference.

U.S. Institute for Theatre Technology, Inc.
1501 Broadway
New York, N.Y. 10036   (212) 354-5360

New York Society of Architects (NYSA)

NYSA publishes handbooks on New York City Codes at the following prices:

	members*	non-members
N.Y. City Building Laws	$16.87	$23.35**
Updating Service (annual)	free	16.20
N.Y. City Electrical Code	6.36	8.52
N.Y. City Fire Prevention Code	6.90	14.46

* Members of NYSA.
** Incl. tax and handling.

Copies of these Code handbooks are also available at the OOBA office for reference.

New York Society of Architects
101 Park Avenue, Room 831 N.W.
New York, N.Y. 10017   (212) 683-2244

the Theatre Row story

project description

Five derelict tenements that once housed massage parlors, pornographic theatres, and peep shows on West 42nd Street have been redeveloped into five 99 seat Off Off Broadway theatres and ten floors of rehearsal and office space, totalling approximately 46,000 sq. ft. Located between Ninth and Tenth Avenues, the tenants of Theatre Row (Black Theatre Alliance, Actors and Directors Lab, Lion Theatre Company, Intar, Harlem Children's Theatre, and South Street Theatre) join two existing theatres on the block, Playwrights Horizons and the Nat Horne Theatre Company. Also included in the project is one residential building with 2,100 sq. ft. of ground floor retail, which is leased to a French restaurant. Construction began in November, 1977. Four-wall construction on all spaces was completed, and some of the theatres were opened, in mid-May, 1978.

Theatre Row's importance is twofold. It is the first development in New York City to provide up-to-Code space for Off Off Broadway theatres. Equally as important is the tax relief given to the project under the Mayor's Business Investment Incentive Program with Urban Development Corporation (UDC) ownership. The granting of this incentive to a not-for-profit developer to develop theatres is the City's imprimatur on the theatres' importance to the economic vitality of the City. City assistance under this program to the 42nd Street Corp. is continuing.

project sponsor

The 42nd Street Local Development Corporation (42nd Street Corp.), a tax-exempt corporation organized under Section 1411 of the New York State Not-for-Profit Corporation Law, is the project developer. 42nd Street Corp. was organized in April, 1977 for the purpose of revitalizing 42nd Street west of Seventh Avenue.

According to state law, a Local Development Corporation (LDC) has broad economic development purposes, i.e. the creation of jobs. The Statute specifies that an LDC is to act "in the public interest" and to "lessen . . . the burdens of government." The 42nd Street Corp., while a private entity, is thus viewed as the project-implementing arm of the local government and as such receives support from the City of New York. This support has taken the form of tax equivalency rentals in lieu of full real estate taxes on Theatre Row.

In its revitalization program for West 42nd Street, the corporation has identified seven projects, with Theatre Row the corporation's first significant development project. Theatre Row—Phase II—the redevelopment of all of the properties on West 42nd Street between Dyer and Tenth Avenues into a restaurant and market complex, theatres, and arts related uses, and the redevelopment of the properties at the corner of Ninth Avenue and West 42nd Street into a restaurant, retail space, and mini-Shubert alley—will complete the upgrading of the Ninth to Tenth Avenue block. In conjunction with Manhattan Plaza, the subsidized apartment complex for the Clinton community residents and performing artists, Theatre Row—Phases I and II create a critical mass to provide an anchor for future redevelopment. Other projects now in the planning stages include a vertical arts center and dance theatre on the Seventh to Eighth Avenue block, a farmers' market and equestrian center.

Theatre Row history

In 1975, Robert Moss, Artistic Director of Playwrights Horizons, was unexpectedly without a theatre space for his next season. Playwrights had to relocate quickly in order not to lose funding which was earmarked for that season. Bob Moss found a space on West 42nd Street and planned to remain there only until a permanent space in a better location could be found. However, Moss found that neither the theatre people nor the audiences objected to the neighborhood. Playwrights' success attracted Lion Theatre Company and the Nat Horne Theatre. With three theatres on the block, Bob Moss convinced Fred Papert, president of 42nd Street Local Development Corporation, that a Theatre Row should be created out of the remaining tenements on the block.

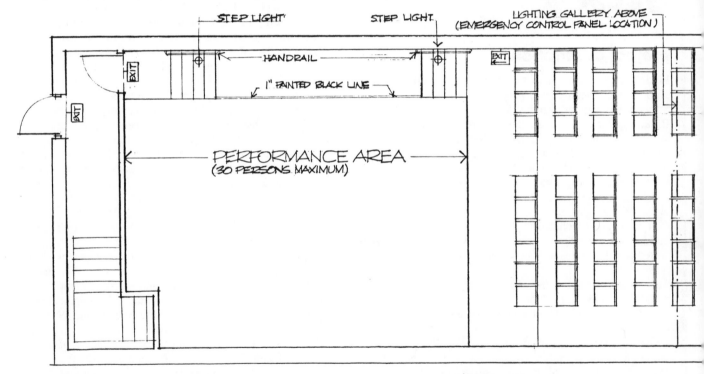

STEP LIGHT   STEP LIGHT   LIGHTING GALLERY ABOVE
(EMERGENCY CONTROL PANEL LOCATION)

EXIT   EXIT   HANDRAIL   EXIT

EXIT   1" PAINTED BLACK LINE

PERFORMANCE AREA
(30 PERSONS MAXIMUM)

NOTE:
POSTED CAPACITY SIGN TO BE AS PER N.Y.C.
BUILDING CODE SECTION C26-801.3 eg:
'OCCUPANCY BY MORE THAN 112 PERSONS IS
DANGEROUS AND UNLAWFUL'. EMERGENCY
LIGHTING AS PER SECTION C26-801.18

The Lion Theatre space is typical of most of Theatre Row—a 22' wide, 5 story brick building converted from residential and business space.

property acquisition

42nd Street Corp. began to acquire the Theatre Row properties in 1976 from Mid-Central Properties and Irving Maidman, the two landlords.

42nd Street Corp.'s tactic in acquisition was to forge a partnership with the mortgagees. 42nd Street Corp. took title to the properties for no cash, subject to all the mortgages and tax arrearages. These mortgages, all of which were in default, had substantial balances. The properties' value was minimal, weighing the tax arrearages and the buildings' derelict physical condition against the outstanding balance of the mortgages.

Both Mid-Central and Maidman transferred title to 42nd Street Local Development Corporation for no cash, subject to all liens, including mortgages.

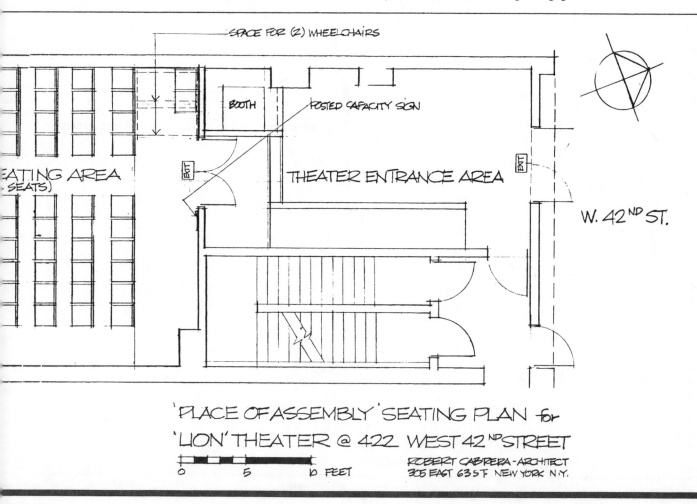

'PLACE OF ASSEMBLY' SEATING PLAN for 'LION' THEATER @ 422 WEST 42ND STREET

ROBERT CABRERA - ARCHITECT
305 EAST 63 ST NEW YORK N.Y.

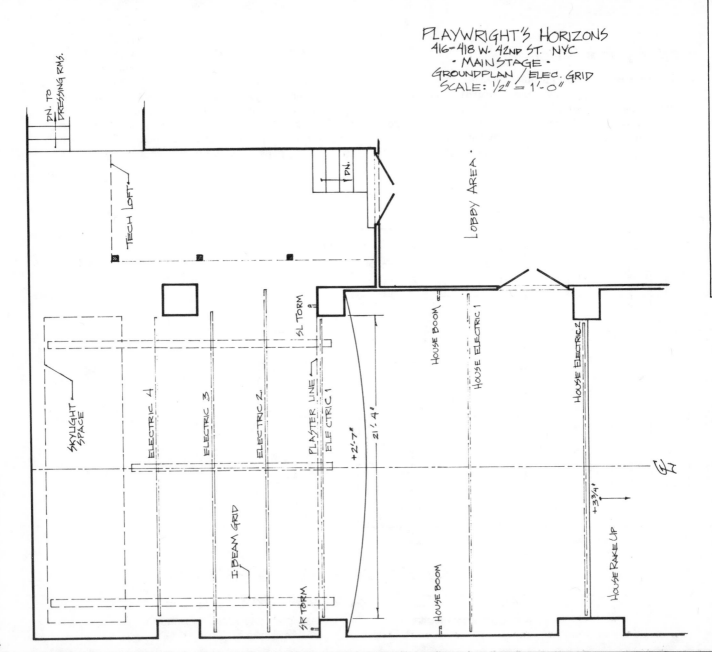

PLAYWRIGHT'S HORIZONS
416-418 W. 42ND ST. NYC
· MAINSTAGE ·
GROUNDPLAN / ELEC. GRID
SCALE: 1/2" = 1'-0"

DN. TO DRESSING RMS.

TECH LOFT

DN.

LOBBY AREA ·

SKYLIGHT SPACE

ELECTRIC 4

ELECTRIC 3

ELECTRIC 2

PLASTER LINE

ELECTRIC 1

SL TORM

I-BEAM GRID

SR TORM

+2'-7"

21'-4"

HOUSE BOOM

HOUSE ELECTRIC 1

HOUSE ELECTRIC 2

+3'4"

HOUSE RAKE UP

HOUSE BOOM

project packaging

The critical element for the success of the project in the planning stage was tax abatement. Based on the expected rents and operating expenses, it was clear that the project could not support full real estate taxes. The project had to be removed from the tax rolls and a tax equivalency rental charged in lieu of full taxes.

This was accomplished through ownership of the properties by the New York State Urban Development Corporation, pursuant to the Mayor's Business Investment Incentive Program, as follows:

● The Mayor's Business Investment Incentive Program assists economic development projects to attain economic feasibility through tax relief. Under this program, which has been in effect since January, 1976, the City negotiates a tax equivalency payment with the developer. In the case of Theatre Row, this is equal to 50% of profits.

City agencies and the Board of Estimate must determine that the project meets the criteria of the Program, as follows: (a) substantial new private investment; (b) job development; (c) substantial impact on an industry or an area; (d) no windfall profits, i.e. the tax relief is no more than is required for feasibility; (e) the City shares in the success of the project; and (f) the project will pay full taxes within a reasonable period of time.

In the case of Theatre Row, extensive negotiations with the City's Office of Economic Development, Office of Management and Budget, Corporation Counsel, and Comptroller's Office began in late 1976 and continued until closing, on November 10, 1977, on the terms and conditions of the project.

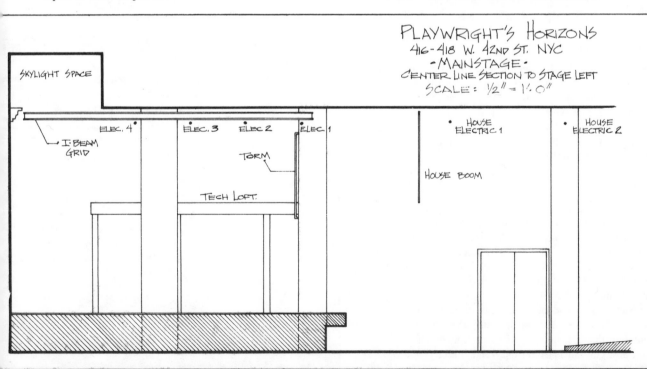

PLAYWRIGHT'S HORIZONS
416-418 W. 42ND ST. NYC
-MAINSTAGE-
CENTER LINE SECTION TO STAGE LEFT
SCALE: 1/2" = 1'-0"

SKYLIGHT SPACE

ELEC. 4 ELEC. 3 ELEC 2 ELEC 1

I-BEAM GRID

TORM

TECH LOFT.

HOUSE ELECTRIC 1 HOUSE ELECTRIC 2

HOUSE BOOM

THE THEATRE ROW STORY

75

The Board of Estimate approved the project by two separate resolutions, dated April 21 and June 23, 1977.

• The New York State Urban Development Corporation is a public benefit corporation authorized by Chapter 252 of the Unconsolidated Laws of New York State. To encourage development, the Legislature gave certain powers to the UDC, including tax exemption on all properties owned by UDC. Through this power, the Theatre Row properties were removed from the tax rolls.

The basic structure of the deal follows:

• A donation of all of the Theatre Row properties by 42nd Street to UDC.

• Ownership by UDC removed the properties from the tax rolls.

• UDC leased the properties to 42nd Street for 30 years for a tax equivalency rental equal to 50% of profits.

• 42nd Street, in turn, sublet the properties to the theatre companies.

• If there is a default under the lease or if certain other conditions are not met, the City will take title to the properties. One of the most significant of these conditions is that the City set a limit on the square footage, excluding 414 West 42nd Street, that may be used for other than theatre uses. The purpose here was to limit the tax relief only to theatre uses.

the tenants

Prior to and during negotiations with the City and UDC, 42nd Street had been soliciting theatre companies as tenants. When the project was first conceived in early 1976, 42nd Street contacted organizations such as the Off Off Broadway Alliance and Black Theatre Alliance for possible tenants. As a result, 42nd Street sent letters to approximately 300 companies.

42nd Street then held two meetings, in late summer, 1976 and November, 1976, with many of these companies to discuss the kind of space that would be provided and general lease terms. 42nd Street provided raw, up-to-Code space in which the theatre companies would make their own improvements.

About 100 theatres expressed interest in leasing space. 42nd Street asked each company to send a letter stating the amount and type of space needed; promotional material on the company; and financial statements for the preceding three years.

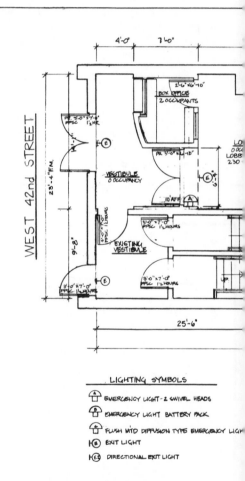

Through interviews, both by 42nd Street and theatre people, this group was narrowed down to 20. By March, 1977, the companies were essentially narrowed down to the tenants that ultimately leased space, Intar, Actors and Directors Lab, Black Theatre Alliance, Lion Theatre Company, South Street Theatre, and Harlem Children's Theatre.

During the summer of 1977, the Board of Directors of the 42nd Street Theatre Row, which had been formed in early 1976 as a collective management entity for all the theatres on the block, interviewed the proposed tenants for their financial capability and artistic credibility. The Board of the 42nd Street Theatre Row recommended each of the tenants.

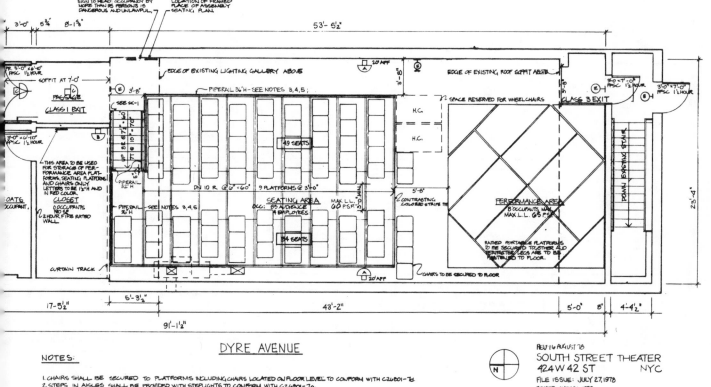

DYRE AVENUE

NOTES:

1. CHAIRS SHALL BE SECURED TO PLATFORMS INCLUDING CHAIRS LOCATED ON FLOOR LEVEL TO CONFORM WITH C26801-7d.
2. STEPS IN AISLES SHALL BE PROVIDED WITH STEPLIGHTS TO CONFORM WITH C26801-7g. EACH STEP WILL BE MARKED WITH A PERMANENT CONTRASTING COLOR STRIPE AS PER C26801-7g.
3. RAILINGS AROUND SEATING SECTIONS AND AT STAIRS SHALL RESIST SIMULTANEOUS LATERAL FORCE OF 50 PLF AND VERTICAL FORCE OF 100 PLF TO CONFORM WITH C26-902-3b.
4. RAILINGS AROUND SEATING SECTIONS SHALL BE AT LEAST 30" HIGHER THAN ADJACENT PLATFORMS AS PER C26-604-8F.
5. RAILINGS AT STAIR SHALL BE IN CONFORMANCE WITH C26-604-8F.
6. SEATS SHALL BE 19" O.C. MINIMUM AS PER C26-801-7(a)(1)(6).
7. EMERGENCY LIGHTING SHALL PROVIDE 5 FOOT CANDLES OF ILLUMINATION AT THE FLOOR LEVEL AS PER C26801.18
8. AISLES AND CROSS AISLES WILL BE PROVIDED WITH AT LEAST ½ FOOT CANDLE OF ARTIFICAL ILLUMINATION BY ELECTRICAL MEANS IN ACCORDANCE WITH SECT. C26801.B(9)

REV 16 AUGUST 78
SOUTH STREET THEATER
424 W 42 ST   NYC
FILE ISSUE: JULY 27, 1978
REVISED JULY 21, 1978
FILING ISSUE: JUNE 2, 1978
REVISED 6 JUNE 1978

1ST FLOOR
THEATER, SEATING PLAN

JOB N°	DATE	SCALE	DWG N°
7130	2 JUNE 78	¼"=1'-0"	

John Chmera Architect

PA-1

project costs

The development costs as of November 10, 1977, the closing date, totalled $948,120. This sum increased to $1,045,730 by May 13, 1978, the opening date, due to construction extras required by a more complete engineering analysis, UDC, the tenants, and 42nd Street

Corp. Many of these extras improved the overall project quality. Tenants had to finance separately their improvements, which included stage, lighting, seating, partitions.

The construction contract for the project, originally bid at $700,000, rose to approximately $850,000 by the end of construction. Additional substantial work was

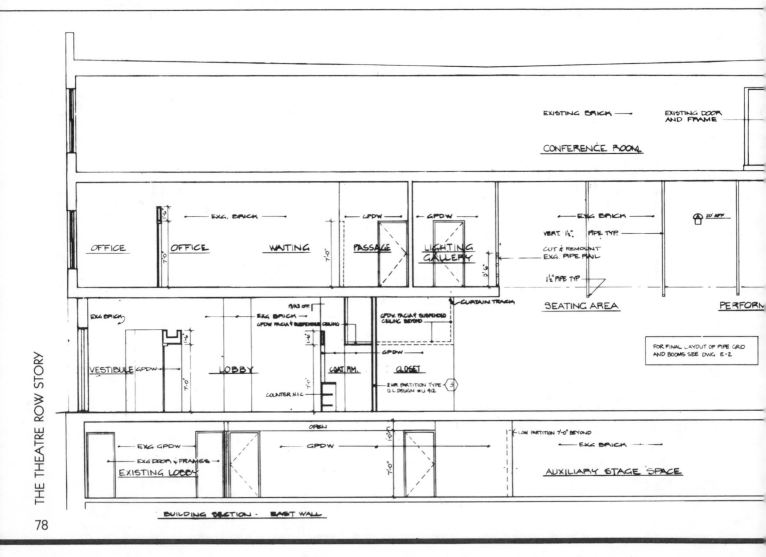

THE THEATRE ROW STORY

necessitated, as an engineering analysis had not been completed by the time the bid was in, and because of requirements of both UDC's construction department and the New York City Department of Buildings.

In addition to professional fees, title insurance, etc., which are included in the soft costs of the development budget, the Theatre Row budget had two items: payment of back taxes and settlement of the existing mortgage.

As the properties were in substantial tax arrears, the City required payment of all back taxes as of the date of closing. Back taxes plus interest and penalties totalled $117,800.

When 42nd Street took title to the properties, it assumed all of the existing mortgages. However, these mortgages had to be paid or converted to second mortgages in order to allow a bank to grant a new mortgage for construction (construction mortgages must, by law, be *first* mortgages). The two existing mortgages affected were treated as follows:

● One mortgage in the amount of $61,000 was settled for a cash payment equal to 50% of the principal, or $30,500.

● The $375,000 mortgage held by the Federal Deposit Insurance Corporation was converted to a second mortgage.

project financing

The renovation work, excluding tenants' improvements, was financed as follows:

● $485,000 mortgage, at 8¾% interest for a term of 24 years, provided by the Bowery, Emigrant, and Franklin Savings Banks

● $250,000 grant from the Port Authority of New York and New Jersey

● $250,000 bridge loan from The Ford Foundation until the Port Authority grant came through (the Ford loan was repaid in full)

● $55,000 grant from Robert Sterling Clark Foundation

● $25,000 grant from Rockefeller Brothers Fund

● $25,000 grant from Jacqueline Onassis

● $25,000 loan from United Broadway Church of Christ

● $22,500 loan from Frederic Papert, president of 42nd Street Local Development Corporation

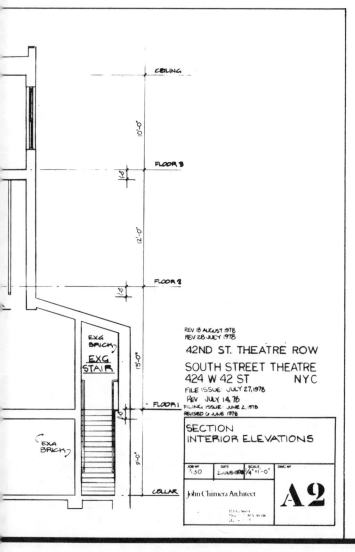

CEILING

10'-0"

FLOOR 3

1'-0"

12'-0"

FLOOR 2

1'-0"

EXG BRICK

EXG STAIR

13'-0"

EXG BRICK

9'-0"

FLOOR 1

COLLAR

REV 18 AUGUST 1978
REV 28 JULY 1978

42ND ST. THEATRE ROW

SOUTH STREET THEATRE
424 W 42 ST   NYC

FILE ISSUE: JULY 27, 1978
REV   JULY 14, 78
FILING ISSUE: JUNE 2, 1978
REVISED 6 JUNE 1978

SECTION
INTERIOR ELEVATIONS

JOB N° 7,30   DATE 2 JUNE 1978   SCALE ¼"=1'-0"   DWG N°

A2

John Chimera Architect

THE THEATRE ROW STORY

79

Port Authority contribution and easement

The Port Authority is prohibited by its charter to give an outright grant. Because of this restriction, the grant was given in consideration of the City's relinquishing its right to the vacant property behind Theatre Row. The $250,000 figure was based in part upon the assessed valuation of the property which fronts on West 41st Street running the full length of the block behind properties between Ninth Avenue and Dyer Avenue.

The Port Authority also granted an easement on this property, which runs behind the theatres to the 42nd Street Corporation, to be used as the secondary means of egress from the theatres as required by fire regulations.

operation of project

Temporary Certificates of Occupancy were granted to all of the buildings except 424 on May 19, 1978. The theatre companies were in possession as of that date.

In addition to rent, the tenants pay an allocable share of the cost of heat, hot water, water charges, and insurance, to the landlord, 42nd Street Corporation, which will manage the project. 42nd Street Corp. provides boiler and structural maintenance. The tenants, however, arrange for their own superintendent.

The initial lease term for all tenants is five years with an option to renew for three years, followed by two additional renewal periods of six years each.

Rent for the initial five years is $1,000 per month for the theatre space and $500 per month for each rehearsal office floor. The rental increase for the three year renewal period is tied to the amount needed to pay the FDIC mortgage. However, a maximum increase of 15% is allowable.

Increases for each of the remaining six year renewal periods are equal to 10% over the preceding year's rental.

The initial tenants of Theatre Row and the space they are occupying are as follows:

Address	Space	Tenant*
410	5 floors, including theatre	Black Theatre Alliance, Inc.
412	5 floors, including theatre	Actors and Directors Lab
414	ground floor	La Rousse (restaurant)
		residential units
420	basement, 1st & 2nd floors, including theatre	Intar
	3rd floor	The Acting Company
	4th & 5th floors	Harlem Children's Theatre
422	2 floors, including theatre	Lion Theatre Company
424	3 floors, including theatre	Theatre Research, Inc. (South Street Theatre)

*As of fall 1978.

part three
design and planning strategies

The overall thrust of this section on design and planning is to present a survey of as many design considerations as possible, including ideas for stretching space through careful planning. It considers design strategies for stage space, audience spaces, and support spaces along with strategies for saving money and getting the most for the least in services and materials. The ideas in this section are intended to be helpful if you are planning your theatre with or without the assistance of a consultant or an architect.

Many of the design ideas included here will not have relevance to the planning of a large, conventional theatre; they are ideas and suggestions that are unique to the small, non-traditional theatre space. Uniqueness of design is one of the most attractive qualities of many Off Off Broadway theatres. The non-traditional environment and ambiance are features that draw an audience to a particular theatre, and the uniqueness of the space will remain as a vivid and graphic expression of the group.

This section does not present a concept for the design and planning of your space, but attempts to survey a wide range of possibilities from which to choose.

8

the stage space

Consideration of the space components of any theatre should commence by examining the design of the stage space, proceed to the design of the audience space with relation to it, then move to examine the necessary support spaces requirements.

The stage space, regardless of size or shape, has these basic components to consider: the floor; the overhead + the rigging; the walls; and the means of access.

Flexibility in stage size and shape can be cheap in small theatres where time and labor are cheap. This is the complete reverse philosophy to the usual thinking with regard to flexible stage space where elaborate,

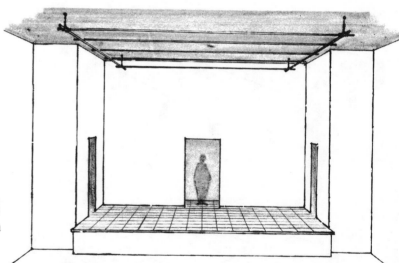

The Stage Space. *Floor, overhead + rigging, walls and access.*

expensive machinery is devised and installed because time and manpower mean money. It should be pointed out that as the small theatre company grows in size, operating budget, and intensive programming, there will be a point in time when this concept of cheap flexibility will cease to be feasible.

stage floor

First, consider some inexpensive design ideas for handling the stage floor. If a simple modular platform system is devised, almost total flexibility in size, configuration, and placement can be achieved. For example, consider a simple system of 4′ x 4′ platform tops "legged up" on 2″ x 6″ stock, and bolted or clamped together.

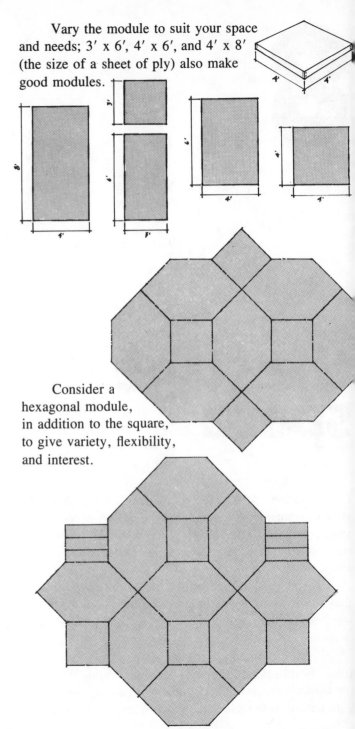

Vary the module to suit your space and needs; 3′ x 6′, 4′ x 6′, and 4′ x 8′ (the size of a sheet of ply) also make good modules.

Consider a hexagonal module, in addition to the square, to give variety, flexibility, and interest.

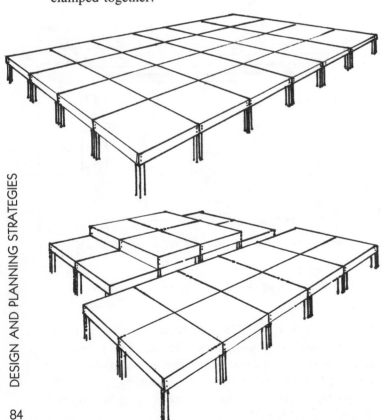

Consider platform modules in rectangles, triangles, and squares. For example: 4'x 8', 4' x 4' and 45°/90° triangles which are 4' on two sides.

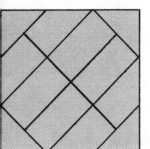

Modular system designed for the South Street Theatre in Theatre Row.

permanent platform stages

With a permanent stage, flexibility at the leading edge may be all that is needed. Modular sections can be added to a permanent stage to achieve this.

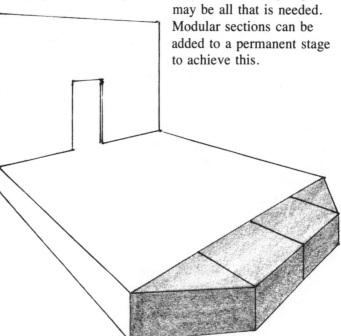

Once the platform modules are together, consider surfacing the platforms with Homosote, Masonite, Ozite underpad, and/or canvas. Face with Masonite, ¼" plywood, velour, or even corrugated cardboard.

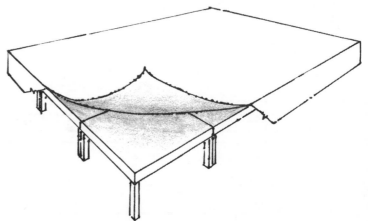

materials and construction

Working directly on the floor of the theatre space provides an inexpensive and flexible solution. However, in many old buildings the floor will be too rough and will require surfacing. Also, the surface of the deck in the performance area should not be too hard or too slippery—concrete, or linoleum laid directly over concrete.

The AMAS Repertory Theatre has developed an inexpensive portable floor: a ¾″ foam base with ¾″ plywood on top of which is an untempered Masonite surface. It is constructed in 4′ x 8′ sections, with the Masonite overlapping each plywood section by half to prevent seams from rising in the event the wood warps.

A variant on this was developed as a temporary outdoor dance floor laid on concrete: a base of ¾″ foam then ¾″ plywood sheets held together with gaffer's tape and covered, first with used battleship linoleum, and then with a top layer of Marley floor.

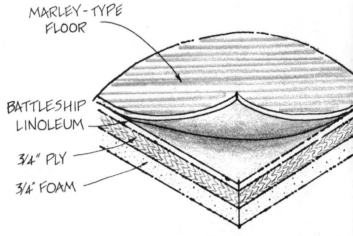

MARLEY-TYPE FLOOR

BATTLESHIP LINOLEUM

3/4″ PLY

3/4″ FOAM

Both of these decks were laid directly over existing concrete floors. They were inexpensive, easy to make, resilient, and portable.

Permanent stage floors should not be laid directly on concrete but should be laid on 2′ x 4′ wood sleepers. A double layer of medium soft pine is most desirable but expensive and hard to get—two layers of ¾″ plywood would be second best.

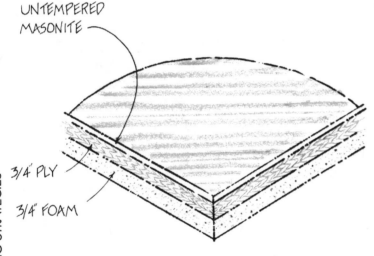

UNTEMPERED MASONITE

3/4″ PLY

3/4″ FOAM

FLOOR SECTION

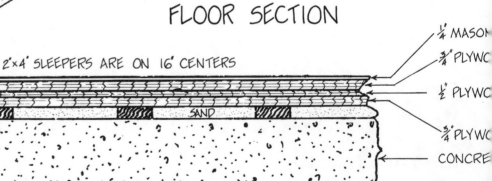

2′x4′ SLEEPERS ARE ON 16′ CENTERS

SAND

¼″ MASON

¾″ PLYWO

½″ PLYWO

¾″ PLYWO

CONCRE

Reverberation can be reduced by lining the underside of hollow platforms with Ozite underpad, fiber glass insulation, or Homosote. Consider gluing or stapling this insulation directly to the underside of the plywood platform top before attaching it to the platform frame. In addition, the frame itself can be wrapped in foam rubber or covered in Homosote. For further noise suppression, Ozite underpadding or rubber padding can be applied to the bottom of each leg of the platform.

Homosote or rug padding (covered in canvas) can, of course, be used on top of platforms to reduce the surface noise.

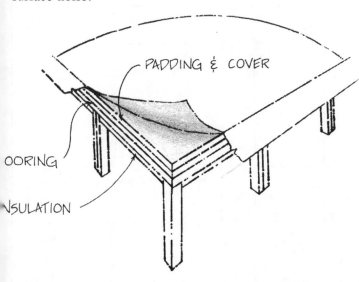

PADDING & COVER

OORING

NSULATION

Resilience is a factor if the stage is used for dancing. Equity prohibits any dancing on marble or concrete floors in either rehearsal or a performance, and suggests the stage floor be constructed of wood. Furthermore, an actor has the right to refuse to jump on or fall upon a marble or concrete floor.

Stage floors must be able to withstand frequent repainting.

stage walls

Usually the walls of the stage want to be as negative as possible. They should remain neutral and "unseen" until such time as you choose to make a feature of them.

Stage walls are often painted matte black for this reason. However even white or grey can become background colors if properly handled, as Peter Brook proved in his productions of *King Lear* and *A Midsummer Night's Dream*.

Bare brick walls can also provide neutrality. Some companies have chosen to strip off old plaster to expose structural brick walls and have found this provides the right background for their productions. If the stage and seating areas form a single space, it will unify the environment to treat all of the walls in the same finish and color.

The wall between stage, or playing area, and backstage should be a sound barrier. Putting two layers of ⅝" sheetrock on one side and one layer on the other is considered a better soundproofing than equal layers on both sides.

When planning the walls, side lighting positions are important and should be part of the initial planning of the space.

exits from the stage

The Building Code requires two means of egress from the stage placed "remote from each other." This is a safety regulation with reference to the actors' access to and from the whole stage space, not just the acting area. Two exits from the stage may serve, but, of course, more than two exits from the playing space or the setting are desirable, often required.

Doors for stage exits are not always practical or desirable; for small stages open exits are usually best. Though hanging curtains can reduce noise transmission from backstage, it may be necessary to create a sound lock behind each exit.

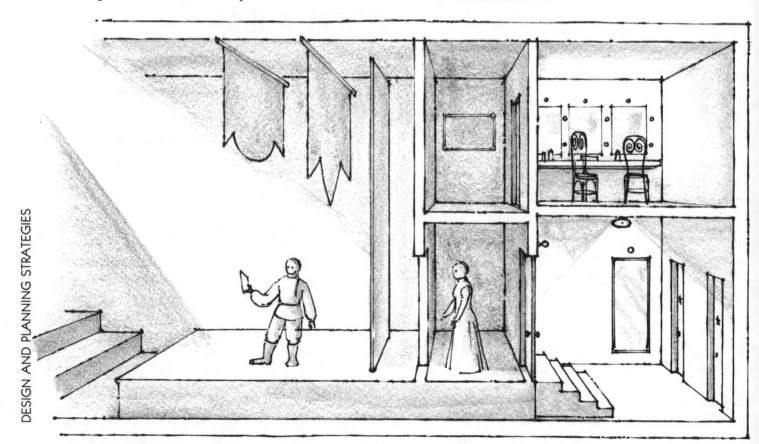

Establish a corridor or sound and light barrier between the stage and backstage.

DESIGN AND PLANNING STRATEGIES

overhead + rigging

The height of the ceiling is an all-important consideration. In principal, the more height the better. The design treatment of the ceiling and overhead space above the stage will be conditioned by the height. The design and planning of stage rigging for handling lighting equipment and scenic pieces will also be affected by height.

Developing a grid system for lighting instruments and scenic pieces can become complex or it can be kept quite simple. If the overhead is less than 30' high, you can probably handle the mounting of lights and scenery from the floor. Mounting positions up to 22' high can be reached with a ladder; a rolling scaffold will be best to reach positions from 22' to 30' in height. A scaffold requires a relatively flat, level deck, of course.

A rolling scaffold is useful where grid height exceeds 22'.

catwalks and counterweight system

If your ceiling is more than 30' which is unlikely in most of the spaces available for small theatre conversion, a catwalk system will be preferable for access to pipes or mounting positions.

In addition to catwalks, a counterweight system or winch system to raise and lower pipes of lights or scenic pieces might be installed.

Be sure to allow sufficient headroom over the catwalk for a person to stand upright—6' to 7' is desirable. Also provide the catwalks with non-skid floors. Be sure the catwalks have rails and consider making them of standard 1½" pipe so they can be used

as hanging positions for lights. If used for lighting, plan for raceways with outlets distributed along the catwalks, or use neatly bundled cables which would be a cheaper, portable solution. Consider the catwalk as a follow spot or projection position.

Easy access from catwalks to the control booth can save time and manpower when focusing and lighting a production.

To make them as unobstrusive as possible, paint the catwalks a flat, dark color—preferably black. To make the catwalks a design feature of your theatre, paint them a bold color in contrast to the theatre ceiling.

fixed grid system

If using a fixed grid overhead, plan it to cover an area of the ceiling adequate for all overhead lighting positions.It may be advantageous or necessary to design a grid for the entire ceiling if the space is planned as a Two- Three- or Four-sided Arena or as a flexible theatre space. In any configuration the grid should be sufficiently larger than the playing area to provide good overhead lighting angles. Positions for front lighting are considered to be best when the angle from the actor's eye level to the lighting instrument is between 30° to 50°. 45° is generally considered to be ideal.

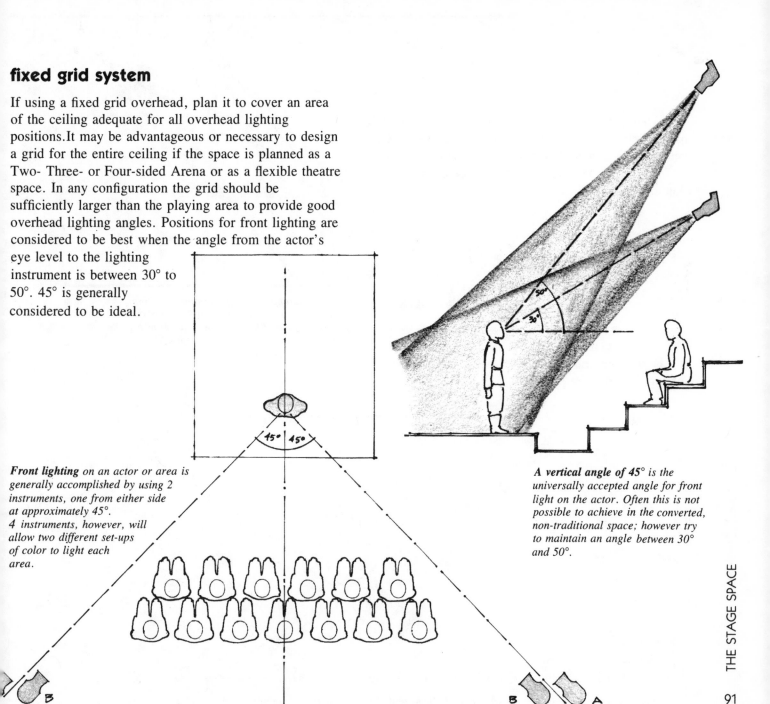

Front lighting on an actor or area is generally accomplished by using 2 instruments, one from either side at approximately 45°.
4 instruments, however, will allow two different set-ups of color to light each area.

*A **vertical angle** of 45° is the universally accepted angle for front light on the actor. Often this is not possible to achieve in the converted, non-traditional space; however try to maintain an angle between 30° and 50°.*

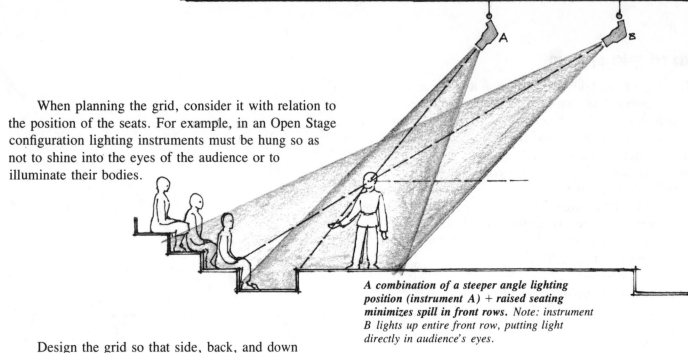

When planning the grid, consider it with relation to the position of the seats. For example, in an Open Stage configuration lighting instruments must be hung so as not to shine into the eyes of the audience or to illuminate their bodies.

A combination of a steeper angle lighting position (instrument A) + raised seating minimizes spill in front rows. Note: instrument B lights up entire front row, putting light directly in audience's eyes.

Design the grid so that side, back, and down lighting positions are provided.

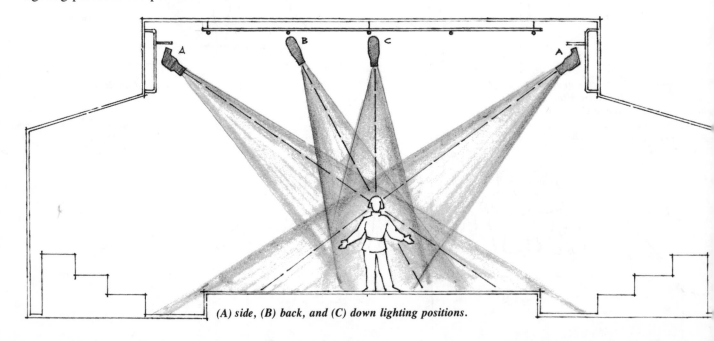

(A) side, (B) back, and (C) down lighting positions.

The layout of the grid may form a regular pattern using a uniform module, or it may vary according to the specific requirements of the space. Use a cross pattern of pipes, spaced approximately 4'x 4', for a normal ceiling height and an average stage size.

If the ceiling height allows, suspend the grid 18″ or more below the ceiling to permit easy mounting as well as over hanging for lighting instruments. Suspend the pipes on steel cable with pipe stiffeners to prevent pipes from rolling.

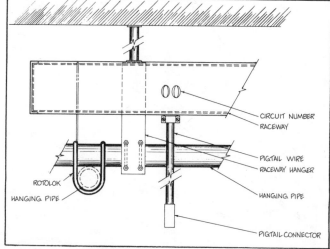

Detail for a permanent raceway system. Designed for the Seattle Repertory's 2nd Stage.

Clamping the pipe intersections together with rotolock type clamps or adjustable swivel clamps will permit sliding the pipes to reposition them for greater flexibility in the placement of equipment. Rotolocks or C-clamps can also be used to secure additional, temporary lengths of pipe to the grid system for special equipment for a specific production.

Remember the weight of the grid will put stress on the ceiling, so have an engineer take a look first. Lighting instruments, cables, and scenery pieces will be additional weight. An engineer will be able to ascertain if the ceiling will safely hold all the weight as well as its own, or will be able to advise an alternate method of suspension.

Use standard 1½″ pipe for easy mounting of instruments. Distribute outlets by means of raceways or bundles of cable.

parallel system of pipes

If the theatre configuration is permanent and one-directional, such as an End Stage, use a permanent system of individual pipes hung parallel to the leading edge of the playing area. Add in shorter intersecting pipes for special hanging positions.

Spacing between pipes will vary; allow for more pipes over the stage or playing area.

A Proscenium Stage without a fly loft can utilize the same type of parallel pipe system over both the audience and the stage to accommodate scenery, masking pieces, and lighting equipment.

If the stage house is high enough to fly scenery and lighting equipment, a rigging system must be part of the design. The rigging for flown scenery can be manually operated hemp lines or steel cable counterweight, or a single spot line system (manually or winch operated), or a combination of these.

If the loft is 30′ or less the sheaves and blocks can be underhung and can be serviced from a scaffold on the stage floor. If more than 30′, it will be important to have a gridiron with space above for top-mounted head blocks, sheaves, and cables, as well as adequate headroom.

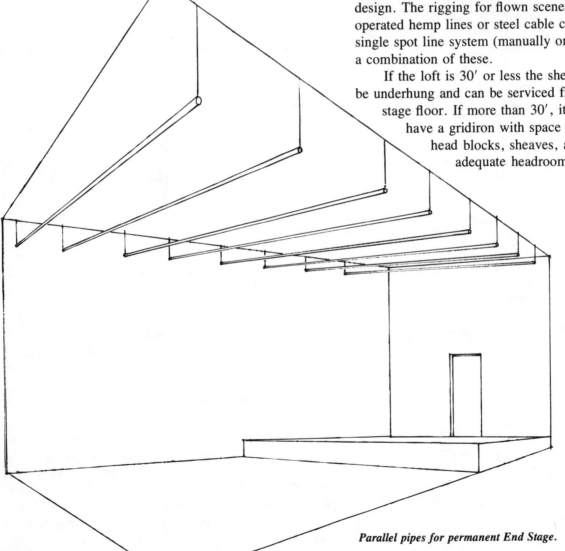

Parallel pipes for permanent End Stage.

Conventional counterweight systems.

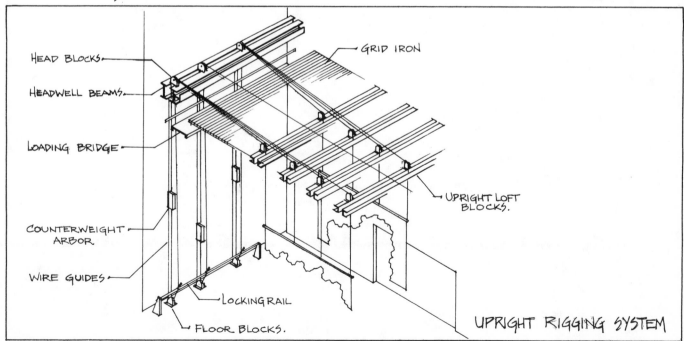

BRACER BEAM

UNDERHUNG HEAD BLOCK

LEAD LINES

CONTROL LINE

WIRE GUIDES

COUNTERWEIGHT ARBOR

LOCKING RAIL

FLOOR BLOCK

LOFT BLOCK

UNDERHUNG RIGGING SYSTEM.

HEAD BLOCKS

HEADWELL BEAMS

LOADING BRIDGE

COUNTERWEIGHT ARBOR

WIRE GUIDES

LOCKING RAIL

FLOOR BLOCKS.

GRID IRON

UPRIGHT LOFT BLOCKS.

UPRIGHT RIGGING SYSTEM

THE STAGE SPACE

95

Three concepts for productions at the Colonnades
Theatre Lab showing imaginative arrangements of
seating modules and playing areas in a flexible theatre
space.

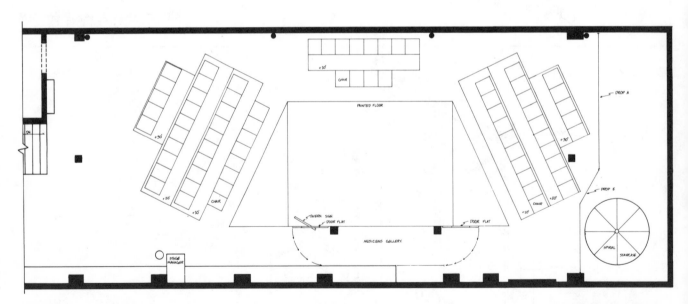

CAUCASIAN CHALK CIRCLE
COLONNADES THEATRE LAB

THE SEAGULL
COLONNADES THEATRE LAB

SCREEN

PROJECTION

SCREEN

the audience space

Seeing and hearing are the primary considerations in the audience space. These are achieved through the successful combination of sightlines, seating, acoustics, and lighting. These elements, together with design, create the audience environment.

sightlines

Good, uninterrupted viewing is usually achieved by a combination of horizontal and vertical sightlines in relation to the stage. The rake of the seating + the staggering of the seats + the height of the stage all affect the ability of the audience to see. The design of these elements should combine to provide an uninterrupted view of the entire performance area.

vertical sightlines

Elevating the rows of seats by sloping the floor or by stepped risers accomplishes vertical sightlines. Theoretically, one-row vision requires sufficient elevation of each row for every member of the audience to see over the heads of the row directly in front. This is frequently not practical and other means, such as staggering the seating, must also be employed.

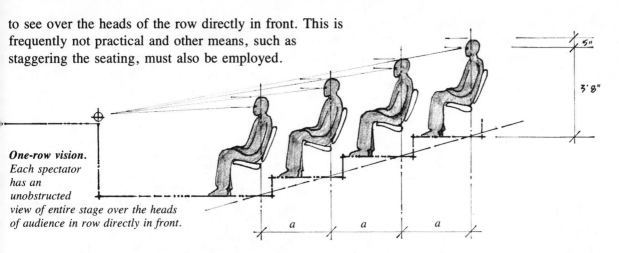

One-row vision. *Each spectator has an unobstructed view of entire stage over the heads of audience in row directly in front.*

horizontal sightlines

Good horizontal viewing is usually accomplished by staggering the seating so that each member of the audience is looking at the stage area between the heads of the two persons in the row in front as well as over the head of the person two rows in front. This plan is especially applicable to conventional Proscenium or End Stage configurations.

Staggered seating to provide two-row vision.

small theatre sightline problems

Basic principles for achieving good viewing will apply, but there are some special problems for small spaces and Arena configurations. Many small theatres in converted spaces use the floor of the building as the stage floor rather than a raised stage. In this situation plan to use a steeply raked system of risers. The lower the stage floor, the steeper the rake of the seating.

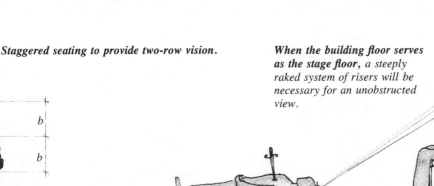

When the building floor serves as the stage floor, *a steeply raked system of risers will be necessary for an unobstructed view.*

Arena sightlines are more complex than the fixed position viewing in a Proscenium or End Stage theatre. Staggering the seats with two-row vision is less effective in Three-sided or Four-sided Arena; so these configurations depend more on vertical sightline solutions. Actors may block one another for different parts of the audience, and the line of vision is no longer directly to the front, as in Proscenium, but at a constantly changing angle. Again a steep angle and stepped risers are required for uninterrupted vision.

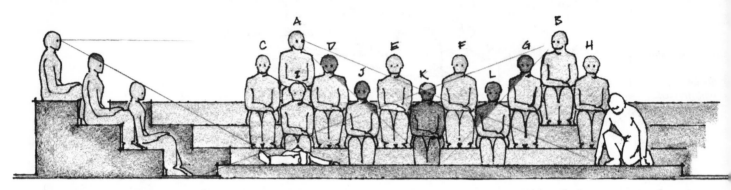

If sightlines providing two-row vision are used for an arena or thrust stage, A *may see* X *between* C *and* D *and over* I, *but will have difficulty seeing* Y *past* D *and* J. B *can see* Y, *but will have great difficulty seeing* X.

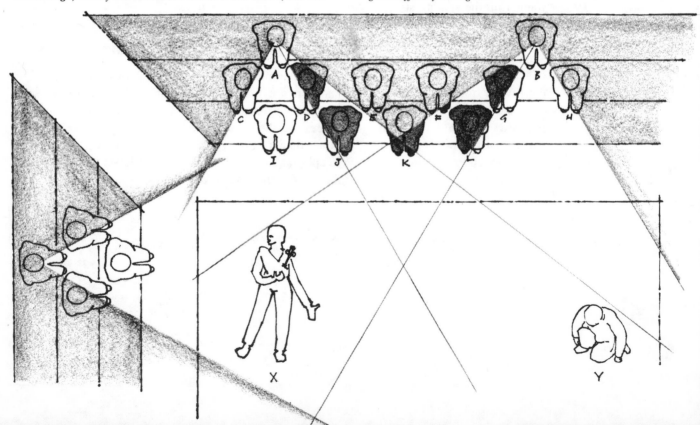

It is unsatisfactory to have too many rows of seats in an Arena; sightline problems increase and intimacy is lost. About seven rows is considered maximum, except perhaps, at the narrow end. Fortunately, three or four rows are all that are usually required for the small, intimate Arena theatre and sightline problems are minimized.

curved rows and staggered seating

In a narrow auditorium the rows of seats may be straight. However, if the audience is wide, it will be necessary to curve the rows to orient all spectators to the stage. Curving the rows also makes staggering the seats easier. Conventional theatre seats are manufactured in varying widths to assist in staggering seats, while maintaining straight aisles that are constant in width.

A system for determining curvature for rows of seats.

BACKWALL OF THEATRE

seats and seating layout

In addition to solving the problems of good viewing and good sightlines, there are esthetic and stylistic considerations to be made with regard to seating. Good seats and a workable seating layout demand careful planning. Good seats are not necessarily expensive seats. Frequently, used theatre seats are available or there are innovative do-it-yourself alternatives such as cushioned risers. Give serious thought to the seating layout, also. Will a permanent layout serve best, or will a flexible seating scheme work best for your type of theatre and productions?

platform modules for seating

For greatest flexibility in a space with a level floor, consider seating risers in modules similar in construction to stage modules. The modules can be constructed of wood, jiffy scaffolding, or other pipe or metal construction systems. There are many commercially prefabricated platform modules to consider. They are predictably more expensive than homemade platform modules.

Any guard rails used for safety should not be allowed to intrude on the view from any seat.

Note: Voids under wooden risers make the fire inspectors go wacky—they will usually require the space to be enclosed in sheetrock. It is not legal to use this space for storage, alas.

fixed vs. movable seats

There are two approaches to seating your audience if chairs are used: *fixed* and *movable*.

Fixed seats—chairs attached to the floor—keep orderly rows, do not require continual straightening before each performance, and keep aisles and exits open in compliance with the Codes. Fixed seats eliminate chair scraping on uncovered surfaces.

Movable seats make it possible to change the basic shape of seating areas and enable this space to be cleared quickly for use during non-performance time. If movable seats are used, the new Building Code bases exit requirements on square footage rather than on the actual number of seats (see Chapter 15).

Whether fixed or movable seats are used, the following features should be considered when choosing seats:

- Seat width—discussed in detail in Chapter 2.
- Seat backs—audience is able to sit for longer periods of time if backs are supported.
- Arm rests—an extra perhaps, but a plus in audience comfort.
- Padding—for seats and/or backs.
- Material—should be easy to clean, durable, and stain repellent. Plastic and metal are easy to clean, but can become uncomfortable.
- Color—should help create appealing but unobtrusive environment. Should not distract eye from stage. Darker colors will absorb light when seats are empty and will not show dirt so quickly.

types of seats

There are numerous variations available on the market worth considering for a small theatre. Brief descriptions follow:

Theatre seats. Permanently installed rows of seats, the traditional seating approach. If ordered new, there are many design options: arms, seat width, color, fabric, back slope, spring seats. Used theatre seats may be purchased from seating companies. Allow ample lead time, especially for reconditioned seats which can sometimes take months for delivery. They may be retrieved from renovations of old theatres or television studios.

Stackable chairs. Plastic or metal, with or without upholstery. Can be placed on risers. Stacks of chairs can be placed on rolling frames for storage.

Folding chairs. Plastic, wood, or metal, with or without upholstered frames. Can be placed on rolling frames for storage.

Stadium seats. Molded plastic, with or without backs. Must be assembled in rows and attached to metal frame or boards. Can be dismantled by the row.

Pull-out seating sections. Available in folding chair or bleacher seat design. Self-contained unit of risers and chairs permanently mounted on metal frames. Whole unit can either collapse into a wall or create storage unit on wheels.

Cushions placed on seating platforms. A cheap and simple solution to seating. Cushions can be cut from foam rubber and covered in a durable, washable fabric such as heavy canvas. If coverings are constructed to be removable, they can be easily cleaned.

Park benches and church pews. Could serve as a non-traditional seating solution. Could be bolted directly to platforms to meet the requirements of fixed seating and later be unbolted and moved. Lines could be painted to indicate individual seat designations and cushions could be added for comfort.

Build your own benches. Designed to be stacked or dismantled for storage. Removable backs and seat cushions could also be added.

Rented seats. As needed per show or for a season. A possible solution to the seating problem but an expensive one. Maintenance problems are solved, however. Most types of commercial seating listed above are available from chair rental companies. OOBA maintains a list of seating suppliers.

acoustics

Acoustical problems encountered in a small theatre are usually minimal. They can often be solved simply by the addition of sound absorptive materials on those surfaces which are reverberant, such as walls, ceilings, floors, seats, and platforms.

In many commercial theatres a noise level of 50 decibels is not uncommon, however the best theatres often maintain a level of 30 decibels or less while acoustical engineers consider 20 decibels as the maximum allowable total background noise.

An occupied theatre seat is more absorbent than an empty one, so consider the use of padding on the chair backs and seats to minimize this difference at those times when theatre is not filled to capacity.

Carpeting of aisles and seating platforms will lessen reverberation. In addition to acoustic tiles for walls and ceiling, consider covering the wall with carpeting, draperies, or wall-hangings to add absorbency to these surfaces.

Make sure all doors located near or within the seating area close silently and are constructed of materials that will decrease noise leakage from adjacent spaces.

It is possible to overdo sound insulation, and in a small space there is danger of deadening the sound *too* much. If there is no reverberation at all, the sound quality becomes unrealistic and it will become difficult to hear the actors.

If you have a space of barn-sized proportions and there are acoustical problems, consider bringing in an acoustical engineer to advise you before the seating and stage layout is planned.

One general note: Any materials used within the seating area must be fireproof or flame retardant and comply with the N.Y.C. Building Code and Fire Prevention Code requirements (see chapters 15 and 17).

lighting

Within the seating space there are three types of lighting to be considered: house lights, work lights, and emergency lights.

house lights

Sufficient visibility should be provided to allow audience members to gain easy access to seats and to read the program. Too bright or too dim lighting will create visual discomfort. Incandescent light should be considered for the light source. House lights should be placed on a dimmer-controlled circuit separate from the stage lighting controls. Place aisle and exit lights on a separate non-dim circuit.

If the seating sections are flexible the house lights and aisle lights must have the flexibility to be repositioned.

work lights

These lights will be necessary during non-performance times to illuminate the house for rehearsals, maintenance, and show preparation. It is desirable that work lights provide maximum visibility, do not require a great deal of electricity, and are controlled by on/off switches. Consider placing house work lights and stage work lights on separate circuits since there will be occasions when both will not be needed.

emergency lights

In most situations the Building Code requires places of public assembly to have emergency lights. The requirements, however, are covered in detail by the Electrical Code, and are discussed in Chapter 16.

10

the support spaces

technical control booth

In Off Off Broadway theatres the technical control booth has often been an afterthought, consuming valuable space in the seating area or backstage area. Plan the control area as an integral part of the stage and seating configuration. When planning the technical control booth, keep in mind the following:

- Provide a good view of the acting area. Install a window of glass or plexiglass.
- Plan a section of the window to slide open for direct contact with stage and seating areas.
- Consider the installation of a monitor speaker to enable technicians to hear as well as see the show when it is desirable to have the window closed.
- Soundproofing will allow the stage manager and technicians to communicate without disturbing the audience.
- If possible, locate near the main power supply. If power cable runs in a direct line to the booth, the installation will be easier and less expensive.
- Supply separate power supplies for sound and lighting control systems, especially if solid state dimmers will be used. The simplest way to do this is to provide separate breaker boxes for sound and lighting.

- Provide adequate number of outlets and disconnect boxes to service all equipment. Allow for additional equipment needs.
- Consider the amount of equipment that will be used both now and in the future—allow for expansion. (See Chapter 2 for suggested minimum size.)
- Consider the booth location and size for use as front projection and follow spot positions.
- Direct access route to backstage other than through the seating area is useful during the performance.
- Doors to the booth should close quietly and be large enough to facilitate moving control equipment in and out of the space.
- Provide both work lights and running lights.
- Provide for ventilation, heating, and cooling.
- Consider supplying an intercom system with master controls located at the stage manager's desk and stations located backstage, front-of-house, and, for technical rehearsals, in the seating area.
- In a flexible theatre, position the booth in an elevated location so that the stage area can be seen using any theatre configuration.

dressing rooms

When planning the dressing room areas, there are a number of considerations which should be taken into account. (Minimum sizes are discussed in Chapter 2).

- If at all possible, locate dressing rooms on the same level as the stage area, avoiding stairs.
- Locate dressing areas within easy access of toilets.
- Provide good, shadowless light for each make-up mirror—incandescent light only, with separate on/off switch for each mirror.
- In addition, provide general illumination for the area.
- Provide at least one full-length mirror for each dressing area.

- Allow adequate hanging space for both costumes and street clothes. (2 running feet of hanging space per actor.)
- Provide lockable drawers and/or small lockers for actor's make-up and valuables.
- Provide convenience wall outlets beside mirrors for hair dryers and electric shavers. Allow one per actor.
- Provide ventilation, heating and cooling.

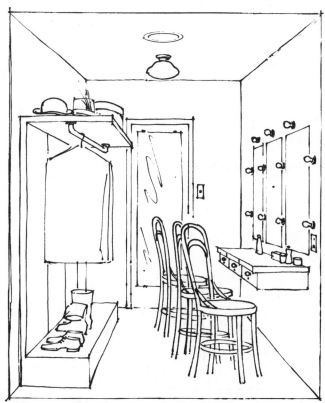

Dressing room. *Use the check list above to determine that minimum space, efficiency, and comfort requirements are achieved.*

To stretch space consider portable dressing table/costume rack units that can either fold up into compact storage or roll out of the way. The units could

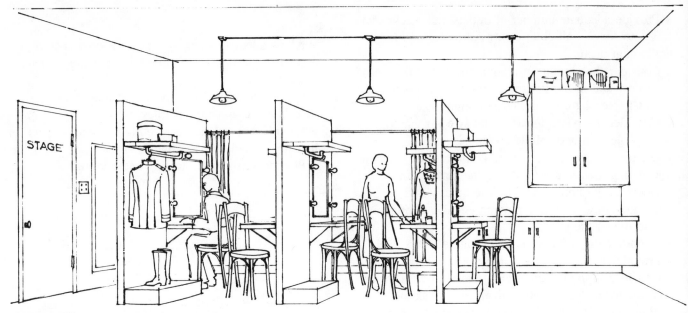

Portable dressing rooms set up.

With dressing room units stacked, *the multi-use space can become a shop, a rehearsal space, or can be used for other activities which do not conflict with the performance schedule of the small theatre company.*

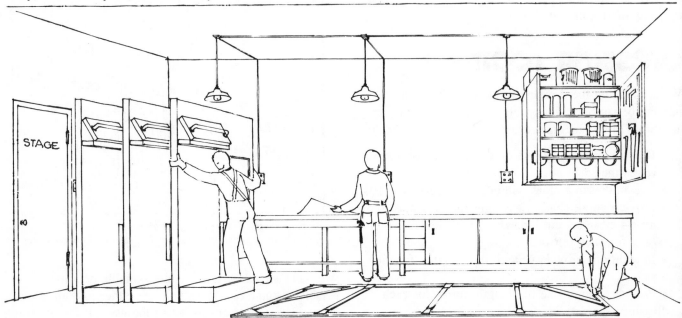

be complete with make-up counter, drawer, mirror, lights, and costume rack that rolls on casters; or they could be designed to collapse. If cleverly designed, the units, when spread out backstage, could form self-contained dressing areas by the addition of folding or stacking chairs.

The obvious advantage to this strategy is that it makes multiple use of precious backstage space. By stacking these dressing room units away when the theatre is dark and they are not in use, the space can be freed for scenery construction, costume construction, or other non-performance related activities.

On a cramped stage, dressing room portability could permit greater flexibility in set design by shifting the dressing room units to accommodate varied ground plans.

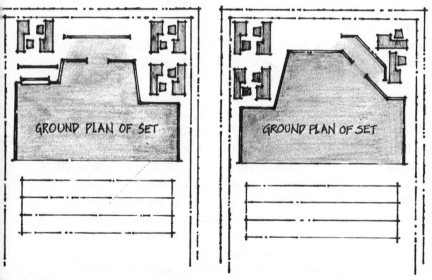

GROUND PLAN OF SET

GROUND PLAN OF SET

In flexible theatre space, portable dressing rooms could allow for a greater variety of configurations.

The Electrical Code makes no provision for wiring a portable dressing room, so the same cable and connectors used for portable lighting equipment should be adequate to bring electrical power to these units.

shops

Most small theatre companies are forced to build and paint scenery, make props, construct costumes, in spaces that must serve other functions. If this will be your situation, consider cabinets or storage rooms for tools, equipment, and supplies. (Mimimum sizes are discussed in Chapter 2.)

Plan your renovation so that these storage areas are near the appropriate work areas. If this is not practical plan for rolling storage units.

Sharing is another possible solution to the shop space problem. The 42nd Street Theatre Row concept includes sharing a central scene shop, for example.

scenic and paint shop checklist

If you are fortunate enough to have shop spaces in your plans, consider the following for the scene construction and paint areas:

- Highest possible ceilings.
- Adequate, glareless light, with protected lamps. Incandescent lights are preferable for the paint area.
- Workbenches and worktables. If workbenches line the perimeter of the shop, it is wise to have at least one free standing worktable with access from all four sides.
- Slop sink with hot and cold water + a large drain. A deep janitor-type sink is best.
- Hot plate or gas burners. Locate this near the sink.
- Adequate electrical outlets. Plan for both present and future equipment needs. Plan distribution to accommodate placement of equipment.
- Fireproof vault or metal locker for paints, dyes, and chemicals to satisfy regulations. It should be well-ventilated and lockable. One theatre satisfied the fire inspector by getting a fireproof paint vault. Once they had the vault, the inspector no longer worried about sprinklers and exhaust requirements.
- A good level work deck. Wood is preferable to concrete.
- Access from loading area to shop and from shop to stage. The size of the loading doors should be sufficient to handle materials; shop to stage doors must accommodate scenic pieces.
- Space to store finished scenic pieces waiting to be moved on stage, or pieces in work.
- Wall telephones. They are out of the way and easier to handle then desk types.
- Lockers for work clothes + personal gear.

prop shop

The prop shop will require all the above and can function in the same space if necessary, although it requires less ceiling height and fewer power tools. If possible, plan a separate space for fabricating props to keep them clear of sawdust and scene paint.

electric shop

This space is needed for storing parts and supplies and for making repairs to sound and lighting equipment. It may be small but needs to be dust-free. Consider a separate space from the scene shop. Plan to keep it locked.

costume shop checklist

During the planning period, consider the following for the costume shop:

- Even, glareless light + outlets for localized light and power equipment. Plan electrical outlets for present and future needs.
- Cutting tables. Allow space for 3' x 6', or 4' x 8', tables with cork tops—either the collapsible type or type equipped with casters that lock.
- Deep sink with hot and cold water.
- Washer/dryer space + electrical outlets and plumbing. Plan it to be adjacent to the sink.
- Hot plate. Place it adjacent to the sink.
- Materials and supplies storage. This should be a lockable space adjacent to the work area.
- Curtained dressing area.
- Racks for costumes in work. These could collapse to save space; or roll to dressing rooms.
- Adequate space for sewing machines and ironing boards. Use the folding type of board to save space.
- Full-length mirror.
- Space for dress forms.
- Wall telephones.

storage

Where building materials, costumes, and props are scavenged and recycled more often than not; where plays may be brought back into the repertory; where labor is often cheaper than materials—storage space becomes crucial. There is never enough. Ingenuity is at a premium in planning the conversion of your space to include maximum storage at minimum cost.

As mentioned in Chapter 2, "lofting," or storage lofts created above other facilities and spaces, is a common way to stretch backstage space. It is especially useful above permanent dressing rooms where the ceiling height is only required to be normal room height, thus frequently creating otherwise unused spaces above them. Consider the convenience of utilizing this space for costume storage. Look for other wasted spaces, or underutilized areas in your plans—over offices, under the control booth, in lobby benches—and devise storage systems to maximize their usefulness.

Consider cheaper spaces for storage, such as a basement. It could help pay for itself in storing re-usable materials or sets and props used in repertory.

Consider the strategy of the Joseph Jefferson Theatre Company which has no costume storage space. They have made an arrangement to give any good period costumes they construct to the TDF Costume Collection as a credit against future rentals from the Collection—an imaginative "storage" solution for a company dedicated principally to doing revivals.

rehearsal space

basic requirements

Some basic requirements to consider in planning a rehearsal space are:

- good heat and ventilation
- good acoustics
- easy access to toilets and drinking water
- sound isolation from shops, stage, and front of house
- rehearsal room equipment: table with light for director and stage manager; lockers, mirrors, and notice board; telephone (should be equipped with a light signal instead of a bell)

(For shape and size requirements see Chapter 2.)

multiple usage

If you are fortunate enough to have a separate rehearsal space, consider designing it for multiple usage:
- as a second stage
- for readings
- for classes
- for public receptions and parties
- as a lounge or lobby
- as a costume shop, prop shop, or scene shop

Full utilization of this space is largely a matter of good scheduling plus speed and efficiency of conversion once the theatre is in operation. If you list the projected multiple uses of the space before making the renovation, the following can be incorporated:

THE SUPPORT SPACES

- provision for the type and number of electrical outlets needed for shop, lounge, or other uses
- necessary storage
- the best floor to serve all purposes
- durable decor to make it an attractive place for public events
- lighting equipment for readings or second stage usage
- lighting control to accommodate multiple uses

shared rehearsal space

Consider the possibility of shared rehearsal space with a theatre or theatres nearby. Interart and Ensemble Studio Theatre, located in the same building, share rehearsal space. The amount of rehearsal space and the number of spaces needed will depend on the production schedule. It has been pointed out by one OOB manager that ''a theatre with multiple production spaces and a heavy production schedule will not fill these multiple spaces for very long if there are not multiple rehearsal spaces; and a repertory theatre cannot continue as a repertory if it has only one rehearsal space.''

box office

Since almost all OOB ticket sales and voucher redemptions are made right before curtain time, the box office or ticket counter must be designed for easy, rapid handling of this crowd in a very short period of time. Much of the rest of the time the box office is little more then a telephone extension, monitored by an answering machine or by a staff person with other duties who provides play information and telephone seat reservation services. This raises questions about the necessity and viability of the conventional box office for the small theatre. Study the problem in terms of projected schedule and needs and decide during the planning period if you actually want and need a traditional box office. Perhaps a booth/counter/table set-up in the lobby would be preferable.

traditional box office

If a traditional box office seems best, here are some design considerations to ponder:

- Be sure to provide adequate space for box office personnel; ticket racks; telephone; and either a safe, a locked cabinet, or a money drawer. If the box office will serve more than one performance space, allow for extra personnel, telephones, and ticket racks If an expansion to include multiple performance spaces is contemplated in the future, provide box office space for this during the planning period. (See Chapter 2 for minimum sizes.)
- Consider locating the manager's office or another administrative office adjacent to the lobby so that, with a connecting window or dutch door, it can double as a box office.
- Try to place the ticket window adjacent to, but out of, the main traffic flow from street entrance to theatre entrance.
- Be sure the box office is heated, ventilated, and adequately lighted. Make sure the adjacent lobby or foyer is also. Light the ticket counter well.
- Consider providing a conspicuous place to post a calendar of performance times and dates.
- Plan the telephones with both bell and light signals if there is any danger that the sound from a bell signal will penetrate the performance space.
- Provide a security system.

ticket booth/counter/table

If a type of ticket counter will serve best, consider these design problems and solutions:

• A ticket counter of this type might be portable or do double duty as a concession or drinks counter during intermissions. One OOB theatre, with limited lobby and box office space, sets up a ticket booth shortly before performances to handle the last minute crush; once the performance has started, the booth is rolled away to allow re-use of this space for the intermission crowd.

• It will be necessary to design storage space for this type of booth or counter. Consider putting it on casters; consider a collapsible unit.

• Consider a lockable telephone or a jack in the vicinity of the counter.
• It will be necessary to have a portable ticket rack which can be relocated for use during non-performance hours and/or locked up when not in use.
• A portable strongbox will be necessary.

Some possible problems of the open ticket counter are:

• theft
• a lack of impersonal separation between box office personnel and the public
• flooding or crowding around, making if difficult for box office personnel to function efficiently

Portable ticket booth/concession counter.

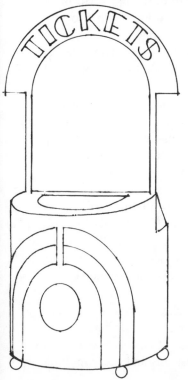
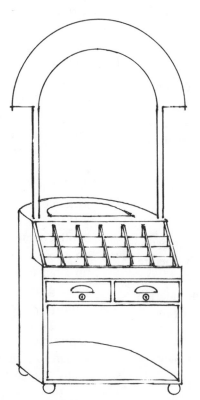
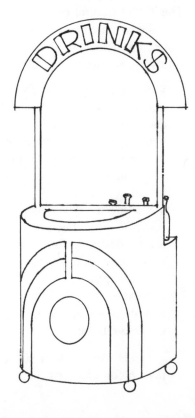

THE SUPPORT SPACES

111

shared facilities

The Ticket Central concept for 42nd Street Theatre Row includes a shared box office located in an adjacent restaurant. This central box office plan provides the following services:

• Phone reservations: Ticket Central will take all ticket reservations for each Theatre Row company and other subscribing companies to a limit to be set with each company in advance and up until 6:00 on the evening of the performance.
• Conducts advance sale and credit card transactions for all companies.
• Mailing list development: Ticket Central will get addresses from each person reserving.
• Provides information, directions, dining suggestions.
• Purchases and provides ticket stock for all Theatre Row companies.
• Provides a central location for promotion materials and an area map identifying the OOB theatres in Chelsea-Clinton.

Ticket Central does not handle last minute sales and reservation pick-ups.

112

lobby and lounge

Multiple uses for the lobby and lounge have already been listed, and minimum sizes are discussed in Chapter 2. Keep the following in mind when planning this area:

• Plan the lobby to be accessible to all front-of-house spaces: rest rooms, public telephone, lounge, offices, and, of course, box office.
• Lobby must have easy access to seating area, but must be designed in such a way that noise and light will not leak in to disturb or disrupt performance or rehearsal. A light and sound lock with two sets of curtains and/or doors is desirable.
• Consider use of the lobby as a ''safe area'' if required by the Building Code to have one (see Chapter 15).
• Adequate general illumination is necessary for safety and for reading programs. Additional specific lighting sources can add interest and accent.
• If there is a bar or counter for concessions and drinks in the lobby or lounge, plan to make it lockable.
• If the concession stand is a temporary booth/counter/table, set up for intermission only, plan on a lockable storage space. One OOB theatre has set up a bar in an elevator adjacent to the lobby for serving intermission drinks—an ingenious multi-purpose space.
• If possible, plan to make a sink and refrigeration accessible to concession counter or bar.
• Plan for ample number of electrical outlets in the lobby/lounge for concessions and other multiple uses.

office space

Plan for future expansion of office staff and for the accumulation of paper that is an inevitable part of the bureaucracy. It is better to design too much than too little office space. Like storage, there is never enough.

During the planning period, consider these design problems:

- If the front entrance of the theatre must serve as a general entrance during the day when the box office is not manned, consider placing administration offices in proximity to front-of-house for security.

- If possible, locate the offices near the box office, the lobby, and the lounge, for convenience.
- Consider placing like functions near each other; such as press/subscription, casting/production, and business/audience development.
- Consider accessibility to rest rooms and drinking water.
- Plan office placement and design so that telephone, typewriter, and conversation noise will not penetrate the rehearsal or performance areas.
- Provide heat and ventilation.
- Provide adequate general light and outlets for localized light at work areas and for office machines.

11

the theatre consultant and the architect

There is little question but that the right architect and theatre consultant will make the design, planning, and renovation a much easier, less painful process. With their knowledge and imagination they should also make a genuine creative contribution. There is a real question with some small groups as to whether these experts are affordable. There is also, quite often, some question about how to make the best use of their expertise. Knowing what to expect from an architect or theatre consultant should help answer some of these questions.

An architect will design the space, coordinate all the consultants and contractors, and will be responsible for holding to estimated costs as well as for the quality of construction. An architect will also be needed for zoning variance procedures and for presenting drawings to the Community Board. A licensed architect's stamp and signature will be necessary for filing any plans with the Department of Buildings.

Few architects have had extensive experience designing theatres, so the theatre consultant will work as your advocate to interpret your theatre needs to the architect. He will provide expertise in planning the stage and seating layout; stage lighting; backstage and support space needs, such as shops, rehearsal spaces, and dressing rooms. The theatre consultant will advise on the specialized theatre equipment and will get cost estimates on this equipment.

The following are some suggestions for making the best use of outside expertise in planning and carrying out your renovation:

• Get an architect and a consultant on your Board of Directors, if possible, and hope they will volunteer their services.

• Make certain their ideas are compatible with your concept.

• Get them early. Get them in on the ground floor of your planning period.

• Seek their expert evaluation of any building you are seriously considering. Let the architect check it out for the problem areas outlined in Chapter 5. Have the theatre consultant assess the space as a potential theatre. Let them both help you assess *how suitable* it is for what you want to do and *how much* it will cost.

• Enlist the help of the architect and consultant in preparing the cost estimate for the renovation.

• Let the architect advise on details of the lease.

• Have your architect assist you in preparing preliminary drawings for submission to the Department of Buildings. The Department of Buildings operates on interpretation of the Code, so before the architect draws up final plans, prepare a preliminary set of drawings to get a reading from them.

• There are some strategies for inexpensive architectural advice and assistance such as using student help and apprentice architects. Remember, however, that only a licensed architect can file plans.

• If you must pay an architect or consultant, arrange for a flat fee without regard to hours. On the other hand, if consultation is required before the space has been selected and work commences, engage these services on an hourly rate which will then be applicable to the fee.

• A theatre generalist sympathetic to your goals is the best consultant. In other words, it is highly unlikely that you will require a specialist, such as an acoustician or a seating expert. If there are special problems, the consultant should advise on getting a specialist. However, most of the spaces are so small they do not require this special expertise.

• It is important to choose a consultant who is strong in lighting.

• A final note: some one person should be given the authority and responsibility to deal with the architect and consultant. It should not be done by committee—no camels, please.

12

sources of materials and equipment

There are many inexpensive ways of getting materials and equipment for renovating, equipping, and operating the not-for-profit theatre.

donations

Like cash donations, remember that donations of equipment and materials can be tax deductible, too. Major corporations can be a source for this kind of donation, in addition to funding. The corporate contact is usually the community relations or public affairs officer.

scavenging

Picking up discarded items can be a lucrative endeavor. Check out areas of new construction or urban redevelopment where streets are lined with dumpsters.

auction sales

In addition to auctions used to liquidate companies going out of business—such as hotels and old theatres, there are a number of agencies within the government that regularly hold auctions.

Post Office. Usually three to four times a year the Post Office will put up notices of auctions in all of their stations. The items for sale are goods which were undeliverable or unreturnable, or damaged items on which the insurance was paid. All goods to be auctioned are on display at the location designated on the notice, prior to the day they will be sold. Just about anything that can be sent through the postal system may end up on the block.

To request placement on the mailing list for notification of these auctions in New York City, send your name and address to:

Claims Inquiry Section
Room 4508
General Post Office
33rd Street and Eighth Avenue
New York, N. Y. 10001

The Post Office also holds auctions on used vehicles—old mail trucks.

To be placed on this mailing list in New York City write or call:

Vehicle Services Branch
4th Floor
General Post Office
33rd Street and Eighth Avenue
New York, N. Y. 10001   (212) 971-7523

Department of Sanitation. In New York City the goods resulting from evictions are auctioned by the Department of Sanitation. There are six different warehouses located in the various boroughs and generally auctions are held twice a week.

To be placed on this mailing list write to:

Department of Sanitation
Chief Clerk—Encumbrance
Room 707
125 Worth Street
New York, N. Y. 10013

Police Department. In New York City, the goods recovered by the Manhattan Transit Authority (items left on buses and subways) are auctioned by the Police Department. Inspections are scheduled a day or so in advance and catalogues of the items for sale are available at the location of inspection. Also for sale are recovered goods which were stolen and never claimed by owners, such as office equipment, sporting goods, bicycles, and motorcycles.

For information call (212) 982-2190.

Surplus personal property. The State of New York periodically auctions off used equipment from state-owned institutions and offices. This may be a shot in the dark, but one never knows what the state may decide to sell. These items are sold in lot or groups by auction or sealed bid.

For a brochure and a mailing list application write to:

Office of General Services
Bureau of Surplus Personal Property
Building No. 18
State Office Building Campus
Albany, N. Y. 12226

wholesale buying and other bargain sources

Joint purchasing. A group of theatres all needing the same supplies and equipment—lumber supplies, stage lighting equipment, lamps and replacement parts, plumbing and electrical supplies, theatre seats—can, by ordering in bulk, purchase these items at below-retail prices. Contact OOBA for information.

Thrift shops. Thrift shops, run by the Salvation Army and other charitable organizations, are often good for used office furniture.

Salvage yards. Salvage yards handle materials from demolished buildings, such as plumbing fixtures, industrial lighting fixtures, and used building materials.

renting vs. buying

There are two schools of thought here; consider which is best for you.

renting

One line of thinking goes as follows: the newly established theatre should rent everything during the first phase. This keeps initial investment to a minimum, keeps the company flexible with options open for change and unfettered by property should they want to move or expand after two or three seasons. The extreme of this point of view is summed up by one theatre consultant, who advises, "A young, new, not-for-profit theatre should start by renting everything—including the toilets."

An additional reason for renting is that many grants will allow rentals, but will not support purchases or capital improvements.

In the case of lighting and sound equipment, one of the largest equipment costs for a small theatre, arguments for renting include:

- Equipment provided should satisfy Electrical Code requirements.
- Responsibility is assumed for certain types of maintenance and repairs during the rental period.
- The equipment can be serviced.
- In the case of lighting instruments and projection equipment, new lamps should be provided with each rental.

Consider renting for the first season or two, testing out various dimmer boards, lighting instruments, and sound systems. If grant money does not prohibit it, a group might work out a rental/purchase plan with a rental company.

buying

The argument for purchase goes: "Why pay out huge sums for rentals and have nothing to show for it several seasons later?" And this can be just as valid.

Perhaps a compromise worth considering would be to purchase all permanent sound and lighting equipment such as control equipment, speakers, work lights, house lights, lighting equipment for permanent concert or reading set-ups; and to rent all the portable equipment used for productions.

buying stage lighting equipment

When buying stage lighting equipment, there are a number of precautions and strategies that can save you money.

comparative shopping

Collect information and price lists from many different manufacturers and dealers. See as much equipment as possible in operation. Check out the types of equipment being used in theatres similar in grid height and stage size to your space.

expert advice

A lighting designer or theatre consultant will be able to point out the advantages and/or disadvantages of any equipment you are considering. They will be able to help you get the best equipment for your money.

used equipment

It is possible to save money by buying used equipment. But, before buying, make sure that replacement parts will be possible to get. Have a lighting technician test all the instruments, put a full load on all the dimmers, and get an estimate if any repairs are necessary.

manufacturers

When buying new equipment, check closely on the manufacturer: reputable manufacturers will offer warranties and will guarantee their equipment. One novice theatre group bought an electronic board from an unknown company for what seemed to be a bargain; they have since spent an equal amount, or more, having it repaired by another company.

packaged lighting systems

There are packaged systems on the market that include a dimmer board, instruments, and cable, for what seems to be a bargain. However, the instruments are sometimes second rate and/or the boards are of poor quality, limited capacity, or outdated. Get a professional opinion before buying one of these bargain packaged systems.

purchasing lamps

When purchasing lighting instruments, it is cheaper to order the lamps separately from a wholesale lamp distributor. You will probably have to order by the case, but the discount off the list price makes it a worthwhile investment.

connectors and cables

It is cheaper to buy new instruments without the connectors. Instrument manufacturers put on the connectors only after receiving an order. Their labor costs, usually at union scale, are added to the price. By ordering the connectors separately and doing the wiring yourself, you can save money.

Consider making up cable. As with connectors on instruments, the supply houses will have the cable made up as orders come in. Someone will have to do the measuring, cutting, and wiring—so you will be paying for the labor as well as the materials. The cable needed can be purchased directly from an electrical supply house. The connectors can be ordered from a theatrical supply house or directly from the manufacturer.

grounded equipment

The cost of buying grounded equipment (3-wire) is not that much more than ungrounded (2-wire) equipment. It is an added safety feature, and since the equipment will eventually be required to be grounded to satisfy the electrical inspector, it is worth the initial investment.

13

general installations

portable vs. permanent

When beginning to plan sound system and stage lighting installations, consider the desirability of portable systems over permanent ones. For a new, small theatre, portable systems have these advantages:

• The Electrical Code's requirements for permanent installations necessitate engaging an electrical contractor and purchasing additional materials not required for portable systems. It is to your benefit to describe the stage lighting circuitry as ''portable'' on all schematic drawings and to explain this to all electrical inspectors. Emphasize that each production is a separate entity and will require all stage lighting instruments and circuits to be repositioned.

• With the possible exception of making the board hook-up, portable systems can be installed without having to hire a licensed electrician.

• Permanent systems are designed for a specific space, therefore it is very difficult to adapt a permanent system to a new space, even if you can manage to move it.

• A portable system is readily adaptable to flexible space. Instruments, circuits, and even control boards can all be moved to new positions to accommodate new configurations.

• With a portable system, it is possible to begin small and to add later as your lighting needs increase and your budget permits. In a permanent system it is wiser to make the complete installation initially.

• Finally, you can take it all with you if you move or if you go on tour.

sound systems

Although the majority of small theatres do not need a sound system to reinforce or amplify the actor's voice, a system is necessary for sound effects. The following considerations apply to the planning of sound systems for small theatres:

speaker location

Plan the number of speakers with relation to the size and configuration of your space. For example, in a traditional Proscenium configuration two speakers may be adequate, whereas in an Arena configuration four speakers may be needed.

Speaker locations should be planned along with the seating and stage layout to avoid interference with audience sightlines and stage lighting positions.

If speakers are hung over the seating area, they must have a minimum clearance of 7' to comply with the N.Y.C. Fire Prevention Code. In addition, they may not block any exits or aisles.

Consider placement of a speaker onstage as a monitor for performers if the configuration being used will make it difficult for them to hear the house speakers.

reel-to-reel tape decks

For theatrical use, reel-to-reel tape decks are preferable to cassette decks. Reel-to-reel machines are easier to edit and all the cues for a show can be stored on one or two reels with leader separating each cue to facilitate running.

An 8-track cartridge loop player is a good and inexpensive alternative to a second reel-to-reel to handle continuous background sound such as surf, crickets, birds, rain, and city ambience. Cassette decks, while good for continuous playing, necessitate separate cassettes for each cue—in a heavily cued show, this becomes impractical and very expensive.

mixers

Mixers should be considered in addition to the basic components of a sound system—tape deck, amplifier, and speakers. Mixers will allow auxiliary tape decks and microphones to be centrally controlled or "mixed."

professional equipment

Rent or purchase professional sound equipment rather than equipment designed for home use. Professional systems are designed for longevity and withstand the abuse of continual use. Home systems are adequate for temporary situations but will not withstand constant use.

electrical installations

Having any electrical work done, or doing it yourself to save money, will require careful planning. There are a number of points to consider to avoid future problems.

- Have a theatrical consultant sit in on the planning of the installation, especially where lighting is concerned. There are wiring problems peculiar to the circuitry used for theatrical lighting equipment that the non-theatre oriented electrician knows nothing about, such as running separate neutral and ground lines for each circuit.

- If you are supplying additional power to your space, allow for future expansion by bringing in more than your present needs require.

- If any rewiring or additional wiring needs to be done, try to bring it up to Code specifications initially to avoid receiving violations later. It may seem costly; however, correcting violations can be more costly and you must hire a licensed electrician to do the work (see Chapter 16).

- If an electrical contractor is hired, get an estimate broken down into labor and equipment. Some contractors make their money on resale of the equipment at a heavy mark-up. It may be cheaper for you to supply all the materials.

security systems

When planning security systems, think like a thief.

Panic bars. Consider installation of panic bars on all exterior doors except primary entrance as a security measure. Panic bars allow free access to exterior—by simply pushing on the bar—and at the same time prevent entry from outside the building. The Fire Department may require removal of all other hasps or locks on fire exits other than primary entrance.

Police locks. For additional security, Fox police locks may be added, to be used when the theatre is closed.

Window gates and shutters. If the theatre is on the ground floor, consider installing window gates or lockable metal shutters.

Alarms. Burglar alarm systems will provide additional security. If the space is broken into, an alarm is sounded both within the space and at the local police precinct. Alarm companies will do the installation. A seven year contract for this service is standard for an annual charge of approximately $400.

Watchman. Consider having a sleep-in technician as a watchman who will make a nightly check and will open up in the morning. This, however, requires a Certificate of Occupancy that includes residence.

Remember, the more secure the theatre, the cheaper the insurance.

the IRT story

Impossible Ragtime Theatre
120 W. 28th Street, New York, N.Y. 10001

Ted Story, Artistic Director/Producer
Cynthia Crane, Producer
Laurice Firenze, Managing Director

the space

The four story commercial loft building, in which the IRT is located, was originally a public school. The second floor, two-thirds of which is currently occupied by the IRT, was formerly rented by a paper and printing company.

the location

In the heart of the wholesale florist district in midtown Manhattan, 28th Street during the day is very busy with the loading and unloading of delivery trucks. At night the activity does decrease, but because many of the merchants have flowers delivered at night, the street is patrolled by a private guard.

Transportation for the staff and audience is excellent—two subway lines stop within easy walking distance of the theatre. Also Penn Station at 34th Street is only six blocks away, helping to bring in a suburban audience. The on-the-street parking, in the evening, easily accommodates the number of patrons that drive. The only drawback to the location is the lack of any other night life in the immediate vicinity; there are no bars or restaurants located near the theatre that are open in the evening.

the story

The IRT, formed in 1974, grew out of a concept for a director's theatre and the belief that "if you want something done right—do it yourself."

The four founding members—Cynthia Crane, George Ferencz, Pamela Mitchell, and Ted Story—were not newcomers to the OOB theatre experience; they had the advantage of having run other small theatres before beginning their own.

In 1972, three of them had functioned as the staff for the Gene Frankel Theatre Workshop at the Mercer Arts Center—Story and Ferencz functioned as the co-managers while each directed shows, and Mitchell acted as an associate producer with Mr. Frankel. When the Mercer Arts Center building collapsed, they moved with Mr. Frankel to a new facility called "Theatre in Space," taking charge of the smaller theatre.

With the Frankel theatre's move to the Lambs Club, they felt it was time to plan for their own theatre, committing themselves to an exploration of the "director's method," a concept theorized by Mr. Ferencz and Mr. Story.

"Most small theatres at the time were terrible places to work," recalls Ted Story. "We decided that we could do a better job." So in the summer of 1974, they began to lay the groundwork, contacting directors, actors, designers, technicians, playwrights, fund raisers, public relations people, and producers. They also began searching for a space and mounted a highly successful membership drive.

About the same time, they were approached by The Actor's Unit, an established not-for-profit theatre started by a group of actors who were in need of help with management, funding, and artistic direction. An alliance between the two groups was formed, placing the IRT in the unique position of becoming immediately eligible for funding, through The Actor's Unit.

THE IRT STORY

123

The commercial loft on 28th Street was found and part of the second floor was rented with a net lease arrangement that only included industrial heating (provided during standard business hours only)—approximately 3,075 sq. ft. for $625 per month. Since the building was originally a public school, all the public corridors and stairways were in compliance with the Building Code's requirements for a place of public assembly and the entire building was sprinklered.

The net lease gave the IRT the freedom to transform the space into a theatre with little restriction from the landlord, and very little help—a $100 paint allowance. The rest of the renovation was accomplished with materials scavenged from the street and from dumpsters located at renovation sites, spending the little cash they had on the necessary hardware to put it all together. The entire crew was comprised of volunteers and the design evolved out of consultations with a number of scenic and lighting designers. Because of financial limitations, the only piece of equipment IRT purchased for the first season was a dimmer board; theatre seats were gleaned from renovations of other theatres such as the Bouwerie Lane and the Vandam.

In 1975, after producing two shows with the Actor's Unit in their new space, the alliance was dissolved and the IRT was left to complete its first season on its own. Funding became of utmost urgency; the IRT—being newly incorporated—was not yet eligible for state and federal grants. Through an intensive fund-raising campaign, the IRT succeeded in maintaining its programs for the next two years, being entirely supported by private and business contributions and its box office receipts.

In order to expand its directors' programs, the IRT found itself in the position of needing a second stage but lacking the necessary finances to rent additional space. Ted Story learned of a small church on the East Side that wanted to convert a basement Sunday school space into a theatre. An agreement was reached with the church, giving the IRT exclusive use of the space 50% of the year for the next two years in exchange for the design and conversion of the space. This arrangement enabled the IRT to present smaller productions at the church space rent-free, while maintaining the larger space on 28th Street for their main productions.

An overbooking of the space, by the church, to other theatre groups left IRT with the short end of the bargain, and after a year this arrangement was dissolved. However, the interaction with other directors in the church space reinforced the belief in a director's laboratory theatre. The diversity of style and the input from other directors appealed to the IRT, but to fully realize this project, it became obvious that exclusive use of a second stage was needed. Fortunately, adjacent space on the same floor of the loft on West 28th Street was vacant, so the IRT rented it and began converting the space to become their Stage II.

As luck would have it, an old building on the corner of 28th and Broadway was being renovated and converted into a McDonald's restaurant. With a bit of persuasive talking and a six-pack of beer, the foreman allowed the IRT's volunteer crew to haul away all the lumber they could salvage! The result was enough building materials to entirely construct the second stage and another lobby space. Theatre seats were gotten through another bit of good fortune—a phone call from a friend at NBC tipped them off to the renovation of a studio theatre and they arrived just in time to liberate the seats from the dump truck! They salvaged enough seats to entirely furnish Stage II.

Currently, the IRT is still located on 28th Street, operating with two heavily scheduled theatres and 14 resident directors. However, they feel that they are rapidly outgrowing their space and have nowhere to expand within the building—the remaining portion of the second floor is rented by another theatre with whom they must share their rest rooms, and the upper floors have been converted into residential lofts. The industrial heating that is provided also creates a special problem during the winter months, since it is shut down at 6 P.M. each Monday through Saturday evening, and on Sunday it is not turned on at all. They are now in the process of finding another space, at least for rehearsals, but hopefully a small three story building which they could entirely take over, giving them the much needed rehearsal and office space they currently lack.

the conversion

STAGE I

Seating—100

Stage—End Stage configuration, with potential to be shifted to a two-sided Arena. Grid system of pipes for hanging scenery and lighting equipment. No curtain. In End Stage set-up, crossover through dressing room/storage area. In two-sided Arena set-up, crossover behind seating section or through lobby.

Stage size—25' × 25', 14' high

Seating area—Conventional theatre seats fixed to risers.

Control booth—Located high on stage right wall at the back of the house. Provides good view of stage.

Lighting equipment—Two 6 × 3600w. autotransformer dimmer packs (IRT owns one board and the other is rented by the season). 24 lighting instruments and some cable is owned by IRT (purchased through a rental/purchase agreement). Additional equipment is rented as needed per production.

Sound equipment—None is owned by the theatre. Speakers and tape decks are borrowed or rented as needed per production. No intercom system.

Dressing rooms—Temporary facilities are set up in storage area behind stage as needed.

Lobby—An adjoining space to seating area serves as lobby for Stage I with an open box office that converts to a concession counter at intermissions.

STAGE II

Seating—65

Stage—Three-sided Arena with a potential crossover behind dressing rooms and through the lobby. Grid system of pipes used for hanging scenery and lighting equipment.

Stage size—23' × 20', 14' high

Seating area—Conventional theatre seats located on two levels, top tier lofted directly over bottom tier, creating a balcony on three sides.

Control booth—Located in one corner of lower seating area, separated from audience with plywood walls. View of stage is adequate for most productions.

Lighting equipment—One 6 × 3600w. autotransformer dimmer board is rented for the season. Lighting instruments rented per production as needed.

Sound equipment—As in Stage I, no sound equipment is owned and must be borrowed or rented as the need arises. No intercom system.

Dressing rooms—Temporary facilities are set up in the storage area behind the stage as needed.

Lobby—An adjoining space separate from the Stage I lobby is used. This lobby is lofted over with the upper level used for storage.

Rehearsal space—No additional space for rehearsals is available. If the theatres are in use, the lobbies and hallways become the only other places to go. When auditions are held, actors waiting to be called line the stairway leading to the second floor!

Shop space—Scenery is built and painted on stage or in the lobbies. A few footlockers are used for storage of personal tools, but there are no tools owned by the theatre. Dressing rooms are used for costume construction.

Offices—One small office, which has been lofted over, is located at one end of the Stage I lobby. It is enclosed and has a lockable door for security and privacy. Every available inch of this office is used for desks and filing and it is not unusual to find meetings taking place in the hallways or lobbies, occasionally even in the men's room!

Storage—As in many small theatres, storage space is at a premium and wherever possible spaces have been lofted over to create additional storage areas. Stage II's lobby is lofted over to provide storage for props and furniture. Beside the dressing room area in Stage I is a lofted area which stores costumes on top and stage equipment and hardware underneath. Lumber is stored backstage in Stage II.

An open box office located in the lobby of Stage I serves for both theatres, and, during intermissions, it is converted into a concession stand.

the program

For the 1976–77 season there were 16 productions in the two theatres. During each season there are also readings and workshop productions which take place when the main shows are not running. In the summer, the stages are dark unless the spaces are rented out to other theatre groups.

Stage I—Equity approved Showcase with special arrangement for an extra 6 performances.

> 4 weeks rehearsal
> 2 weeks, 4 performances/week
> 2 weeks, 5 performances/week
> 18 performances total

Stage II—Equity approved Showcase.

> 4 weeks rehearsal
> 4 weeks, 3 performances/week
> 12 performances total

the costs

In the 1976–77 season, the IRT produced 16 shows in their two spaces with a total of 197 performances. Their total operating expenses for the year were $53,340; included in this figure is $12,660 for rent, $2,430 for electricity, and $1,898 for telephone. This budget was met through a number of grants: NYSCA $5,000, NEA $3,000, foundations $6,700; donations from individuals and private businesses: $16,000; and from income earned through subscriptions, box office, concessions, program advertising, and rental of the theatres: $19,500. It was also necessary to make up part of the deficit through a small bank loan.

Currently the IRT can only afford to pay two members of its staff, the Managing Director and the Technical Director. All others serve in a volunteer capacity.

The IRT, as does many small theatres, finds the funding cycle difficult to deal with: "You are forced to make a budget before you even know how much money you are getting and by the time all the money has come in from the grants—it is already owed! It's never there when you need it. . . it's hard to get a big hunk of money all at once."

the MTC story

Manhattan Theatre Club
  321 East 73rd Street, New York, N.Y. 10021

Lynne Meadow, Artistic/Executive Director
Barry Grove, Managing Director

the space

Built in the 1890s, the five story building occupied by the MTC was originally the home of the Bohemian Benevolent Society, a not-for-profit organization serving as an umbrella for a small group of Eastern European Societies. The building was designed as a clubhouse and included a bar, a restaurant, a gym, a rifle range, a bowling alley, club rooms, and a dormitory. After World War II, European immigration was on the decline and the building no longer served as a stopping off point for immigrants after Ellis Island. The gymnasium on the first floor was converted into a 176 seat auditorium and rented out as a legitimate Off Broadway theatre, known as Stage 73. The new theatre housed such productions as *Best Foot Forward,* in which Liza Minnelli made her New York debut, and *Fortune and Men's Eyes* starring Sal Mineo.

the location

The Manhattan Theatre Club is one of the few theatres situated on the Upper East Side of Manhattan, a predominantly residential section of the city. The community is an erudite one, populated for the most part by the affluent upper middle class. The majority of the MTC audience comes from this community, although the convenience of nearby transportation has helped attract a suburban audience from as far away as New Jersey and Philadelphia. The subway is not convenient to the theatre; however, bus service is excellent and the FDR Drive is only two blocks away. As for parking, there are two 24-hour garages on the same block as the theatre.

the story

Unlike the majority of Off Off Broadway theatres, the MTC was founded by a Board of Directors and not by an artistic director. The group of private citizens comprising the charter Board in 1969 were dissatisfied by Broadway and modeled the MTC after the Arts Threatre Club of London, a forum where new and innovative theatre could be presented and developed. The Board raised the money to start the theatre without producing a single play. Two different artistic directors managed the MTC for short periods before Lynne Meadow took charge as artistic/executive director in 1972–73.

The Board acquired the building by assuming the leasehold for $59,250. This included a heavy furniture and fixture fee, which they later realized they should not have paid. Fortunately, a settlement was eventually made for the real worth of the fixtures and improvements. Much of this first money was the Board's donations. Some of it was in the form of loans, which have since been converted to contributions.

After the acquisition of the lease, private funding sources were exhausted. Revenue was supplemented by renting out space not used by the MTC for rehearsals or productions. Not ready artistically or financially to assume Off Broadway status in order to use the 176 seat Stage 73, the MTC leased that space to other performing groups. It was not until the 1976–77 season that the MTC had a sufficiently large audience and the financial means to take back the large theatre for their major productions and commence producing plays under their own banner.

The building's Certificate of Occupancy already allowed for the performance of theatre, and previous Place of Assembly Permits had been issued. The theatre, therefore, had only to reactivate and renew these licenses.

The MTC also re-established the liquor license previously held by the Bohemian Benevolent Society for approximately $3,000. The income from the bar, though minimal, helped ease the cash flow problem.

By the time Lynne Meadow took charge, the organization was two years old and therefore eligible for public funding. In 1972–73, Miss Meadow's first season, the MTC raised $52,400. Of that amount $19,900 came from the New York State Council on the Arts and $32,500 from foundations. This support, in addition to revenue from box office, bar sales, and rentals made it possible for the MTC to amortize its initial $59,250 debt in four years.

In the first season, the MTC opened every room and Lynne Meadow produced a prolific season of 65 events. "With an Equity Showcase limit of 12 performances and a $2.50 top, you have to do a lot of plays to take in money!" As Barry Grove pointed out, "The MTC presented many of these plays, as opposed to producing them. Now MTC produces all its own work. The season has gradually been trimmed from 65 to 15 productions. In the first years, production costs were nil. However, there is a threshold where a not-for-profit theatre begins to spend more money on production in its effort to upgrade quality."

the conversion

DOWNSTAGE THEATRE (formerly Stage 73 and before that a gym)

Seating—155
Stage—An End Stage configuration. No fly loft. No curtain. No crossover unless the actors take to a fire escape.
Stage Size—19′ deep; 30′ wide; 14′ high, stage to ceiling.
Auditorium—Fixed seating. Conventional theatre seats.
Control booth—High on right wall of auditorium, a less than ideal position for viewing the stage.
Lighting control—18 dim 3/2500w. 6-pack autotransformer boards (very old, built to last, over 15 years old, but MTC owns them outright), 72 lighting instruments (half rented, half owned), cable rented.
Sound—Two reel-to-reel tape decks and one 8-track going into a 6-channel mixer (new). Also head set communication.
Projection booth—Small room at rear of auditorium. Best for 35mm carousel still projections and followspot.
Dressing rooms—Two at stage left. One eight-person and one six-person.
Small lobby—Adjacent to larger corridor serving entire complex.

Downstage Theatre has launched such productions as *Ashes, Catsplay,* the Athol Fugard plays, and many others.

UPSTAGE THEATRE

Seating—100 seats, folding chairs on fixed wood risers.
Stage—22′ wide; 16′ deep; 11′ high. A simple raised platform. No fly space, no grid, no curtain.
Control booth—At back. Minimal space for two persons.
Lighting control—Two 6-pack luxtrol autotransformer units, which MTC owns.
Sound—One reel-to-reel tape deck, same as Downstage for interchange of parts. No head set communication.

Ain't Misbehavin' was performed here and in the Cabaret Theatre at alternate performances.

CABARET THEATRE (formerly a restaurant with liquor license)

Seats at tables—65 persons total.
Stage space—14′ wide; 6′ deep.
Lighting control—Two house dimmers, three stage light dimmers controlled by the stage manager, who runs the show from behind the bar.
Dressing rooms—Temporarily set up in Marble Worker's Union offices one flight above the cabaret. (MTC pays rental for the use of this space in the evenings.)

STUDIO 39—A rehearsal room (former clubroom) on the third floor, equipped with risers. MTC has rented out this space on a four wall rental deal, but is now taking it back for MTC in-house readings, rehearsals, and the like.

OTHER REHEARSAL SPACES (used by MTC but also rented, when not needed by MTC)

Studio 38—Also on the third floor. The largest rehearsal space can handle rehearsals for a Broadway show. Good wooden floors, mirrors on one wall. MTC uses it for Downstage Theatre rehearsals.
Two small studios on the second floor.
One small audition studio on the second floor.

SUPPORT SPACES

Scenic and paint shop—In basement under the Cabaret (formerly the restaurant kitchen). They can fabricate any scenic pieces that will go in a small freight elevator—12′ high flats. Otherwise scenery must be built and painted onstage.
Scenery storage—Formerly the bowling alley.
Prop storage—Large basement caged section.
Electric shop—Basement room.
Costume storage—Inadequate, almost nonexistent.
Costume shop—Third floor, converted from a rehearsal room over theatre. (It was not good for rehearsal because of noise.)

Day box office—Remote location off lobby for Downstage Theatre. Used for advance sales only. Small; adequate for one person only. Just enough room for telephones.
Evening portable box office—Set up in outer lobby before show time for current performances. Ticket pick-up for all theatres.
Administration offices and production offices—Scattered throughout the second and third floor of building.

the program

15 productions per season in three theatres. Slowly expanding.

Downstage Theatre—Equity Off Broadway contract, arrived at after heavy and lengthy negotiation.

    4 weeks rehearsal
    5 weeks, 8 performances/week
    40 performances total

Upstage Theatre—Equity Showcase contract.

    originally a 12 performance run
    1977–78—20 performances/4 weeks
    1978–79—24 performances/4 weeks

Cabaret Theatre—Equity has had no jurisdiction.

    3½ weeks rehearsal
    4 weeks, 7 performances/week—Wednesday through Sunday with 2 late night performances on Friday and Saturday evenings
    28 performances total

the costs

It costs the MTC $8,000 a month just to keep the doors open. Annual space costs are $30,000 rent; $20,000 utilities and maintenance; $10,000 improvements—$60,000 total. The total budget for the 1978–79 season is $700,000 up from $500,000 the year before.

MTC has a net leasehold on the building until 1984 with an option to renew. The MTC has a four wall lease, although the landlord pays for heat and the elevator operator.

MTC continues to rent out space for other productions although it is often the case that the poor quality of the rental production reflects badly on the MTC. Though the MTC is not listed anywhere on the program, patrons often assume the work is the MTC's. Now rentals are required to post a $200 bond against the use of the MTC's name. The production manager is responsible for renting space since he is the most knowledgeable about MTC rehearsal needs and coordinates rehearsal schedules.

There are still two other tenants in the building that rent directly from the landlord. One, a photographer, occupies the fourth and fifth floors. Because MTC occupies a multiple tenant building with common access, the MTC cannot get theft insurance.

All other insurance policies cost the MTC $6,000 per year. This includes fire, plate glass, and liability. The MTC owns its own telephone equipment which realizes approximately a $20,000 savings over five years, at which point it will be owned outright. From then on it will be free.

Each year Barry Grove tries to hold out about $1,500 to $3,000 to make improvements during the dark summer months, to renovate one more space in the maze of rooms. Recent improvements include a renovated lobby and expanded office space. Each year the MTC has begun to use more of the space for its own needs and rentals have decreased sharply. Now the MTC is looking ahead to finding another space—300 seats at least—in order to further expand its operation.

The building has, to a great extent, shaped the artistic development of the MTC. The Downstage Theatre (Stage 73) houses fully staged productions, many of which are considered for subsequent commercial productions. The Upstage, a 100 seat theatre, operates under a Showcase Code where the emphasis is on works in progress. The Cabaret, with small stage, bar, and tables, presents an intimate setting for the work presented by both new and established composers and lyricists. Because of the varied and unique performing spaces in the building, the MTC has developed into a performing arts center where drama, music, and poetry are presented at varying levels of development. Matching the right space to the right project has helped mold the artistic policy of the MTC.

part four
making it legal:
an interpretation of regulations and Codes

The chapters that follow are an interpretation of New York City's Zoning Resolution and its Building, Electrical, and Fire Prevention Codes, and deal only with the sections of these Codes that apply specifically to small theatre spaces. Theatres outside of New York City will have to comply with the zoning laws and the codes of the areas in which they are located. While these differ from place to place, the general principles involved, those of use and safety, will be similar.

The zoning laws and the Codes affecting small theatres in New York are complicated. Don't expect to grasp all the details at once. Most architects and other trained professionals refer to the Codes again and again for specifics. Keep in mind that all requirements do not apply to every theatre situation. The presentation in the following chapters should help to clarify which requirements apply to a specific group or a specific theatre space.

Chapter 18, Procedures, outlines the steps that must be taken to apply for a Certificate of Occupancy, file building plans, and obtain any other permits, certificates, or licenses needed to legally occupy a space.

Following the Procedures chapter is an appendix that lists government agencies and their locations. These agencies can provide any additional information needed on zoning, Codes, permits, and services.

implications of zoning and the Codes

Spending the time to look for the right space, in terms of legal requirements, will be well worth the effort. Finding a space that meets most of the requirements, one that has the proper number of exits, the right live load rating, the proper zoning, and so on, will save a great deal of time, labor, and expense.

If you don't intend to bring a space up to Code requirements, be aware of the possible consequences. In the past several years there have been a number of serious nightclub fires, primarily due to the owners' disregard for Code requirements and the illegal use of spaces. As a result, the Building and Fire Departments have cracked down heavily on their requirements for places of public assembly and issue violations more frequently for illegal and nonconforming uses of space in the City. Depending upon the seriousness of the violation, you may receive written notification and a certain amount of time in which to comply or you may be threatened with a shut-down of operations.

It is the experience of Off Off Broadway theatres that the main concern of an inspector is safety. Correcting hazardous violations should, in any event, be your first concern. If you can show that your theatre is safe, and that you are attempting to keep it up to Code, chances are you will not be excessively bothered by inspectors.

routine on-site inspections

The Fire Department, Department of Buildings, Department of Consumer Affairs, and the Bureau of Gas and Electricity all have the authority to make routine, on-site inspections. Past practice, however, indicates that small theatres are most likely to be routinely visited only by the Fire Department and an occasional electrical inspector.

The Fire Department does routine inspections of all buildings within its geographical jurisdiction. Even such establishment places as Carnegie Hall and Avery Fisher Hall are visited on a regular basis. So it will be in the normal course of affairs that they will visit your space. Although they make inspections daily, it could be that you will operate for a year without being visited. You could also receive a visit the day after you open. It is likely, since you are a theatre, that you will be visited at night when you are in operation.

The inspector will be checking to see that there are no violations of public assembly or fire prevention regulations, such as more people than permitted, obstructed aisles or exits. Should you be questioned by an inspector, have ready for inspection a complete set of all the records, drawings, and permits.

If temporary changes have been made for a particular production, explain that they are temporary, and that the space will be changed back to what was originally approved. The inspector may let the matter pass. But, if he returns six months later and finds these same changes, a lengthier explanation will be required.

It is best to handle inspections and inspectors in a friendly way, developing a relationship that lets the inspector know that every effort is being made to comply, and that the safety of the public is a mutual concern. Keeping a fire inspection log (see Chapter 17 for procedure) and presenting it to the inspector along with all the records, statements, and permits you should have, will prove your good intentions.

If you are visited by an inspector, *don't panic*. Nothing catastrophic is going to happen. Walk around with him and answer any questions he may have, but don't volunteer any information that's not requested. If violations are found, ask what is wrong, why, and how they can be remedied. Depending on the inspector, you may either get some very good advice, or a quote from the applicable Code book.

One Off Off Broadway theatre manager regularly gets an 8 × 10 glossy and bio of the fire inspector's nephew. The inspector is perennially distressed that the theatre does not call his nephew to audition, but there are no written violations either.

14

zoning

use groups and zoning districts

Zoning is a way of separating certain activities that go on in a city, so that they do not conflict with one another. Under the City of New York Zoning Resolution, which is primarily enforced by the Department of Buildings, these activities are divided into categories called Use Groups. Theatre falls into Use Group 8.

The city is broken down into areas, or zoning districts, where the various Use Groups are permitted. There are three basic zoning districts: Residential (R), Commercial (C), and Manufacturing (M).

numerical designations

Density. Each of these districts is further broken down by a numerical designation which generally indicates *density*, or how much of that activity can take place. For instance, a Residential district may be designated R1—single family detached houses—or R8—high rise apartment buildings; and a Commercial district may be designated C1—small retail and service shops—or C8—heavy commercial services, such as warehouses.

Use Group 8, which includes theatre activities, is permitted, by right, in zones designated C2, C4, C6, C8, M1, M2, and M3. This means that should you want to rent or buy a space located in one of these zones, for theatre use, the use cannot be contested and no zoning variance is required. Theatre can sometimes be located in another zone, but not as a matter of right, so a zoning variance would be required. Generally, a zoning category can be upgraded—that is, a Commercial use can go into a Manufacturing zone—but it is more difficult to justify downgrading a category—putting a Commercial use into a Residential zone.

Restrictions and requirements. To make matters even more complicated, each sub-category (C2, C4, etc.) also carries another numerical designation (C2-1, C4-5) which indicates other restrictions, such as maximum allowable floor area (the total floor area of a building permitted on a zoning lot) and building size, and requirements such as parking spaces and the amount of open area on a zoning lot. Parking requirements will vary with the district and the use. In some cases they may be waived by a modification granted by the Board of Standards and Appeals and reviewed by the Department of Buildings.

(For information on restrictions and requirements for specific numerical designations, call the Department of City Planning, listed in Appendix.)

zoning maps

When looking for a space, check the zoning maps of the areas in which you are interested to see where the C2, C4, C6, C8, M1, M2, and M3 districts are located. Once you have found a space, check the location again to make doubly certain that it is in one of these zoning districts. (Zoning maps are available from the Department of City Planning. If the information on the map is not clear, call the Department of City Planning zoning information, listed in Appendix.)

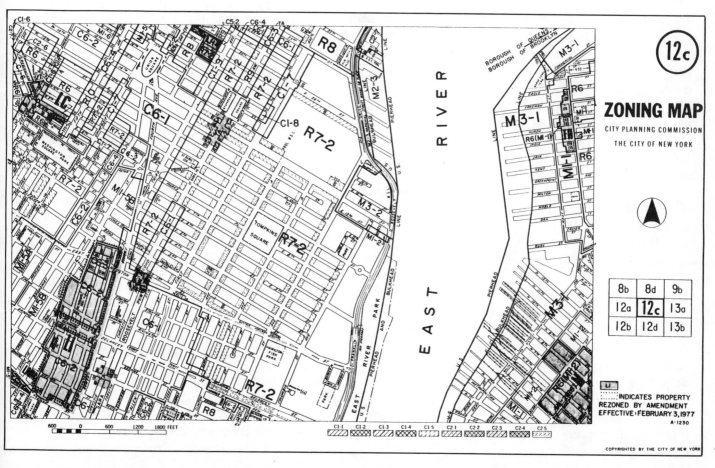

ZONING

135

getting a zoning variance

If, despite all efforts, the space you finally choose is in a non-theatre zone, then, by law, you must file for a zoning variance. This can be a long process and there are no guarantees that you will receive it.

appearing before Community Board

The first step is at the local level and is primarily for political reasons. It requires contacting the Community Board in your district and explaining to them who you are, what you are doing, and that you would like to get on the agenda for the next meeting of the Board. You will then be given the date and place of the meeting and placed on the agenda under "new business."

When you appear at the meeting you will be asked to present your intentions, explain who you are, your artistic directions, your past experience in theatre, your financial viability, and so on. If you have drawings of what you plan to do with your space, it is a good idea to present them at this time.

The matter will be disposed to committee for consideration and, no doubt, you will be asked to come to a committee meeting to talk again in more detail.

Next, a public hearing will be held and notice posted in the community that the issue will be open to public debate. Any interested community people will attend and voice their objections or support of your plan. The Community Board, taking public opinion into account, will move on the request by voting either favorably or unfavorably.

(See Chapter 6 for more information on Community Boards and for specific Community Board districts, addresses and phone numbers.)

filing with Department of Buildings

The next step is one of formality. You file plans with the Department of Buildings for the issuance of a new Certificate of Occupancy. Since your theatre is not a legal use you will be "officially rejected." You must be officially rejected in order to appeal for a zoning variance before the City's Board of Standards and Appeals.

Board of Standards and Appeals hearing

The appeals process is a legal hearing. You will need to be represented by either the architect who submitted the plans, or a lawyer, or both. The Board of Standards and Appeals will consider such things as the alteration of the character of the neighborhood, impaired use of the adjacent property, and the effect of your use of public welfare.

If the Community Board has favorably advised the Board regarding your zoning variance, it is likely that it will pass.

Board of Estimate hearing

You may further be required to appear before the City's Board of Estimate. This hearing will be necessary only if your project involves City money—City funding or tax abatement for example. The Board of Estimate must rule on such items before a variance is granted.

15

the Building Code

Building codes are written to insure the safety of all structures and the people who inhabit them. They establish requirements for such things as material, construction, number of exits, emergency lighting, ventilation, and plumbing.

The Building Code of the City of New York is probably one of the most comprehensive building codes in the country, having just been entirely rewritten in 1968. It will serve well in providing examples of the kinds of requirements that must be met in constructing or renovating spaces for use as small theatres in urban communities.

The Building Code is law and, like most other law, is subject to interpretation by those who administer it. Precisely how it is interpreted will not be known until plans are presented to the Department of Buildings for approval. The simpler the ideas for a space, the less difficulty there should be with approval.

definitions

Familiarity with the following terms will be helpful in understanding Building Code requirements.

Access stairs. Stairs between two floors which do not meet requirements for an exit.

Assessed value. The value of the building as determined by the City for purposes of taxation. It does not necessarily reflect what the building may sell for on the open market.

Certificate of Occupancy (C of O). The document, issued by the Department of Buildings, which authorizes the use of a certain space for specified activities by a certain number of people.

Corridor. An enclosed public passageway providing access from rooms or spaces to an exit.

Dead load. The weight of all permanent materials, equipment, and construction supported by a building, including its own weight.

Exit. A means of egress from the interior of a building to an open exterior space which is provided by the use of the following, either singly or in combination: exterior door openings, stairs or ramps, exit passageways, horizontal exits, interior stairs, exterior stairs, or fire escapes; but not including access stairs, aisles, corridors, or corridor doors.

Exit passageway. A horizontal extension of stairs or ramps, or a passage leading from a yard or court to an open exterior space.

Fire-resistance rating. A rating, given in hours, which indicates the amount of time a wall, floor, or ceiling must remain intact under conditions of fire. Following are ratings mentioned in this text with definitions as applied to wall construction.

- *1 hour*—⅝″ sheetrock, both sides of wall on wooden studs
- *2 hour*—two ⅝″ sheets of sheetrock, both sides of wall on steel or aluminum studs
- *3 hour*—6″ masonry wall with plaster both sides, or 8″ masonry wall without plaster

The principal concern a theatre has with fire ratings is to be certain that the means of egress from the space conform to the ratings required for theatre use.

Fire-retardant. Materials that have been pressure impregnated with chemicals so as to reduce combustibility.

First story. The first story above grade. However, if the building has a full basement, then the basement is considered the first story.

Flameproof. Materials that have been externally treated with chemicals, in order to reduce combustibility.

Grade. The finished surface of the ground, either paved or unpaved.

Live load. The weight of all occupants, materials, and equipment that are likely to be moved or relocated in a building, and that must be supported by the building in addition to the dead load. Live load is rated in pounds per square foot.

Means of egress. The path of exit. This can be a door; a door and stairwell; or a door, stairwell, and passageway.

Occupancy. The type of activity for which a building or space is used and/or the number of persons using a space. In a theatre space this includes audience, actors, and employees.

Place of Assembly Permit. Permit required by and obtained from the Department of Buildings if you have 75 or more persons using a space.

Safe area. An interior or exterior space that serves as a means of egress by providing a transitional area from an assembly place, and that also serves as a normal means of entry to the assembly place.

Old Code or New Code

The first thing to clarify about the Building Code of the City of New York is that, at present, there are actually two different codes in effect, referred to as the Old Code and the New Code.

The New Code went into effect as of December 6, 1968. If an application for a building permit was filed with the Department of Buildings before December 6, 1968, or within 12 months after that date, the owner had the option of filing under either Code.

Which Code governs a specific space presently depends on the following circumstances:

• If a building was built under the New Code, then any renovation in that building must conform to the New Code.

• If a building was built under the Old Code, but the cost of renovation is 60% or more of the assessed value of the building, then the entire building must comply with the New Code, even if only a part of it is being changed.

• If a building was built under the Old Code, but the cost of renovation is between 30% and 60% of the assessed value of the building, then only that part which is being changed must comply with the New Code.

• If a building was built under the Old Code, and the cost of renovation is 30% or less of the assessed value of the building, the renovation can be filed under the Old Code.

Cost of renovation is only the cost of materials and labor and does not include any fees or money spent on furnishings or electrical work. Doing most of the work yourself will not exempt you from adding the cost of labor into the job, even though it may be a minimal number of hours figured at the minimum wage.

Although architects feel there are advantages to each of the Codes, for the type of space required by small, not-for-profit theatres, there seem to be few advantages to filing under the New Code. For example, wall, ceiling and floor fire ratings, which may have met the Old Code requirements for theatre use, may not be satisfactory to the New Code specifications. This will depend upon the building's classification, your occupancy group, and the occupancy groups located directly above, below, and adjacent to your space.

Try by every means possible to renovate under the Old Code. This means keeping the renovation budget at 30% or less of the assessed value of the building. An experienced architect can be of extreme value in helping to convince the Department of Buildings that the renovation will not exceed this 30% mark.

The assessed value of a building can be checked at the Bureau of Real Property Assessment. (See Appendix.)

occupancy

One of the main differences between the Old Code and the New Code is that of occupancy categories and their related requirements. This difference is significant for the small theatre in terms of bringing a space up to Code, and should be noted.

Under the Old Code, there are two occupancy categories applicable to the small theatre: *74 occupants or less* and *75 occupants or more*. The second of these categories actually covers occupancies of between 75 and 298.

For *299 occupants or more*, the Old Code has a third category, designated Special Occupancy.

The New Code has only two categories: *74 occupants or less* and *75 occupants or more*.

Under either Code the requirements for *74 occupants or less* are the easiest to satisfy and a Place of Assembly Permit is not required.

It is when a theatre has an occupancy of more than 75 that it is of great advantage to be under the Old Code. Under the Old Code, only theatres with an occupancy of 299 or more need comply with the requirements for large theatres, those in the Special Occupancy category. Under the New Code, however, any theatre in the second category, *75 occupants or more*, must meet all the requirements laid out for large theatres. Whether the occupancy is 75, 300, or 1,000, the requirements are the same—the New Code shows no mercy.

building classification

The first concept that the Old Code deals with is building classification. It is important to be familiar with this when looking at spaces. A classification is assigned to a building depending on the type of materials used in its construction.

The building classifications are given below, followed by a brief description:

Class 1—Fireproof. The exterior and interior are all masonry or concrete including interior columns.

Class 2—Fire-protected. All masonry or concrete interior and exterior, very similar to Class 1. The difference between these two classes will be difficult to see. It has more to do with how much of a material was used and therefore how long the structure is protected from fire. Many loft buildings, if they have concrete floors and columns, fall into this category.

Class 3—Non-fireproofed. The exterior is masonry but the interior has wooden beams and floors with interior columns of wood or cast iron. Loft buildings with tin ceilings are likely to be Class 3 buildings; the ceilings were put up to cover the wooden beams.

Class 4—Wood frame. All wooden exterior and interior.

Class 5—Metal or fireproofed wood structure. Walls are metal or asbestos panels. Interior is fireproofed wood.

Class 6—Heavy timber. Exterior is usually masonry, interior is heavy timber construction with columns and beams not less than 10″ to 12″ in size.

These classifications cover every type of building built in New York City and the law permits a theatre use in any of them. However, where in the building the theatre can be located, and how much square footage it can occupy, differ according to the building classification:

Class 1. Theatre is permitted on any floor of the building without any limitation in size.

Class 2. Theatre is not permitted above 32' or the third story and is limited to 7,500 sq. ft. in size.

Class 3. Theatre is permitted only on the first story of a multi-story building, but on either story of a two story building, and is limited to 5,000 sq. ft. in size.

Class 4. Theatre is permitted on the first story of a one story building and is limited to 600 sq. ft. in size.

Class 5. Theatre is permitted on the first story of a one story building and is limited to 600 sq. ft. in size.

Class 6. Theatre is permitted only on the first story and is limited to 6,000 sq. ft. in size.

Obviously, Class 4 and 5 buildings are out of the question for a theatre of 100 seats because of the space limitations. Fortunately these two classes of buildings, along with Class 6 buildings, are not very common in the City. Most likely you will be looking at Glass 1, 2, or 3 buildings.

It is important to know the classification of the building because of the location and square footage restrictions among the various classes, but you cannot know this just by looking at the structure. The only way to be certain is to check on the classification of the building. This should be indicated on the current C of O for the space. If the C of O is not available, the classification of the building may be found at the Department of Buildings (see Chapter 18). The square footage limitation for theatres includes all support spaces, even offices. It is possible, however, to locate offices or other support spaces on additional square footage within the same building if they are entirely separate entities.

Before renting a space, make sure that theatre is permitted on the available story and that the square footage is not in excess of what is allowable for that particular classification, otherwise you will be paying for unusable space.

means of egress

74 occupants or less (on first story)

Whether the theatre occupies the entire floor of a building, or shares the floor with other tenants:

- Only 1 means of egress is required.
- Minimum door size is 3' 8". It must swing in the direction of egress; if it opens in, it will have to be re-hung so that it opens out.

74 occupants or less (above the first story)

If the theatre occupies the entire floor of a building:

- 2 means of egress are required.
- Both exit stairs must have a 2 hour fire rating, be a minimum of 3' 8" wide, and lead directly to the street. In some instances the door to the street will not be located at the foot of the stairs, but an exit passageway will lead from the stairs to the exterior door. This is fine as long as the passageway has the same fire rating as the stairs.

If the theatre shares a floor with other tenants:

- Only 1 means of egress from the space is required.
- This means of egress must be a minimum of 3' 8" wide, and lead from your space into a public corridor which leads to 2 exit stairs.

The following are the requirements for the corridor and stairwell for tenants sharing a floor above the first story. While they are the responsibility of the landlord, check to make certain they are fulfilled for the purposes of your theatre:

- The public corridor must have a 1 hour fire rating.
- Minimum width of the public corridor must be 3′ 8″; this will accommodate 50 persons. The width must be increased 6″ for every additional 50 persons occupying the floor.
- Both exit stairs must have a 2 hour fire rating.
- Minimum width of each exit stairs is 3′ 8″. This width will accommodate 120 persons per stairs or a total of 240 persons for both stairs. Be certain that your occupancy and the number of other people on the floor does not exceed 240. Even if the other tenants use their space during the day and you use yours at night, capacity is figured on the assumption that everyone is there at once.
- In a Class 1 building, above the third story or the 32′ line, the capacity for a 3′ 8″ exit stairs drops to 60 persons per stairs. Make sure that the total occupancy for the floor does not exceed 120.

75 occupants or more (occupying entire floor)

If the theatre occupies an entire floor, on the first story or above the first story:

- 2 means of egress are required.
- Minimum door size is 3′ 8″ and must swing in direction of egress.
- Exit stairs (for spaces above first story) must have a 2 hour fire rating and be a minimum of 3′ 8″ in width.

75 occupants or more (more than one tenant per floor)

If the theatre shares a floor with other tenants on the first story:

- 2 means of egress are required.
- Minimum door size is 3′ 8″ and must swing in direction of egress.

If the theatre shares a floor with other tenants above the first story:

- 2 means of egress are required, a minimum of 3′ 8″ each; these must lead from theatre space into a public corridor which leads to 2 exit stairs.
- The requirements for the corridors and stairwells are the same as those for *74 occupants or less, above the first story*.

other requirements for means of egress

The following requirements apply to all means of egress regardless of occupancy categories:

Distance between exits. Where 2 means of egress are required, they must be a certain distance apart in your space: the second exit must be a minimum distance of one-third the depth of the building from the first exit. In other words, if the building is 100′ deep, the 2 exits must be at least 33′ apart.

Handrails. All stairs must have handrails on one side. If they are wider than 3′ 8″, they must have handrails on both sides.

Doors. All doors opening onto exit stairwells must have a ¾ hour fire rating, be self-closing, and open in the direction of egress. A ¾ hour fireproof, self-closing door should have an Underwriter's label or a label from the Board of Standards and Appeals. If a new door is needed, make sure you ask for a ¾ hour, fireproof, self-closing door that is labeled.

Exit stairs. In order for stairs to be used as exit stairs they must be enclosed in fire-rated construction and separated from any adjacent uses by a fire-rated door. Open stairs, of the type found in brownstones and in many Class 3 loft buildings, and those which are not separated from the common hallway, are not acceptable as exit stairs.

upper floor spaces

If you are considering a space on the upper floor of a Class 3 loft building, be cautious. Many of these buildings do not have the required 2 means of egress from the upper floors. Also, many were built with wooden stairs that have winders, steps that are wedge-shaped and turn a corner. Wooden stairs are never legal and winders are not permitted on stairs used as a means of egress.

Don't rent a space on an upper floor of a Class 3 loft building that has only one stairwell. There is no practical way to provide a second means of egress. It is best, in these types of buildings, to find a ground floor space.

If a building does have 2 means of egress from the upper floors (mostly Class 1 and Class 2 buildings) then, in all likelihood, if the stairs are enclosed in concrete, they will already have the proper fire ratings and the correct door swings, and will lead to the right places in terms of egress requirements.

Note: Elevators are not permitted as means of egress.

exit lighting

Exit signs. Illuminated exit signs must be used over all exits. (See *Electrical Code,* Chapter 16.)

Lighting on stairs. Lighting must be provided on all exit stairs. This should be the responsibility of the landlord, but make sure he replaces the bulbs when they burn out.

emergency lighting

Emergency lighting, required by the New Code for public assembly spaces, is retroactive to old buildings. The location of emergency lighting must be shown on architectural drawings and the electrical service must be run on a separate circuit. (See *Electrical Code,* Chapter 16.)

ventilation

Some means of providing fresh air and removing the stale air must be provided in any building, be it an apartment occupied by a single person or an assembly hall occupied by several thousand people. The amount of ventilation required depends upon the size of the space and the number of people occupying it, as well as on the number of operable windows located within the space.

Following are the formulas and tables used to calculate the amount of ventilation required. Also given are a list of the terms used, with explanations; and sample calculations.

THE BUILDING CODE

143

terms

Cubic feet. The volume of the space. It is found by multiplying the width by the depth by the height.

Cubic feet per person. The volume divided by the number of persons in the space.

Floor area (or square footage). Found by multiplying the width by the depth of the space.

Floor area per person. The floor area divided by the number of people in the space.

Window area. Found by multiplying the width of the window by the height of the window.

Window area per person. Found by dividing the window area by the number of persons in the space.

formulas

The first step is to calculate the Ventilation Index for the space. There are two formulas, one for a space with windows, one for a space without windows:

$$\frac{\text{Cubic feet per person} \\ 10 \times \text{the floor area per person} \\ + 100 \times \text{the window area opening per person}}{\text{Ventilation Index for spaces with windows}}$$

$$\frac{\text{Cubic feet per person} \\ + 10 \times \text{the floor area per person}}{\text{Ventilation Index for spaces without windows}}$$

examples

space width: 25′
height: 50′
depth: 20′
4 windows: 4′ × 8′
occupancy: 74 persons

$$25' \times 50' \times 20' = \frac{25{,}000 \text{ cu. ft.}}{74} = 337 \text{ cu. ft. per perso}$$

$$25' \times 50' = \frac{1{,}250 \text{ sq. ft.}}{74} = 16.8 \text{ (floor area per person)}$$
$$\times 10 = 168 \text{ sq. ft.}$$

If space has windows:

4 windows: 4′ × 8′ each
4′ × 8′ = 32 sq. ft. each window
32 × 4 = 128 sq. ft. for 4 windows

$$\frac{128 \text{ sq. ft.}}{74} = 1.72 \text{ (window area per person)}$$
$$\times 100 = 172 \text{ sq. ft.}$$

337 (cu. ft. per person)
168 (10 × floor area per person)
+172 (100 × window area per person)
677 Ventilation Index for space with windows

If space does not have windows:

337 (cu. ft. per person)
+168 (10 × floor area per person)
505 Ventilation Index for space without windows

tables

Once the Ventilation Index is calculated, the tables below can be used to check the required supply of fresh air and the required exhaust for the space.

table A – spaces with windows

Index #	Supply (per sq. ft. of floor area)	Exhaust (per sq. ft. of floor area)
0–300	2.5 cubic feet per minute (cfm)	2 cfm
301–520	2 cfm	1.5 cfm
521–850	1.5 cfm	1.25 cfm
851–1250	None Required	1 cfm
1251–1650	None Required	.67 cfm
Over 1650	None Required	None Required

table B – spaces without windows

Index #	Supply (per sq. ft. of floor area)	Exhaust (per sq. ft. of floor area)
0–300	2.5 cfm	2 cfm
301–520	2 cfm	1.5 cfm
521–850	1.5 cfm	1.25 cfm
851–1250	1 cfm	1 cfm
1251–1650	.67 cfm	.67 cfm
Over 1650	.33 cfm	.33 cfm

Using the example of the space with windows, the calculated Ventilation Index was 677. Using Table A, the required supply of fresh air is 1.5 cfm for every square foot of floor space.

$$25' \times 50' = 1{,}250 \text{ sq. ft.} \times 1.5 \text{ cfm} = 1{,}875 \text{ cfm}$$

The required exhaust for the same space can be calculated in the same manner:

$$1{,}250 \text{ sq. ft.} \times 1.25 \text{ cfm} = 1{,}562 \text{ cfm}$$

To calculate the required supply and exhaust for a space without windows, Table B is used. In the example given for the same space without windows, the Ventilation Index was 505, so the required supply is 2 cfm for every square foot of floor space.

$$25' \times 50' = 1{,}250 \text{ sq. ft.} \times 2 \text{ cfm} = 2{,}500 \text{ cfm}$$

The exhaust required is 1.5 cfm for each square foot of floor space.

$$25' \times 50' = 1{,}250 \text{ sq. ft.} \times 1.5 \text{ cfm} = 1{,}875 \text{ cfm}$$

THE BUILDING CODE

145

complying with requirements

Once you have calculated the Ventilation Index for a space and figured the required amount of supply and exhaust, this information can be applied practically:

Check the cubic foot per minute (cfm) rating of any current ventilation system installed in the space to determine if it will meet the new cfm requirements for the theatre's occupancy.

If no ventilation system is present, light industrial or commercial fans can be installed to meet the Code requirements. This will avoid the expense of a mechanical ventilation system and its installation. Light industrial or commercial fans are rated in cfms.

Using the example of the space with windows, the required supply was 1,875 cfm, so a fan rated for 1,900 cfm will be needed, and the required exhaust was 1,562 cfm, so a fan rated for 1,600 cfm will also be needed.

The Code requirements for supply and exhaust present many problems to the small theatre. Obviously the simplest and cheapest way to comply is to install the properly rated fans in existing windows in a space, but these fans are often very noisy and distracting, and the open windows will bring in street noise. Also, fans do not cool or warm the outside air before bringing it into the space as a mechanical ventilation system does.

If the space does not have windows, then the fans can be placed in windows located elsewhere in the building and sheet metal ducts can be run into the theatre space. If these ducts are not large enough the air moving through them will create noise.

One alternative is to find a windowed space that has a Ventilation Index of 1650 or over (see Table A). In this situation, so long as the windows are operable, no additional means of supply and exhaust is required.

plumbing and sanitary requirements

Under the Old Code, commercial establishments have to provide at least 1 water closet for employees.

For places of public assembly accommodating large numbers of persons, the Old Code states that a sufficient number of water closets and urinals must be supplied as directed by the Borough Superintendent. They have to be in an accessible location and be provided with signs clearly indicating their purpose. For a small theatre of 74–100, usually 1 facility for each sex will suffice.

seat and row spacing

No more than 7 seats in a row are permitted if there is an aisle on only one side of the row. If there are aisles on both sides of the row, up to 14 seats are allowed in any one row.

There is no minimum front-to-back dimension required by the Old Code between rows of seats. Common sense should be followed here. A good rule of thumb: allow 3' of space from the back of one row to the back of the row behind it. Anything less is very cramped for an audience.

live load

Live load is the number of pounds per square foot that a given floor can support. The Code is concerned with live load as a safety factor. Each use or activity is assigned a minimum value, described in pounds per square foot.

- Theatre is required to have a 60 pounds per square foot live load value if there are fixed seats.
- If there are movable seats, a 100 pounds per square foot live load value is required.
- The stage area is required to have a live load value of 100 pounds per square foot.

The floor of the space you rent must meet the live load requirement for theatre use. This is not something you have to calculate. The building was originally assigned a live load value. Check to make sure it is equal to, or more than, what is required for your use.

Most manufacturing and loft buildings have a live load of 120 pounds per square foot, so that space found in one of these buildings would present no problem. Also the first floors of most commercial structures were designed for 100 pounds per square foot of live load; so, generally, spaces that were originally stores, supermarkets, banks, and the like, will have the necessary live load rating. Structures designed for residential or office use usually have live load values of 40 pounds and 50 pounds per square foot, respectively; these will not conform to theatre requirements.

To check the live load value of a structure, request the Certificate of Occupancy for the previous use. If it doesn't exist, the information will appear on the last alteration application. This can be found in the Plan Room at the Department of Buildings, filed under the proper address.

sprinklers

The Old Code does not require that theatre spaces with 299 seats or less be sprinklered. However, past practice has been that sometimes sprinklers are required in storage areas and in dressing rooms. This requirement will not come from the Department of Buildings when plans are initially submitted, but from the Fire Department, after a routine on-site inspection.

fire-retarding and flameproofing

All materials used in the construction of the space must be fire-retardant or flameproof. If wood is used to construct platforms, stages, or walls, it must be fire-retardant wood meeting the standards of the Department of Buildings. Fire-retardant wood may not have a flame-spread rate greater than 25 and must bear a label from the manufacturer stating this. Flame-retardant paint is not an acceptable means of fire treatment for ordinary wood purchased through the lumber yard.

All draperies and other fabrics must be treated with a standard flameproofing compound available from any theatrical paint supply company. It is a dry chemical that is mixed with water and sprayed on.

To comply with flameproofing requirement:

- Save receipts showing the date of purchase and the quantity purchased.
- Flameproofing treatment is good for a year, so each year flameproofing will need to be repeated. When this is done, a statement should be written including the date and the calendar number on the can. This statement should be notarized and kept among other records. (See *flameproofing affidavit*, Chapter 18.)

THE BUILDING CODE

147

NEW CODE REQUIREMENTS

occupancy classification

Under the New Code, occupancy classifications have been established. (These should not be confused with the Use Group classifications of the Zoning Resolution.) Two categories of occupancy classifications apply to theatre:

F1-A. Includes buildings and spaces in which scenery or scenic elements are used.

F1-B. Includes buildings and spaces in which scenery or scenic elements are *not* used.

Scenery or scenic elements are defined as anything movable or temporary, but do not include movable seats; non-scenic elements are any permanent part of the theatre construction, such as stage walls.

Once a theatre is filed as an F1-B, the Fire Department can issue a violation if they inspect and find any temporary scenic elements or props being used on stage. Even a chair placed on stage is defined as a temporary scenic element.

Choosing the F1-A or F1-B category is an important decision to make before drawing up plans and filing under the New Code, so consider their limitations carefully.

requirements for theatres with scenery or scenic elements (F1-A)

If scenery is used, the following requirements apply to the stage areas and to the scenery:

- All scenery or scenic elements must be constructed of non-combustible materials and be rendered flameproof or have a flame-spread rating of 25 or less.
- Any scenery or scenic elements placed in the seating area cannot be placed so as to obstruct exit

signs, exit doors, or the path of travel to exits.

- The stage construction must meet the same fire ratings as that of the building's floor. This also applies to any trap doors set into the stage floor. In addition, the rooms or spaces beneath the trap doors must also meet the same fire rating as that of the building's floor. These rooms or spaces cannot be used for workshops or storage areas—the only storage that is permitted is scenery which is used during a performance.
- The stage area must have 2 means of egress, remote from each other, which means on opposite sides of the stage.
- Emergency ventilation is a Code requirement for the stage area. However, this requirement was written with relation to the traditional Proscenium theatre so the specifications cannot be directly applied to other theatre configurations such as Arena and Thrust stages. This does not mean that these types of stages are exempt from the emergency ventilation requirement but rather that the Department of Buildings must interpret these specifications and their application on an individual basis.

requirements for theatres without scenery (F1-B)

If you file under this category, your Certificate of Occupancy will designate an F1-B use only, but the requirements are far less stringent than the ones for theatres with scenery.

- Raised platforms may be built as stages when they are supported on floors having the required fire-resistance ratings. In addition, the area below the platforms must be enclosed on all sides with solid construction.
- The stage area must have 2 means of egress, remote from each other, which means on opposite sides of the stage.
- There are no requirements for emergency ventilation

building classification

Buildings filed under the New Code are classified according to construction groups: Class I structures are non-combustible and Class II structures are combustible. The following are the classifications, with a run-down on where theatre can be located and how much space it can occupy. Be certain to check the classification before signing a lease.

Descriptions of building classifications have not been provided. Specifications are very detailed and it is extremely difficult to distinguish visually between classifications. Any buildings classified under the New Code, having been built in the last decade, will have a classification listed on the current Certificate of Occupancy.

Class IA. Theatre is permitted on any floor without any limit on square footage.

Class IB. Theatre is permitted on any floor without any limit on square footage.

Class IC. Theatre is permitted up to 85', or seven stories, without any limit on square footage.

Class ID. Theatre is permitted up to 75', or six stories, and is limited to 17,500 sq. ft.

Class IE. Theatre is permitted up to 40', or three stories, and is limited to 10,500 sq. ft.

Class IIA. Theatre is permitted up to 75', or six stories, and is limited to 14,700 sq. ft.

Class IIB. Theatre is permitted up to 75', or six stories, and is limited to 14,700 sq. ft.

Class IIC. Theatre is permitted only if building is sprinklered and then up to 50', or four stories, and limited to 12,600 sq. ft.

Class IID, Class IIE. Theatre is not permitted in either class.

means of egress

74 occupants or less (on first story)

If the theatre has fixed seats:

- Only 1 means of egress is required, a minimum of 3' 8" in width, and opening directly onto the street. Egress requirement is based on number of seats.

If the theatre has movable seats:

- For an audience area not exceeding 740 sq. ft., only 1 means of egress is required, a minimum of 3' 8" in width, and opening directly onto the street.

Egress requirement is figured on an occupancy based on 10 sq. ft. per person. If you intend to have 74 or less in a space, be certain your audience area does not exceed 740 sq. ft. If you have 750 sq. ft. of audience area, your occupancy would be considered 75 (750 divided by 10), and 2 means of egress would be required, even if only 74 people were using the space.

74 occupants or less (above the first story)

Whether the theatre has fixed or movable seats:

- 2 means of egress are required.
- If there are other tenants sharing the floor, only 1 means of egress is required from the theatre, into a public corridor; but 2 means of egress are required from the public corridor.

75 occupants or more

Under the New Code, as under the Old Code, 2 means
of egress are required when the occupancy is over 74,
but, unlike the Old Code, the means of figuring out
what kinds of exits and *where* they are located is more
complicated. Take your time in reading over this section
and refer to the illustrations where they are noted as
they will help to clarify the requirements.

Primary and secondary egress. Under the New Code,
if you have more than 74 persons, you are required to
have 2 means of egress, whether you are on the first
story or above.

There are two types of egress defined under the
New Code: one is *primary,* the other is *secondary.*
These terms refer to the distance a member of the
audience must travel to reach one or the other.

The maximum travel distance to a primary exit is
85'.

The maximum travel distance to a secondary exit is
120'.

In any theatre space, every member of the audience
must be seated within 85' of one exit and 120' of
another exit.

These travel distances are measured in *legs*. Each
time a person is required to change direction along the
path of egress (make a turn), this becomes another leg
of travel. These legs are measured in the following way:

- first leg = the actual distance
- second leg = the actual distance
- third leg = 1.25 × the actual distance
- fourth leg = 1.40 × the actual distance
- any leg with 4 or more steps = 1.25 × actual
distance

The first leg is always measured from the seat to
the aisle, if the seat is not on the aisle. To compute the
travel distance from any one seat, use the table above
and add up the distances. Remember that from any one
seat, the distance to one exit can not be more than 85'
and to the other exit not more than 120'. According to
the formula, if you make the path of travel complicated
you are penalized for it. The simpler and straighter the
path the better. When there are too many turns or too
many steps, the *1.25 ×* or *1.40 ×* factor forces you to
place your exits closer. A 40' distance on a third leg
becomes 50' on the formula.

Classification of exits. The New Code also classifies
exits according to where they lead people or how they
lead people. There are three different types of exits
under the New Code, as follows:

- *Class 1*—exits which are normally used for
entrance or exit. They must open directly to the
outside or to a safe area.
- *Class 2*—exits which are used just for egress, not
for entrance, and which lead directly to the outside or
to a safe area.
- *Class 3*—exits which open directly onto a corridor,
a stairwell, or an exit passageway, leading to the
outside.

DIAGRAMS OF EXIT CLASSIFICATIONS

NEW CODE

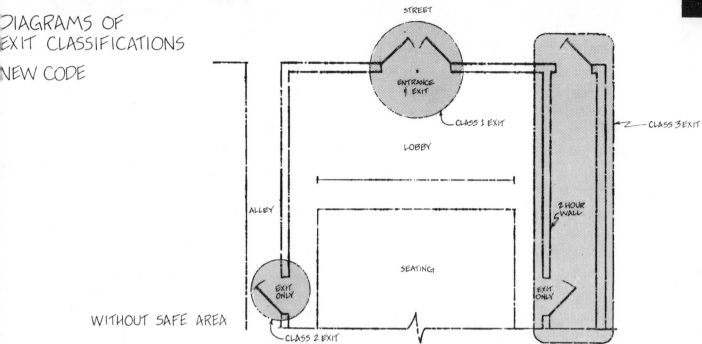

WITHOUT SAFE AREA

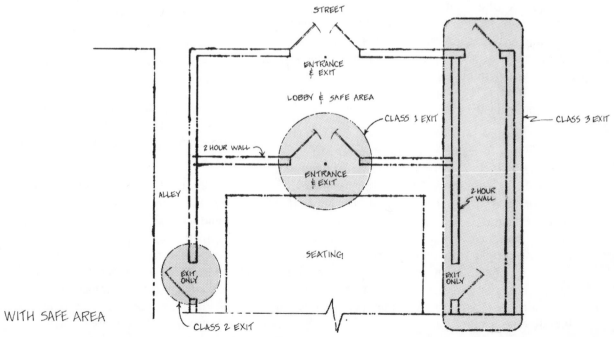

WITH SAFE AREA

Safe area. The concept of *safe area,* or an "area of refuge," as it is sometimes called, was introduced in the New Code. It is a means of holding a number of people who are waiting to exit in an area that is separate from the main space of assembly and, theoretically, away from the fire or other disaster. A safe area is created by constructing a 2 hour fire-rated wall between the area and the assembly space. A lobby can function as a safe area if the wall you build between the two spaces has a 2 hour fire rating. There are other requirements which a safe area must meet:

- The area must provide at least 2 sq. ft. per person, not including furnishings, for the number of people using that exit. If 75 persons are using it, there will have to be at least 150 sq. ft. of clear floor area. If 100 persons are using it, there must be 200 sq. ft. of clear floor area.
- The minimum width of a safe area is 8′ and is measured at right angles to the direction of travel.
- No space containing hazardous uses—such as paint shop, scenery or costume shop, or storage space for mechanical, electrical or A/C equipment—can open directly onto a safe area.

Number of exits. The New Code requires different numbers of the different classes of exits depending on varying circumstances. The theatres with which this book is concerned will never require more than a total of 2 exits. Listed below are only those requirements that will be needed by these theatres in typical situations:

If the theatre has fixed seats and an audience area of more than 12 sq. ft. per person:

- Both exits can be of any class.

If the theatre has movable seats or fixed seats and an audience area of less than 12 sq. ft. per person:

- A theatre on the first story will be required to have 1 Class 1 exit and 1 Class 2 exit, or, if preferred, 2 Class 1 exits.
- A theatre on the second or third story will be required to have 1 Class 1 exit and 1 Class 2 exit or, if preferred, 2 Class 1 exits.
- A theatre above the third story must have all Class 1 exits.

Relationship between travel distaces, safe areas, and exits. The easiest way to illustrate how these requirements relate to each other is through examples and drawings.

- *Above the ground floor.* Above the ground floor you are required to have 2 exits. Since both Class 1 and Class 2 exits must open onto a safe area, or directly onto the street, you will have to make a safe area. The most expedient way to do this is to use your lobby space. In this situation, your primary and secondary travel distances are measured from the seat in the audience to the doors leading from the theatre space into the safe area.

LOBBY & SAFE AREA
WITH EXIT STAIRWELLS-
2ND & 3RD FLOORS-NEW CODE

ELEVATOR

ELEVATOR

2 HOUR WALL

LOBBY & SAFE AREA

EXIT STAIRS

EXIT STAIRS

PRIMARY & SECONARY TRAVEL PATHS MEASURED TO HERE

2 HOUR WALL

SEATING

PRIMARY & SECONDARY TRAVEL PATHS

WITHOUT SAFE AREA - GROUND FLOOR SPACE

NEW CODE

EXIT ONLY

ENTRANCE & EXIT

LOBBY

2ND LEG

96 SEATS

PRIMARY PATH
MAX 85'

1ST LEG
SECONDARY PATH - MAX 120'

● *On the ground floor.* If you are on the ground floor, you have a few options. Your exits can open directly onto the street, so you do not need to have a safe area. But if you do choose to have exits opening directly onto the street, you must measure your primary and secondary travel distances from the seat to these exterior doors. If you decide to create a safe area, and use your lobby, your primary and secondary travel distances are measured to the doors leading from the theatre space to the safe area.

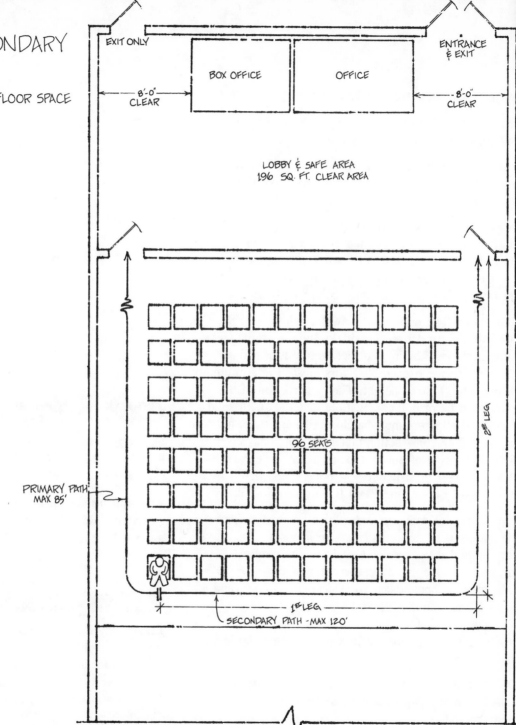

PRIMARY & SECONDARY TRAVEL PATHS

WITH SAFE AREA - GROUND FLOOR SPACE

NEW CODE

EXIT ONLY

ENTRANCE & EXIT

BOX OFFICE

OFFICE

8'-0" CLEAR

8'-0" CLEAR

LOBBY & SAFE AREA
196 SQ. FT. CLEAR AREA

96 SEATS

2ND LEG

PRIMARY PATH MAX 85'

1ST LEG

SECONDARY PATH - MAX 120'

other requirements for means of egress

The following requirements apply to all means of egress regardless of occupancy categories:

Distance between exits. When more than 1 exit is required from a floor of a building, each exit shall be placed as remote from the other as is practicable.

Doors. Exit doors and doors providing access to exits shall be self-closing, swinging doors with a 1½ hour fire rating, except that doors leading into stairs and exit passageways, and corridor doors, shall have a ¾ hour fire rating. The minimum door height shall be 6' 8".

Exit stairs. The minimum allowable width is 3' 8". The maximum vertical rise of a single flight of stairs between floors, landings, or between a floor and a landing may not exceed 8'. Stairs must have a minimum clearance of 7' head height. The construction of the stairs must be of non-combustible materials with solid treads and all risers must be closed. These stairs must be enclosed with construction materials which have a fire-resistance rating of not less than 1 hour, except as follows: Class IA structures—4 hour, Class IB structures—3 hour, and Class IC structures—2 hour.

Corridors. Internal corridors which are used as part of the means of egress must be constructed of non-combustible materials that have a minimum fire rating of 1 hour, except as follows: Class IA structures—4 hour, Class IB structures—3 hour, and Class IC structures—2 hour.

    The corridor height must be a minimum of 7' 6" for at least 75% of the floor and at no point may be less than 7' in height.

Distance from stage. No exit opening may be closer than 12' to any part of a stage using scenery or scenic elements (F1-A).

exit lighting

Exit signs. Illuminated exit signs are required over all exit doors. Requirement is the same as in the Old Code. (See *Electrical Code,* Chapter 16.)

Lighting on stairs. Lighting must be provided on all exit stairs. Requirement is the same as in the Old Code.

emergency lighting

Emergency lighting must be provided over the entire public assembly space.

    The location of emergency lighting must be shown on architectural drawings and the electrical service must be run on a separate circuit. (See *Electrical Code,* Chapter 16.)

ventilation

While the Ventilation Index formula and the tables are the same as for the Old Code, the problems are more complicated. Many newer buildings do not have operable windows, as they were built with air handling systems designed to heat, cool, and ventilate. These systems were installed throughout the building and, no doubt, there will be one already in your space. The problem, however, is that since the densities of the other occupancies in the building are usually lighter, the system was probably designed to handle a much smaller capacity than a theatre requires. For example, an office space is generally calculated as 1 person per 100 sq. ft., whereas a theatre's density is more likely to be 1 person per 10 sq. ft.

One solution to this problem is the installation of your own mechanical ventilating system, which can be very costly.

Some theatres in this situation have used the existing system, although it was not sufficient. One theatre has an air conditioning system but no ventilation system, as the ducts for one look identical to the ducts for the other.

calculating required ventilation

The amount of ventilation required depends upon the size of the space and the number of people occupying it. As the requirements for ventilating the general areas of the theatre are the same as those under the Old Code, the same calculations can be used. (See Old Code Requirements, *ventilation*.)

plumbing and sanitary requirements

The New Code does have requirements for public toilets, determined by the number of people who occupy the space. They are as follows:

Toilets. 1–100 people, 1 water closet; 101–200 people, 2 water closets.

Urinals. 1–200 people, 1 urinal; 201–400 people, 2 urinals.

Sinks. For every 1–200 people, 1 sink.

Drinking fountains. For every 1,000 persons, 1 drinking fountain; if more than one level or tier of theatre, 1 drinking fountain per level.

THE BUILDING CODE

157

seat and row spacing

The New Code does not give a maximum number of seats permitted in any row, however it does require the following for space between rows:

- A minimum of 12″ between the back of the seat in one row and the front of the seat in the next row.
- For every seat over 7 that must be passed to reach an aisle, the 12″ space between rows must be increased by ¼″.

Platforms for folding chairs. If instead of fixed seats, platforms for folding chairs are used, make sure that the size of the platform is large enough to permit the proper back-to-front row spacing (given above) for the number of seats in that row.

Stepped platforms for seating. If stepped platforms, without chairs, are used for seating, the Code requires:

- A minimum of 18″ in width for each individual seat space.
- At least 28″ in depth, from front to back, for each platform.
- For every seat over 7 that must be passed to reach an aisle, the platform depth must be increased ¼″.

steps

If there are risers or steps in a space, the following requirements apply:

- Risers cannot be less than 4″ or higher than 8″.
- There can be no variation in this height within a run of steps. In other words, if one riser is 4″ high, all risers must be 4″ high.
- Treads cannot be less than 9½″ in width.

live load

As under the Old Code, New Code requirements for live load are a safety factor. Each use is assigned a live load value, described in pounds per square foot.

- If there are fixed seats, a 60 pounds per square foot live load is required.
- If there are movable seats, a 100 pounds per square foot live load is required.
- The stage area is required to have a live load of 150 pounds per square foot.

When considering a space, check the live load rating of the building to make sure it meets the requirements for theatre use. (See Old Code Requirements, *live load,* for how to get this information)

fire protection and finish

The materials used for, or on, walls, floors, and ceiling of a theatre space must meet certain flame-spread ratings.

Under this requirement materials are rated with relation to the amount of time it takes them to burn.

The reference standards for flame-spread ratings are set by the National Board of Fire Underwriters and are used by the New York City Building Code. Most manufacturers of commercial building materials and interior-finish materials provide this data with the products they sell.

Any commercial goods purchased for use in a theatre should have a flame-spread rating between 26 and 75. Since most consumer goods are not required by law to furnish this information, materials purchased from a local hardware or fabric store may not have this rating. In this case, it is a good idea to check with the manufacturer before purchasing.

zoning* and Building Code checklist

(Supplement to *evaluation checklist* at end of Chapter 5.)

notes

zoning

zoning district: C2   C4   C6   C8   M1   M2   M3

Other: _____ (Variance required)

Subclassification: _____

Requirements and restrictions (check with Department of City Planning)

Building Code

classification

Old Code: 1   2   3   4   5   6

New Code: IA   IB   IC   ID   IE   IIA   IIB   IIC   IID*   IIE*

(*theatre not permitted)

Floor location of space: _____ **Is theatre permitted?** _____

Sq. ft. available: _____ **Sq. ft. allowed:** _____

Assessed value of building: $ _____

Renovation estimate: $ _____

Building can be renovated under: Old Code   New Code

Live load rating of floor(s): _____ lbs. per sq. ft.
   Meets theatre requirements: yes   no

Ventilation requirements: Supply _____ cfm   Exhaust _____ cfm

Will present system (if any) meet requirements?   yes   no

Number of existing exits: _____ width: _____

Fire-rating _____

**Will existing exits comply with means of egress requirements
   for theatre's proposed occupancy?**   yes   no

Number of existing urinals: _____ **waterclosets:** _____
                                   sinks: _____ **fountains:** _____

Meet requirements: yes   no

* See Chapter 14 for zoning information.

16

the Electrical Code

The Electrical Code of the City of New York is one of the most stringent in the country. At present, it is being used as a model for electrical codes being updated by many cities throughout the country.

Licensed electricians and electrical engineers use this Code as a reference for all electrical work, and it does cover everything from plug types to transmitting stations! Much of the Code deals very technically with electrical installations and equipment, and will not be discussed here. This chapter will discuss only the sections of the Electrical Code which deal directly with theatres, and will describe briefly what is required to keep your system up to Code standards.

Article 27 of the Electrical Code is the section that deals specifically with theatre. Theatre is defined by the Code as follows: ''any building or part of a building fitted and used for dramatic, operatic, motion pictures, or other performances or shows, or which has a stage for such performances used with scenery or other stage appliances.'' In other words, no matter how small a theatre may be, it will be required to meet the Electrical Code's specifications.

stage lighting equipment and installations

The Electrical Code divides all electrical equipment, wiring, and installations into two principal categories: *permanent* and *portable*.

Permanent refers to anything attached to the wall and not intended for repositioning. In a theatre this would refer to all internal (in-house) wiring, including fuse boxes, outlets, disconnect boxes, and patch panels.

For permanent theatre installations, all wiring must be run in conduit, electrical metallic tubing, or surface metal raceways, both on stage and in the house (over seating area), as per Article 27 of the Electrical Code; and, in addition, must comply with many other specifications listed throughout the Electrical Code. If you are planning a permanent installation, it is advisable to hire a licensed electrician to help you since the Code has many technical specifications for permanent wiring.

Portable is defined by the Code as any electrical equipment which is capable of being readily moved due to its use. In a theatre this refers to lighting instruments, all rented equipment and cable, and any installations which must remain flexible. (All of the stage lighting equipment and boards used in Broadway houses are considered to be portable by Code standards.)

portable switchboards

Portable switchboards (dimmer boards) must have an outlet specially designed for this purpose, with enclosed fuses capable of handling the total amount of power used by the board, and must have an externally operated switch. This outlet is commonly referred to as a "disconnect box" since it is capable of switching off or disconnecting all the power going to the board. This box must be mounted on the wall at a location near the board in order to provide easy access to it.

There are other specifications (wiring methods, connector types, etc.) too technical to detail, with which a manufacturer must comply. If circumstances are such that you will be constructing your own boards, it is a good idea to obtain a copy of the Electrical Code and to get advice from someone who has had experience in this area.

portable cable

Portable cable or any non-permanent wiring has many specifications for theatrical use. The cable must be flexible, which means that the outer covering will be rubber, thermoplastic, or asbestos, and the insulation for each conductor (wire) will be rubber or thermoplastic. The cable must be rated for hard usage and for use in damp places. The gauge (size) of the conductors cannot be smaller than #18, which means no zip cord is permitted. (#14 and #12 are most commonly used in theatres.)

The plug connectors used on portable cables cannot cause mechanical strain on the connections. (Pin plug or twist lock connectors are most commonly used in theatres and will meet this specification.) In addition, the female half of the connection must be attached to the live end of the cable.

If the cable is purchased or rented from a theatrical supply house then all these specifications will be met, but if you plan to make up your own cables, read the Code and double check with an electrician before you purchase the supplies.

There is no mention in the Code regarding the running of cable, but, from previous experience with inspectors, theatrical electricians agree that neatness counts. This means tying or taping the cable every three to five feet along the pipe on which it runs. It will also relieve strain on the plugs. If an inspector sees sloppily run cable, he may require that it be redone or that metallic tubing or raceways be installed through which the cable must be run.

portable strips, plugging boxes, and arc lamps

Portable strips, portable plugging boxes, and portable arc lamps are all mentioned in Article 27 of the Code. The requirements for all of these will be taken care of for you if you are either renting or purchasing this equipment. Again, as with portable boards and cables, if you plan to make your own, first read the Code and get advice.

dressing rooms

The Code requires that conduit, electrical metallic tubing, or surface metal raceways be used for the wiring method in dressing rooms, which is the same requirement applied to permanent installations.

The Code further specifies that the lamps in a dressing room be protected by guards sealed or locked in place. These are usually metal or plastic baskets specially made to cover the light bulb and help to prevent contact with flammable materials.

house lights and work lights

House lights and work lights are not specifically dealt with in the Electrical Code section on theatres. Depending upon the situation, they could either be classified as portable or permanent, and should be wired accordingly.

grounding

A fairly recent change in the Electrical Code requires that all buildings, commercial and residential, have grounded wiring. The change is retroactive, so it applies to both old and new structures. As the old wiring of so many buildings is not grounded, this requirement is not being strictly enforced as yet since it would mean rewiring over half the buildings in New York City! Grounding, in its simplest form, means the addition of a third wire (ground) where previously two wires have been acceptable. An inspector can, however, require that a 2-wire system be grounded if he deems it necessary—usually where safety is involved.

Grounding is required if any rewiring is done or if new wiring is added to the old ungrounded system. This need not be any great additional expense—grounded cable and the corresponding electrical hardware is not appreciably more expensive than their 2-wire counterparts. The expense lies in not doing it right the first time and then receiving a violation. Redoing all the work will cost you roughly the same amount you originally paid, so you will end up paying twice for the same work.

It is also a good idea to keep the grounding requirement in mind if you plan to buy equipment. You may be able to get a bargain on 2-wire equipment and cable, but if you receive a violation for non-grounded equipment it will not be much of a bargain by the time you have finished getting it all grounded.

emergency lighting

Emergency lighting, which is also a Building Code requirement for public assembly spaces, is dealt with in much more specific terms in the Electrical Code's Section 32.

Emergency lighting includes the exit lights and any additional lights necessary to properly illuminate, in an emergency situation, any portion of a theatre to which the public has access during the performance. Although not required by the Code, it is a good idea to also include the areas used by the actors and technicians.

alternate power supply

Emergency lighting systems must have an alternate power supply in the event of an electrical power failure such as a blackout or fire. There are two basic ways in which to provide this alternate power supply:

- Generator-powered system, supplied by a source other than the main electrical power supply.
- Battery-powered system. Many small theatres find this the most practical solution.

general provisions

All emergency lighting systems must comply with the following:

- All wiring for emergency illumination must be entirely independent of all other wiring.
- The system must be capable of automatically switching to the alternate power supply (generator or batteries) in the event of electrical power failure.
- Emergency lights cannot be controlled by any stage light controls (dimmer boards).
- The only switch or manual cut-off allowed in the emergency lighting system is at the main service. This switch must be accessible only to authorized persons and should be located in the lobby or another convenient place at the front of the building.
- The emergency lighting system must be tested frequently to assure it is in proper operating condition. Electrical and fire inspectors on routine inspection may ask that this system be tested.

There are many emergency lighting systems on the market. If you need to purchase and install one, it is a good idea to seek expert advice first to make certain that the system being installed will comply with the Code in your situation.

THE ELECTRICAL CODE

163

17

the Fire Prevention Code

The New York City Fire Prevention Code has a number of regulations specifically designed for theatres and does enforce these regulations by means of routine inspections. When to expect your first inspection will depend upon whether or not you choose to obtain your Consumer Affairs License. Legally, you must obtain this license to operate a theatre within New York City. Upon application to the Department of Consumer Affairs, the various City agencies will be notified, including the Fire Department's Division of Fire Prevention. You must pass an inspection by the Fire Department in order to receive your license.

Even if you do not apply for a Consumer Affairs License, it is only a matter of time until the Fire Department will make an inspection, as they do patrol their district systematically and are aware of newcomers.

There are some regulations of the Fire Prevention Code which the Building Code also covers; these will not be mentioned again in this chapter.

The Fire Prevention Code is probably the easiest with which to comply. Its requirements are based mainly on common sense and are designed for the safety of the public.

inspection checklist

The Fire Department inspectors have two different sets of checklists, which they use for inspecting theatres, depending upon the size. The following items make up the checklist that applies to theatres with less than 300 seats. Each checklist item is followed here by a brief explanation. Some suggestions from the Fire Department are given as well.

good housekeeping

All rubbish and debris should be disposed of, especially around the stage, backstage, and seating areas. Any storage areas should be maintained in an orderly fashion. It is strongly suggested that all paints and flammable liquids be kept in a closed, but ventilated, metal cabinet. Also, it is suggested that electrical cables be run overhead and not on the floor, especially where there is heavy traffic and a chance that the cable may be worn through.

portable extinguishers

A 2½ gallon water type extinguisher should be provided for every 2,500 sq. ft. and should be placed on a hook or shelf at least 2', but not more than 4½', off the floor. The extinguishers must be tagged with the last date of inspection. It is also advisable to place a CO_2 extinguisher in the area where the dimmer boards are located, in case of electrical fires.

sprinkler heads in each dressing room

It is advisable to wait until you are inspected by the Fire Department before going to the expense of installing sprinklers, if your dressing rooms do not have them. If your space was built under the Old Code, sprinklers were not required. It may be possible, if extinguishers are located within this area, that you will not be required to install a sprinkler system; however, it is up to the discretion of the inspector whether or not to waive this requirement.

"no smoking" signs

"No Smoking" signs must be placed in the areas of a theatre where smoking is not permitted, such as dressing rooms, backstage, and seating areas. If you do have a smoking area, it should be so designated and the proper receptacles provided. The inspector has the authority to take away smoking areas if deemed hazardous.

locked and blocked exits

Any exits to be used in case of an emergency situation must be left open during all public performances and the access to them must remain clear and unobstructed.

theatre log book

Keeping a log book is required. Reproduced on the following pages are the instructions for keeping a log book as issued by the Fire Department and a page from a log book used by one small theatre.

DIVISION OF FIRE PREVENTION

FIRE DEPARTMENT

February 15, 1974

Facsimile of:
F.P. Directive
10-62 (Revised)

The following is hereby promulgated for the information and guidance of members:

THEATRE INSPECTION LOG BOOK

The following instructions are for the guidance of theatre managements for the purpose of standardizing Theatre Inspection Log Books and entries therein and it is recommended that:

In order to standardize the "Theatre Inspection Log Book" the following instructions were sent to all theatre agencies for distribution to the various theatres throughout the City;

"In order to standardize the "Theatre Inspection Log Book" and entries therein, it is recommended that:

1. Each theatre provide and maintain a journal of the following specifications;

a. Bound book with pen ruled lines and a red ruled margin;

b. Pages to be 8½" x 11", and consecutively numbered on the top at the corner;

c. The face of the cover shall have the inscription "Theatre Inspection Log Book: and the name of the theatre;

d. The inside front cover shall have a copy of the "Theatre Inspection Guide" affixed.

2. Daily entries in the journal are to be made by owners or managers as per the following samples, whichever applies;

a. Date and Time. Mr. John Doe, Manager, inspected all parts of theatre in accordance with stipulations of the Fire Department "Theatre Inspection Guide" and found all applicable items complied with and/or in good condition.
Certified standpipe operator on duty:

Mr._____ Certificate No._____

Person designated to prevent any undue excitement or possible panic conditions:

Mr._____(Not applicable to Motion Picture Theatres).

Nearest street fire alarm box corner of _____and_____

Signed: John Doe - Title

b. Date and Time. Mr. John Doe, Manager, inspected all parts of theatre in accordance with stipulations of the Fire Department "Theatre Inspection Guide", and found all applicable items complied with except the following: (Indicate conditions referred to and action taken, e.g. exit lights over north side door out-bulb replaced, etc.)
Certified standpipe operator on duty:

Mr._____ Certificate No._____

Person designated to prevent any undue excitement or possible panic conditions:

Mr._____and_____

Nearest street fire alarm box corner of

Signed: John Doe - Title

3. The book shall be used for no other purpose and shall be kept in Manager's office for inspection by members of this Department. Failure to maintain this book as indicated above will result in the service of a violation order."
Chief Officers, when making visits, investigating complaints, etc., shall examine subsequent entries made in the "Theatre Log Book", since the previous inspection was made by a chief officer, and shall record the results of such examinations therein; also conditions found and action taken if required.
All other Department members inspecting theatres shall enter their name, purpose of visit and action taken if required.

AUGUSTUS A. BEEKMAN
Fire Commissioner

Please note: Under #2a and #2b, the references to standpipe operators do not apply to theatres under 300 seats.

Sample page from a log book

DATE: _____   TIME: _____

_____, Manager, inspected all parts of theatre in accordance with stipulations of the Fire Department "Theatre Inspection Guide," and found all applicable items complied with and/or in good condition. The person designated to prevent any undue excitement or possible panic is _____.

The nearest fire alarm box is at the corner of _____and _____.

The Theatre Inspection Guide to which this entry refers is reproduced here. Both the instructions and this Guide should be attached to the inside of the log book for easy reference.

This guide can be used to help maintain a violation-free theatre. Again, the references to standpipes and standpipe operators do not apply to theatres that have under 300 seats.

THEATRE INSPECTIONAL GUIDE

1. Note the location of street fire alarm box nearest to stage door for immediate transmission of alarms of fire.

2. Building alarm box on stage shall be maintained in proper working order at all times. This alarm may be transmitted in addition to street fire alarm box. Telephone on premises may also be used to transmit alarm.

3. Inspect all emergency exits, stairways, courts and passageways to determine condition, availability for use and compliance with law.

4. Cause asbestos curtain to be lowered at the close of each performance.

5. Examine all automatic fire doors to determine operative condition and availability for use.

6. Inspect all portions of standpipe and sprinkler systems, including pumps and tanks; also all fire appliances to determine condition and readiness for immediate use. Certified standpipe operator to be present at all times when theatre is open to the public.

7. Report unserviceable standpipe or sprinkler systems, to officer of company in whose district theatre is located.

8. Examine automatic skylight to determine operative condition and readiness for use.

9. Inspect all parts of theatre, particularly backstage and under the stage for accumulations of rubbish, and maintain free of same at all times.

10. Require all doors in proscenium wall to be kept closed during performances.

11. Prohibit smoking in all portions of backstage, under the stage, in dressing rooms and other rooms or space related to stage portion of theatre.

12. Require necessary extinguishers to be readily available when materials of a hazardous nature are used in performance.

13. Required Fire Department permits to be obtained and kept available for inspection.

14. Require necessary precautions to be taken when articles of a hazardous nature are used.

15. Designate responsible person to be prepared at all times to take a position in front of the audience to prevent any undue excitement or possible panic conditions in the event of an emergency.

16. During each performance inspect all portions of auditorium. Note any obstructions in aisles or passageways or violations of law relative to standees, and take immediate corrective action when violations are found.

17. At conclusion of stage performance, require stage trap doors closed and stage elevators made flush with stage floor.

18. Air conditioning system fresh air intakes to be kept clear of rubbish and/or combustible materials at all times.

19. Provide a log book and record daily the inspections made as indicated above; violations observed and action taken. This book to be kept available at all times for inspection by members of this department.

NOTE: The above items applicable to Motion Picture Theatres shall be observed and records kept as indicated above.

By Order of,

AUGUSTUS A. BEEKMAN
Fire Commissioner

theatre license from Consumer Affairs division

Obviously, if you are being inspected by the Fire Department following your application to Consumer Affairs, this will not apply.

If you do not have a license and are inspected, you may be in for a bit of trouble. It is part of the inspector's checklist to request proof of this license. If you are not able to produce this proof, you will be reported, in all likelihood, to the Department of Consumer Affairs. The result may be a shut-down of operations until you obtain this license. However, if you begin the application process with Consumer Affairs within 24 hours of receiving the violation, you are considered legal, as long as you have no other outstanding violations with any other department.

flameproofing affidavit for show scenery and house draperies

For each show that your theatre produces, you are required to have a sworn affidavit stating that all the materials used in construction of the scenery are flameproofed. This affidavit should be filed with the Fire Commissioner and a copy should be kept on file by you so that you may show it to the inspectors. Below are reproduced the latest regulations from the Fire Department governing flameproofing and an example of the standard affidavit used.

DIVISION OF FIRE PREVENTION

FIRE DEPARTMENT

F. P. Directive 1-78   February 3,

The following is promulgated for the information and guidance of all personnel:

REGULATIONS RELATIVE TO THE FLAMEPROOFING OF DECORATIONS, DRAPES, CURTAINS AND SCENERY

(Filed with the City Clerk on November 1, 1977)

A. SCOPE:
    These regulations shall be applicable to the testing, certification and approval of detions, drapes, curtains and scenery used for artistic enhancement in any building of a p character, except those premises exempted in Section C19-161.1 of the Administrative Cod
B. AUTHORITY:
    Vested in the Fire Commissioner by Section 489 of the City Charter and Section C19-1 of Chapter 19 of the Administrative Code of the City of New York and Rule 6.1 of the R of the Board of Standards and Appeals for Tests of Fire-Resistive Flameproofed Materials as Textiles, Paper, Similar Materials and Adhesives Used for Decorative Purposes and Tre Acoustical Draperies, Carpets and Similar Material for Use in Places of Public Assembly Special Occupancy Structures.
C. REGULATIONS:
    1. *Affidavits Relative to Flameproofed Materials:*
        a. The owner, lessee or proprietor of any building or occupancy of a public charac as defined in Section C19-161.1 of the Administrative Code shall attest to the flameproing of combustible decorations, drapes, curtains and scenery used for artistic enhanceme in such building or occupancies by filing an affidavit with the Fire Commissioner.
        b. The required affidavit shall be sworn to by the person, firm or corporation th flameproofed the combustible materials and shall state in such affidavit that the flan proofing method complies with the approval of the Board of Standards and Appeals a the Board of Standards and Appeals Cal. No. of the flameproofing compound. T affidavit shall include the date of treatment and the warranted period of flameproofi effectiveness.
        c. A copy of the affidavit of flameproofing shall also be maintained on the premis for inspection by field inspectors of the Fire Department.
    2. *Affidavits Relative to Non-Combustible Decorations:*
        a. If non-combustible decorations are used for artistic enhancement in building occupancies of a public character, as defined in Section C19-161.1 of the Administrati Code, the owner, lessee or proprietor shall file an affidavit of non-combustibility with Fire Commissioner.
        b. The required affidavit shall indicate the manufacturer or supplier of the materi the type of material and the non-combustibility characteristics of the material.
        c. A copy of the affidavit of non-combustibility shall be maintained on the premi for inspection by field inspectors of the Fire Department.
    3. *Fire Department Acceptance:*
        a. The acceptance, by the Fire Department, of decorations, drapes, curtains a scenery in buildings or occupancies of a public character, shall be contingent on the ex ence and filing of the required affidavit of flameproofing or non-combustibility and satisfactory passage of a field flame test executed by a Fire Department Inspector.
        b. The acceptance, by the Fire Department, of combustible decorations that have be flameproofed shall be limited to one (1) year periods.
        c. The acceptance, by the Fire Department, may be renewed after the initial one ye acceptance period, provided that the original affidavit is filed with the Fire Commission and a copy on the premises and the materials satisfactorily pass a field flame test execut by a Fire Department Inspector.
        d. Each renewal of acceptance shall be limited to a one (1) year period or until next dry cleaning or washing process. A record of each dry cleaning or washing shall maintained on the premises for inspection by the Fire Department.
        e. Renewal of acceptance shall not be extended more than two (2) years beyond original one (1) year acceptance.
        f. Flameproofed combustible decorations accepted for three (3) consecutive ye shall not be field tested or acceptable. Such decorations shall be the subject of a violat order with a compliance time of sixteen (16) days, to remove or have same flameproo and file a new affidavit of flameproofing.

Fire Department Disapproval:

a. No combustible or reported non-combustible decorative material shall be acceptable [re]quired affidavits are not filed and on the premises, or does not pass the field flame test [exe]cuted by a Fire Department Inspector.

b. Decorative materials disapproved due to failure of a field flame test shall be the [subj]ect of a violation order for forthwith removal.

c. Decorative materials disapproved due to the lack of required affidavits shall be the [subj]ect of a violation order to remove such decorative material or have same flameproofed [and] file a flameproofing affidavit. Compliance time shall be forthwith, except as provided [in] f above.

Decorative Materials Approved by the Board of Standards and Appeals for Use in Occupancies of a Public Character:

a. Decorative materials approved by the Board of Standards and Appeals shall be [acce]ptable to the Fire Department provided that the owner, lessee or proprietor files an [affi]davit with the Fire Commissioner and maintains a copy thereof on the premises at[test]ing to the fact that such decorations have been approved by the Board of Standards [and] Appeals and includes therein the Board of Standards and Appeals Cal. No. for the [mat]erial.

b. Acceptance, by the Fire Department of such material, shall also be dependent on [a] satisfactory passage of a field flame test executed by a Fire Department Inspector.

c. Enforcement procedures as described above for unacceptable decorative materials [shall] be executed for failure to provide affidavits or the failure of field flame testing.

6. *Modifications:*

Whenever circumstances, conditions, limitations, or surroundings are unusual, or are such as to render it impracticable to comply with all the foregoing requirements, the Fire Commissioner may waive or modify such provisions over which he has jurisdiction to such extent as he may deem necessary consistent with public safety.

7. *Saving Clause:*

If any clause, sentence, paragraph, section or part of this article shall be adjudged by any court of competent jurisdiction to be invalid, such judgment shall not affect, impair or invalidate the remainder thereof, but shall be confined in its operation to the clause, sentence, paragraph, section or part thereof directly involved in the controversy in which such judgment shall have been rendered.

AUGUSTUS A. BEEKMAN
Fire Commissioner

STATE OF NEW YORK
COUNTY OF NEW YORK

Gentlemen:

We flameproofed the following:

Date: 2/14/72   Materials: All fabric on wings, velour fireproof lumber, downstage apron all lumber fireproofed.

Used for: "Any Show" Production at
Anybody's Theatre
Any Street
New York, New York

With approved flameproofing compound approved by the Board of Standards and Appeals, for use in New York City under Cal #539-53-SM.

This flameproofing compound is guaranteed for a period of one year from the above date, in accordance with the rules of the Board of Standards and Appeals providing fabric is not impaired either by wetting or being subject to excessive moisture.

Anybody's Theatre Inc.

_____

Sworn and subscribed to before me

This ____ day of _____ 19__

Mr. John Doe
Notary Public, State of New York

permits

The Fire Department issues permits for iceboxes. A permit is $5 per each icebox over ¼ horsepower (hp) but under 3 hp and is renewable annually. The rate increases as the horsepower increases.

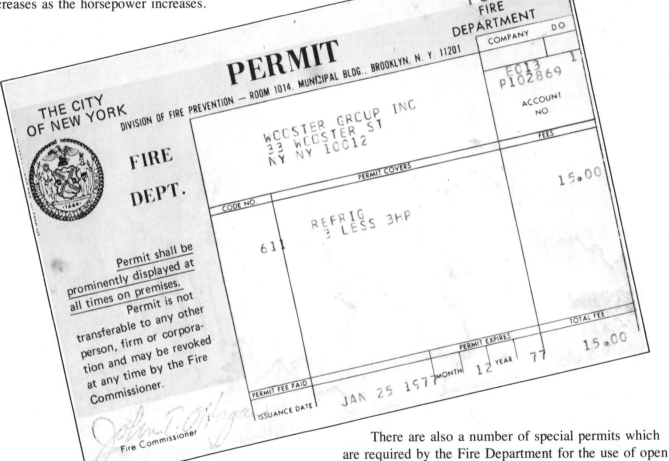

PERMIT

164588
FIRE DEPARTMENT

THE CITY OF NEW YORK
DIVISION OF FIRE PREVENTION — ROOM 1014, MUNICIPAL BLDG., BROOKLYN, N.Y. 11201

FIRE DEPT.

Permit shall be prominently displayed at all times on premises.
Permit is not transferable to any other person, firm or corporation and may be revoked at any time by the Fire Commissioner.

John T. Hogan
Fire Commissioner

COMPANY   D.O.
EC13   1
P102869
ACCOUNT NO.

WOOSTER GROUP INC
33 WOOSTER ST
NY NY 10012

PERMIT COVERS

CODE NO
611

REFRIG
3 LESS 3HP

FEES
15.00

PERMIT EXPIRES
MONTH 12 YEAR 77

TOTAL FEE
15.00

PERMIT FEE PAID
ISSUANCE DATE   JAN 25 1977

There are also a number of special permits which are required by the Fire Department for the use of open flame, flash paper, flash pots, etc. on stage. There is a $25 fee for these permits and the accompanying special inspection. All of these permits must be kept on file and shown to the Fire Inspector upon request.

18

procedures

preliminary procedures

Before committing yourself to a space, go through the following steps:

check zoning map

(1) Go to the Maps and Publications Room at the Department of City Planning and get a zoning map of the district in which the building is located. Double check the zoning designation, making sure that theatre is permitted.

(2) Check with Zoning Information regarding the sub-designations to find out what restrictions or requirements are placed on this location.

check Certificate of Occupancy

(1) Look on the existing Certificate of Occupancy (C of

O), which should be on file with the building's manager, to check the building's classification. If the C of O is not available, take the exact address and go to the Index Room at the Department of Buildings.

(2) At the Index Room you will be told if a C of O exists for the building.

(3) If a C of O exists, you will be sent to the C of O Room where you will be issued a number used to look up the building's classification.

(4) If a C of O does not exist, you will be given a block and lot number, to be used at the Plan Desk.

(5) At the Plan Desk, fill out a slip stating the information desired and the building's folder will be released to you. On the last Altered Building Application for the building, the classification will be listed.

(6) Even if a C of O exists, go to the Plan Desk and fill out a slip to find out the building's last legal use, the live load rating of the floor, and if any outstanding violations on the building exist.

(7) Double check all information, using the checklist provided at the end of Chapter 15 to make sure that theatre is permitted in the building and that all the necessary requirements for theatre use are met.

application procedures

The entire process of filing plans and applications for the various permits and licenses a theatre will need to legally operate within the City can take anywhere from two months to half a year!

A lot of this time can be saved by hiring an architectural firm that does their own expediting with the Department of Buildings. Because of their familiarity with the Codes and the procedures, they can help you organize the filing of the applications, keep track of their progress, and help insure that they will not become lost in the red tape.

Occasionally, you may find an architect who does not do his own expediting and in this situation you may wish to also hire a professional expeditor. The architect can usually recommend an expeditor with whom he is familiar; however, if the architect is carefully chosen it will not be necessary to hire an expeditor.

If you must do your own expediting, be prepared for a great deal of phone calling and running around within the various departments. The application procedures in this section involve a considerable amount of red tape, so patience and perseverance will also be necessary.

Altered Building Application

This form, which is obtained from the Department of Buildings, must be filed, even if no alterations or renovations are to be done, in order to indicate a change of use so that a new C of O may be issued.

The filing fee is $33 minimum. If renovation work is to be done, the fees will be based on the cost of the renovation, but may not exceed 30% of the total. (See *table of filing fees*.)

If renovations are to be done, written permission from the building's owner must be obtained and plans must be filed showing the proposed alteration. These plans must be filed by a licensed architect or engineer, who will stamp them to verify their accuracy.

The plans for renovation filed with this application will be reviewed by a plan examiner to see if all the Building Code requirements are met. The architect who has stamped and filed these plans will be notified if the examiner has any objections. If either you or the architect feel the examiner's interpretation of the Code with regard to your plans is not accurate, a reconsideration may be requested. The Chief Engineer of the Department of Buildings will then review the arguments and the plans, and will determine the validity of the interpretation. If he decides in the examiner's favor, then the appropriate changes must be made and the plans refiled.

Once the plans are approved, a work permit will be issued. The construction work can only be done by a licensed general contractor, or by yourself—if you state that you will be acting as your own general contractor. You will be required to sign an affidavit stating this, as well as stating that you will be responsible for the proper liability coverage on anyone who will be working on the construction.

As the end of construction approaches, arrangements must be made for a final inspection by a construction inspector from the Department of Buildings. He will be checking to make sure that all the construction conforms to the plans submitted with the Altered Building Application. If any changes have been made, they must be in compliance with the Code, and a new set of plans, indicating all these changes, must be submitted before the final approval is given by the inspector.

Once the final approval is given, a new Certificate of Occupancy will be issued by the Department of Buildings.

THE CITY OF NEW YORK
HOUSING AND DEVELOPMENT ADMINISTRATION

DEPARTMENT OF BUILDINGS

MANHATTAN ☐
Municipal Bldg.
New York, N.Y. 10007
Tel.: 566-2383

BROOKLYN ☐
Municipal Bldg.
Brooklyn, N.Y. 11201
643-7943

BRONX ☐
1932 Arthur Avenue
Bronx, N.Y. 10457
583-5520 Ext. 6

QUEENS ☐
126-06 Queens Blvd.
Kew Gardens, N.Y. 11415
520-3268

RICHMOND ☐
Boro Hall
St. George, N.Y. 10301
390-5202

Notice — This Application must be TYPEWRITTEN and Filed in QUADRUPLICATE

ALTERED BUILDING APPLICATION

APPLICATION FOR APPROVAL OF PLANS

(No work may be started until a separate
Work Permit is obtained.)

1. (a) BLOCK _____

   (b) LOT _____

2. LOCATION _____ House Number, Street, Distance from Nearest Corner and Borough

3. ZONING: (a) District _____ (b) Map No. _____

4. PROPOSED WORK UNDER:

   (a) (OLD) 1938 BUILDING CODE

   (b) (NEW) 1968 BUILDING CODE

5. (a) HEIGHT _____ (b) No. of Stories _____

6. CLASSIFICATION OF BUILDING:

   (a) PROPOSED: Occupancy Group _____ Construction Class _____

   (b) EXISTING: Occupancy Group _____ Construction Class _____ Classified _____ (Year)

7. Will a New Certificate of Occupancy be Required?   Yes ☐   No ☐

8. OCCUPANCY IN DETAIL:

STORY (Include cellar & basement)	(a) EXISTING LEGAL USE						(b) PROPOSED OCCUPANCY					
	Apts.	Rooms	USE				Zoning Resolution			Building Code		USE
				No. of Persons	Live Load (PSF)		Dwelling - or Room-ing Units	Use Group		Habit-able Rooms	Occu-pancy Group	

9. EXISTING CERTIFICATE OF OCCUPANCY NUMBER _____

PROCEDURES

173

B Form 141 (Rev. 6/69) 100M 140203757

10. OPEN SPACES (Sq. Ft.)
(a) PARKING: _____
(b) LOADING BERTHS: _____
(c) OTHER OPEN SPACES: _____

11. LIMITATIONS OR RESTRICTIONS:
(a) BOARD OF STANDARD AND APPEALS CAL. NO. _____
(b) CITY PLANNING COMMISSION CAL. NO. _____
(c) OTHERS: _____

12. DESCRIBE IN WHAT MANNER THE BUILDING WILL BE ALTERED:

13. ARE THERE ANY OTHER BUILDINGS ON LOT?   YES ☐   NO ☐

14. (a) IS APPLICATION MADE TO REMOVE VIOLATIONS? _____ (b) IF YES, STATE VIOLATION NUMBERS _____

15. IS BUILDING IN URBAN RENEWAL AREA? _____

16. WORK AND EQUIPMENT TO BE INSTALLED:

(a) FENCE ☐   (b) SIDEWALK SHED ☐   (c) VAULTS ☐

(d) PLUMBING ☐   (e) ELEVATORS ☐   (f) CURB CUT ☐

(g) LENGTH IN FEET OF CURB CUT(s) _____
(INCL. SPLAY):

17. REQUIRED FIRE DETECTION AND EXTINGUISHING SYSTEMS:

(a) STANDPIPE SYSTEM ☐   (b) AUTOMATIC SPRINKLER SYSTEM ☐

(c) YARD HYDRANT SYSTEM ☐   (d) FIRE ALARM AND SIGNAL SYSTEM ☐

(e) STANDPIPE FIRE TELEPHONE AND SIGNALING SYSTEM ☐   (f) SMOKE DETECTOR ☐

(g) OTHER FIRE EXTINGUISHING SYSTEMS ☐   STATE TYPE _____

18. IF VOLUME OF BUILDING IS TO BE CHANGED, GIVE THE FOLLOWING INFORMATION

(a) TOTAL FLOOR AREA (EXISTING) _____ SQ. FT.   PROPOSED _____ SQ. FT.

(b) ADDITIONAL CUBIC CONTENTS _____ SQ. FT.

19. (a) ESTIMATED COST OF ALTERATIONS: _____

(b) ESTIMATED COST, EXCLUSIVE OF ANY ENLARGEMENT: _____

table of filing fees for Altered Building Application

COST	FID*	FULL FEE	COST	FID*	FULL FEE
1,000	33.00	33.00	26,000	43.80	146.00
2,000	33.00	43.00	27,000	44.70	149.00
3,000	33.00	53.00	28,000	45.60	152.00
4,000	33.00	63.00	29,000	46.50	155.00
5,000	33.00	73.00	30,000	47.40	158.00
6,000	33.00	78.00	31,000	48.30	161.00
7,000	33.00	83.00	32,000	49.20	164.00
8,000	33.00	88.00	33,000	50.10	167.00
9,000	33.00	93.00	34,000	51.00	170.00
10,000	33.00	98.00	35,000	51.90	173.00
11,000	33.00	101.00	36,000	52.80	176.00
12,000	33.00	104.00	37,000	53.70	179.00
13,000	33.00	107.00	38,000	54.60	182.00
14,000	33.00	110.00	39,000	55.50	185.00
15,000	33.90	113.00	40,000	56.40	188.00
16,000	34.80	116.00	41,000	57.30	191.00
17,000	35.70	119.00	42,000	58.20	194.00
18,000	36.00	122.00	43,000	59.10	197.00
19,000	37.50	125.00	44,000	60.00	200.00
20,000	38.40	128.00	45,000	60.90	203.00
21,000	39.30	131.00	46,000	61.80	206.00
22,000	40.20	134.00	47,000	62.70	209.00
23,000	41.10	137.00	48,000	63.60	212.00
24,000	42.00	140.00	49,000	64.50	215.00
25,000	42.90	143.00	50,000	65.40	218.00
			Over 50,000	+.90	+3.00

*Initial fee paid with the filing of the Altered Building Application.

plans for the Department of Buildings

It is possible to save money by drawing up the required plans for the Altered Building Application yourself. You will need to have a licensed architect or engineer review, stamp, and file them, but the cost for this service will be considerably less than if professionals have done all the drawings.

Another alternative to having the plans drawn up by a professional is to hire an apprentice or student

---

B Form 17 (Rev. 6/75)-55M-714026(75) -346

THE CITY OF NEW YORK
HOUSING AND DEVELOPMENT ADMINISTRATION
DEPARTMENT OF BUILDINGS

☐ MANHATTAN
Municipal Bldg.,
New York, N. Y. 10007
Tel.: 566-2383

☐ BRONX
1932 Arthur Avenue,
Bronx, N. Y. 10457
583-5520 Ext. 6

☐ BROOKLYN
Municipal Bldg.,
Brooklyn, N. Y. 11201
643-7943

☐ QUEENS
126-06 Queens Blvd.,
Kew Gardens, N. Y. 11415
520-3268

☐ RICHMOND
Boro Hall,
St. George, N. Y. 10301
390-5202

STATEMENT "A"

BLOCK .... LOT ....

LOCATION ....
House Number   Street   Distance from Nearest Corner   Borough

TO THE COMMISSIONER:

APPLICATION IS HEREBY MADE FOR APPROVAL OF THE PLANS AND SPECIFICATIONS HEREWITH SUBMITTED FOR THE ERECTION OR ALTERATION OF THE STRUCTURE HEREIN DESCRIBED SUBJECT TO THE FOLLOWING CONDITIONS:

THIS APPLICATION SHALL BE DEEMED TO HAVE BEEN ABANDONED 12 MONTHS AFTER DATE OF SUBMISSION UNLESS IT HAS BEEN DILIGENTLY PROSE-CUTED AFTER REJECTION IN WHOLE OR IN PART (ADMINISTRATIVE CODE, C26-109.9)

WORK WILL NOT BE COMMENCED UNTIL THE WORK PERMIT IS OBTAINED (ADMINISTRATIVE CODE, C26-109.1).

APPROVAL OF PLANS SHALL BE VOIDED IF A WORK PERMIT APPLICATION IS NOT SUBMITTED WITHIN 12 MONTHS OF THE DATE OF PLAN APPROVAL (ADMINISTRATIVE CODE, C26-108.8)

AN APPLICATION FOR A WORK PERMIT SHALL BE ACCOMPANIED BY SATISFACTORY EVIDENCE OF COMPLIANCE WITH THE PROVISIONS OF THE STATE WORKMEN'S COMPENSATION LAW (ADMINISTRATIVE CODE, C26-110.1, C26-111.1, C26-112.1).

A WORK PERMIT SHALL EXPIRE BY LIMITATION IF THE PERMITTED WORK IS NOT COMMENCED WITHIN 12 MONTHS OF THE DATE OF ISSUANCE (ADMINISTRATIVE CODE, C26-118.6).

WORK WILL BE INSPECTED BY ARCHITECTS, ENGINEERS AND DESIGNATED PERSONS IN ACCORDANCE WITH ADMINISTRATIVE CODE C26-106.3.

....
(Typewrite Name)

states that he resides at ....

in the Borough of .... ; in the City of .... ;

in the State of .... ; that he is making this application for the approval of .... plans and

....
(Architectural, Structural, Mechanical, Etc.)

specifications herewith submitted and made part hereof.

Applicant further states that he has prepared or supervised the preparation of such .... plans and that to

....
(Architectural, Structural, Mechanical, Etc.)

the best of his knowledge and belief, the plans and work shown thereon comply with the provisions of the building code and other applicable laws and regulations, except for the following where there are practical difficulties, as set forth in accompany-

ing documents:

architect, engineer, or draftsman.

The drawings must indicate the existing structure and any proposed changes being made, including the materials to be used in construction. They must be accurate and drawn to scale. The plans will need to include the following information: the designated stage area, designated audience area with a seating arrangement, designated exits and aisles, the location of the exit lights and emergency lights. Also include plans of the rest of the space including the location and size of

---

.... (Name of Owner)

who is the owner in fee of all that certain lot, piece or parcel of land, shown on the diagram annexed hereto and made a part hereof, to make application for the approval of such detailed statements of specifications and plans, elevator or plumbing work (if any) and amendments thereto, in the said owner's behalf.

Applicant further states that the full names and residences, street and number, of the owner or owners of the said land, and also of every person interested in said building or proposed structure, are as follows:

Owner's name .... Address ....
(If a corporation, give full name and address of at least two officers.)

Lessee .... Address ....

Architect .... Address ....

Engineer .... Address ....

Superintendent .... Address ....

EXAMINED AND RECOMMENDED
FOR APPROVAL ON ...., 19......

APPROVED ...., 19......

.... Examiner

.... Borough Superintendent

NOTICE—This statement must be TYPEWRITTEN and filed in QUADRUPLICATE

That the said land and premises above referred to are situated, bounded and described as follows:
(NOTE—See diagram below)

BEGINNING at a point on the .... side of

distant .... feet .... from the corner formed by the intersection of

.... and ....

running thence .... feet; thence .... feet;
(Direction)   (Direction)

thence .... feet; thence .... feet;
(Direction)   (Direction)

to the point or place of beginning, being designated on the map as

Block No. .... Lot No. ....

(SIGN HERE) .... Applicant

Affix Seal of Registered
Architect or Professional
Engineer Here.

AUTHORIZATION OF OWNER: I hereby state that I have authorized the applicant to file this application for the work specified herein.

....
(Signature of Owner or Officer of Corp.)

the dressing rooms, lobby, offices, rest rooms, shops, and storage areas. It is important that the drawings are accurate.

It should be noted that all final approved drawings must be submitted on mylar or cloth. Don't panic, however—paper drawings can be easily transferred to cloth or mylar by a blueprinting company.

FALSIFICATION OF ANY STATEMENT IS A MISDEMEANOR UNDER SECTION 643a-10.0 OF THE ADMINISTRATIVE CODE AND IS PUNISHABLE BY A FINE OF NOT MORE THAN FIVE HUNDRED DOLLARS OR IMPRISONMENT OF NOT MORE THAN SIX MONTHS OR BOTH.

BRIBERY IS A CRIME: A PERSON WHO GIVES OR OFFERS A BRIBE TO ANY EMPLOYEE OF THE CITY OF NEW YORK, OR AN EMPLOYEE WHO TAKES OR SOLICITS A BRIBE IS GUILTY OF A FELONY PUNISHABLE BY IMPRISONMENT FOR UP TO SEVEN YEARS OR A FINE, OR BOTH. PENAL LAW SECTION 200.00 AND 200.10.

Above Block and Lot Verified .... 19........

.... Department of ....

House Number .... Dated .... 19 .... Bureau of

PLOT DIAGRAM must be drawn to indicated scale, showing the correct street lines from the city plan; the plot to be built upon in relation to the street lines and the portion of the lot to be occupied by the building; the legal grades and the existing grades, properly identified, of streets at nearest points from the proposed buildings in each direction; the House numbers and the block and lot numbers. Obtain this data in each borough office. Show dimensions of lot, building, courts and yards.

Status of Street: private— ; public highway— ; other

The legal width of .... is......ft.; sidewalk width should be .... ft.
The legal width of .... is......ft.; sidewalk width should be .... ft.

The street lines as shown in the diagram are substantially correct. Proposed changes in street lines and grades, if any, are indicated on the diagram thus: Legal Grade, 25.00. Existing, 24.00. Above house numbers, street status, street lines and grades shown below verified.

Dated .... 19 .... Bureau of

DIAGRAM

N. ←

The north point of the diagram must agree with the arrow

(For New Buildings give information below:)

SIZE OF BUILDINGS: At street level............feet front ....feet deep............feet rear
At typical floor level............feet front ....feet deep............feet rear

Certificate of Occupancy application

Although a C of O will not be issued by the Department of Buildings until all renovations, plumbing, and electrical work has been inspected and approved, you should file for a new C of O immediately to set the procedure in motion. You will need the building owner's authorization to file.

It should be noted that if your space is located in a building of three stories or less, a new C of O will need

B Form 24 (Rev. 7/76) 48M-806079(77) 346

THE CITY OF NEW YORK

HOUSING AND DEVELOPMENT ADMINISTRATION

DEPARTMENT OF BUILDINGS

MANHATTAN □
Municipal Bldg.,
New York, N. Y. 10007

BROOKLYN □
Municipal Bldg.,
Brooklyn, N. Y. 11201

BRONX □
1932 Arthur Avenue,
Bronx, N. Y. 10457

QUEENS □
126-06 Queens Blvd.,
Kew Gardens, N. Y. 11415

RICHMOND □
Boro Hall,
St. George, N. Y. 10301

APPLICATION FOR CERTIFICATE OF OCCUPANCY

TEMPORARY □   AMENDED □   AMENDED FINAL □   FINAL □

APPLICATION No. ....19......   BLOCK .... LOT..........
                    (N.B. Alt. B.N.)

PERMIT No. ....19......

LOCATION ....
              House Number   Street   Borough

                         Date .... 19 ....

TO THE COMMISSIONER:

Application is hereby made for a Certificate of Occupancy to be issued to the undersigned who states that he is the owner □. or is authorized by the owner □, to make such application.

Owner or Lessee.. Address ....

Applicant .... Address ....

(Signed) .... Address ....

Mail to ....

INSTRUCTIONS: THE NAME AND ADDRESS OF THE OWNER OR LESSEE OF THE BUILDING, AND ARCHITECT OR OTHER REPRESENTATIVE MUST BE STATED. IF OWNER IS A CORPORATION, STATE NAME AND ADDRESS OF ONE OF THE EXECUTIVE OFFICERS. THIS APPLICATION MUST BE TYPEWRITTEN AND SIGNED BY OWNER, LESSEE OR ANY PERSON AUTHORIZED BY OWNER OR LESSEE.

STORY	LIVE LOAD LBS PER SQ. FT.	MAXIMUM NO. OF PERSONS PERMITTED	ZONING DWELLING OR ROOMING UNITS	BUILDING CODE HABITABLE ROOMS	ZONING USE GROUP	BUILDING CODE OCCUPANCY GROUP	DESCRIPTION OF USE

to be obtained for the entire building. If your space is located in a building of four or more stories and the amount of space occupied is less than 20% of the entire building, then you will only need a C of O for the space you actually occupy; however if you occupy 20% or more of the building then a new C of O will need to be obtained for the entire building.

OPEN SPACES (Sq. Ft.)

PARKING: _____

LOADING BERTHS: _____

OTHER OPEN SPACES: _____

LIMITATIONS OR RESTRICTIONS:

BOARD OF STANDARD AND APPEALS CAL. NO. _____

CITY PLANNING COMMISSION CAL. NO. _____

OTHERS: _____

Affidavit is herewith submitted for the issuance of a certificate of occupancy for the structure herein mentioned. (Administrative Code C26-121.9)

STATE AND CITY OF NEW YORK } ss.:
COUNTY OF

.... (Typewrite Name)

being duly sworn, deposes and says that he resides at .... in the City of

.... in the Borough of .... in the State of ....

that he has supervised the .... of the building at location indicated above.
                          (Construction or Alteration)

The deponent further states that his relation to the above mentioned construction is described in paragraph .... (a, b) below.

(a) That he was the .... who supervised the construction work.
                      (Licensed Architect or Professional Enigneer)

(b) That he was the Superintendent of Construction who supervised the work.

The deponent further states that he examined the approved plans and specifications of the building herein referred to for which a certificate of occupancy is sought and that to the best of his knowledge and belief the building has been erected or altered in accordance with the approved plans and specifications and any amendments thereto and as erected or altered complies with the provisions of the building code and all other applicable laws and regulations except insofar as variations or variances therefrom have been legally permitted or authorized and herein noted:

Sworn to before me this ....

day of .... 19 ....   } .... (Signature)

....
(Notary Public or Commissioner of Deeds)

N.B. OR ALT. NO.   DATE OF COMPLETION: CONSTRUCTION CLASSIFICATION:
BUILDING OCCUPANCY GROUP CLASSIFICATION: HEIGHT: STORIES: FEET

STATE WHETHER ANY OF THE FOLLOWING EQUIPMENT IS IN THE BUILDING. MARK ITEMS WITH "X"

☐ Gasoline Tank Installation
☐ Fuel Oil Installation
☐ Sprinkler System
☐ Stand Pipe System
☐ Fire Alarm and Signal System

☐ Other Fire Extinguishing Systems
   (State Type)
☐ Yard Hydrant System
☐ Heating Equipment Requiring Approval of the Dept. of Air Pollution and Boiler Division
☐ Smoke Detector

FOR DEPARTMENT USE

Final Report   Construction .... Date ....
                Plumbing .... Date ....
                Iron and Steel .... Date ....
                Plastering .... Date ....
                Elevator .... Date ....
                Multiple Dwelling .... Date ....

Fire Department Approval .... Date ....
Curb Cut .... Date ....

REMARKS:

THE FINAL SURVEY (C26-121.7) WAS APPROVED ON _____ (Date)

INDEX CLERK WILL NOTE ALL N.B., ALT. AND OTHER APPLICATIONS TOGETHER WITH PENDING AMENDMENTS, VIOLATIONS, U.B.'S, EXIT ORDERS, RECENT SPECIAL REPORTS AND DEPARTMENT OF RENT AND HOUSING MAINTENANCE ORDERS.

I HAVE EXAMINED THE ABOVE PAPERS AND FIND NOTHING WHICH WILL PREVENT A CERTIFICATE OF OCCUPANCY BEING ISSUED:

_____   _____
(SIGNED)   TITLE

RTIFICATE OF OCCUPANCY NO. _____   DATE ISSUED _____

application for permit for a Place of Assembly

Although this permit, commonly known as a "PA License," will not be issued until after the new C of O is issued, you should again begin the filing procedure with the Department of Buildings at the same time the

---

B Form 97 (Rev. 10/70)-11M-703095(72) 346

THE CITY OF NEW YORK

HOUSING AND DEVELOPMENT ADMINISTRATION

DEPARTMENT OF BUILDINGS

☐ MANHATTAN Municipal Bldg., New York, N. Y. 10007

☐ BROOKLYN Municipal Bldg., Brooklyn, N. Y. 11201

☐ BRONX 1932 Arthur Avenue, Bronx, N. Y. 10457

☐ QUEENS 120-55 Queens Blvd., Kew Gardens, N. Y. 11424

☐ RICHMOND Boro Hall, St. George, N. Y. 10301

APPLICATION FOR PERMIT FOR A PLACE OF ASSEMBLY

DO NOT WRITE IN THIS SPACE

_____ on _____ story

C.O. # _____

BLOCK _____ LOT _____

ZONING DISTRICT _____

LOCATION _____ _____
House Number   Street

_____
Borough

Distance from Nearest Corner _____

1. Location of space or room _____

2. Type of occupancy _____

3. When was above occupancy established? _____

4. Max. No. of persons to be accommodated: PATRONS _____ EMPLOYEES _____ TOTAL NO. _____

5. State number of different seating arrangements to be used _____

6. Classification of building: (Construction) _____ (Use) _____

7. Application No. under which work (if any) is to be performed _____

VERIFIED BY _____ DATE _____

Fee payment — (see C26-34-0) _____

STATE AND CITY OF NEW YORK ⎫
COUNTY OF _____ ⎬ SS.:
                    ⎭

Sworn, deposes and says: That he resides at _____ Borough of _____ being duly

_____
(Typewrite Name of Applicant)

Altered Building Application is filed. You will need to file for this permit only if your proposed occupancy will be 75 or over.

Another set of plans will need to be filed with this application, indicating seating plans, any alternate seating plans, and the location of the exit signs. Again these plans must be submitted on mylar or cloth.

The Fire Department will be notified when this

application for the approval of the plan and specifications herewith submitted, and made a part hereof, for the work to be done in the building therein described, with the understanding that this application shall be deemed to have been abandoned 12 months after date of submission, if after it has been rejected in whole or in part, he takes no further action; and the applicant agrees to comply with all provisions of the Administrative Code and all laws and regulations applicable to the use and maintenance of such space in effect at this date; that any work to be done is duly authorized by the owner.

Deponent, further says that the full names and residence of the owners or lessees of said premises are:

OWNER: _____ ADDRESS: _____

LESSEE: _____ ADDRESS: _____

Sworn to before me this

day of _____ 19___   (Sign here) _____

_____   *Applicant*
Notary Public or Comm. of Deeds   If Licensed Architect or Professional Engineer, affix seal.

EXAMINED AND RECOMMENDED

FOR APPROVAL ON _____, 19___   _____, Examiner

APPROVED _____, 19___   _____, BOROUGH SUPT.

NOTICE—This Application must be TYPEWRITTEN and filed in QUADRUPLICATE

For instructions as to the requirements and filing of this application, see the other side of this sheet.

SELECTED PROVISIONS RELATING TO PLACES OF ASSEMBLY

1. Sec. C26-201.0 defines a "place of assembly" as an enclosed room or space in which 75 or more persons gather for religious, recreational, educational, political or social purposes, or for the consumption of food or drink, or for similar group activities, but excluding such spaces in dwelling units; or an outdoor space in which 200 or more persons gather for any of the above reasons. Every tier of seating shall be considered a separate assembly place.

2. A seating plan (and any alternate seating plans), not smaller in size than required for $\frac{1}{8}$ inch scale plans, shall be filed providing the information required by C26-801.4. When such seating plan has been approved by the Department, duplicates on cloth shall be filed. Copies of approved seating plans and approved alternative seating plans shall be kept on the premises and shall be readily available for inspection. (C26-801.4).

3. If seating is not fixed, or if standee spaces are provided, indicate on the plan the location of the "CAPACITY SIGN", at least 12 inches wide and 16 inches high, indicating the maximum number of persons to be accommodated (C26-801.3).

4. Indicate on plan the location of directional and "EXIT" signs, at least 8 inches in height with strokes at least $\frac{3}{4}$ inches wide, complying with all the requirements of sub-article 606.0, C26-801.10(e), and C26-801.17.

application is submitted. An inspection of the space must be made before the permit is approved.

This permit must be renewed annually. The filing fee is $27.50.

5. Signs shall be of the internally lighted type in all assembly spaces where the general illumination is reduced to less than 5 foot candles during a performance or during occupancy. Signs shall be lighted at all times during occupancy. (C26-801.17)

6. Where revolving doors are permitted as exits, the owner shall be responsible for their operation and maintenance and shall have the doors inspected at intervals not to exceed six months. Inspection reports shall be kept on file at the premises for at least two years. (C26-604.4 (m) (3)).

7. a. The entire exhaust system for cooking equipment, including ducts, hoods and fans shall be inspected periodically, and thoroughly cleaned.

   b. Grease filters shall be serviced and replaced regularly by qualified employees of the owner or by a cleaning agency. A record indicating the name of the person, or firm doing the servicing and the dates when filters were cleaned or replaced shall be kept on the premises and shall be available for inspection by the Commissioner. They shall be cleaned or replaced as frequently as necessary, but at least once every three months.

   c. At least twice a year, the automatic fire damper located at the hood outlet, release devices and fusible links, if employed, shall be replaced or properly cleaned.

   d. At least once every year, the automatic valve operation and the extinguishing system shall be tested. A record of such tests shall be kept on the premises and shall be available for inspection by the Commissioner of Buildings and the Fire Commissioner. (C26-1300.7(d) and RS 13-3).

8. A permit shall be secured from the Department of Buildings. An annual fee of twenty dollars shall be paid to this Department upon the issuance of a permit. (C26-34.0)

9. Drapes, curtains decorations and scenery having flame spread ratings exceeding 25, shall be flameproofed in compliance with C19-161.1 of the Fire Code. (C26-802.2)

10. In F1 and F2 places of assembly (Theaters, Auditoriums, Churches, Synagogues, etc.), emergency control panels shall be manned in accordance with the provisions of C26-802.2(b) (10)a, C26-802.3(4)a, and C26-803.1(c)(4)a.

11. Section 643a-11.0 of the Administrative Code provides that every person who shall violate any of the provisions of any Building Laws, Rules or Regulations enforceable by the Department, shall be guilty of an offense, and upon conviction thereof, shall be punished by a fine of not more than one thousand dollars. Such person shall also be subject to the payment of a civil penalty of not more than $250.

TO THE BOROUGH SUPERINTENDENT:

I inspected the premises described in this application on _____, 19___ and I found that it complies with the approved plans and specifications.

Signed _____

Inspector

applications for sign permits

This application, obtained from the Department of Buildings, will cover any sign which is to be erected.

With this application, plans must be submitted showing the size and location of the sign, the materials used in its construction, and the means of supporting and anchoring the sign.

A licensed rigger must file this application, stating that he is either doing the work or that he is supervising the work.

If the sign is to be illuminated, an additional application from a licensed electrician will have to be filed with the Department of Gas and Electricity, stating that he is either doing the wiring or that he is supervising the work, and a schematic plan of the wiring must also be filed. (See *application for inspection of electrical work*.)

The fees for sign permits are based on the installation costs, and upon the square footage of the sign.

permits for awnings and canopies

Applications for awning or cloth canopy permits must be filed with the Department of Highways because they extend over the sidewalk.

Marquees and solid canopies are considered to be permanent construction and therefore part of the building. The Building Code is very restrictive governing their construction and erection.

Awnings and canvas canopies, on the other hand, can be either fixed or retractable. The stringent requirements regarding the construction and the materials used in the manufacturing of awnings necessitate the filing of a notarized letter from the manufacturer stating that the awning conforms to these requirements. Make sure the application for this permit has been approved prior to purchasing or setting up the awning. This way you will be guaranteed that the manufacturer is complying with the requirements; otherwise you may not be permitted to set up the awning you just bought.

This permit will also apply to any signs, banners, or pennants that project from the wall.

This permit, once obtained, must be renewed annually.

application for inspection and certification of electrical work

To be in strict compliance with the Electrical Code, for any electrical work that is to be done—installation, alteration, or repairs—an application for a Certificate of Electrical Inspection must be filed by a licensed electrician with the Bureau of Gas and Electricity. The licensed electrician will describe in detail the work to be done and submit wiring diagrams in duplicate. The application must be filed before the work is begun.

If the electrician is filing an application for work which is to be done by an unlicensed contractor, he is required to state this fact on the application.

There are filing fees involved: an initial filing fee of $2, payable upon application, and an additional fee based upon the type and amount of work to be completed (rates are listed on the application). This

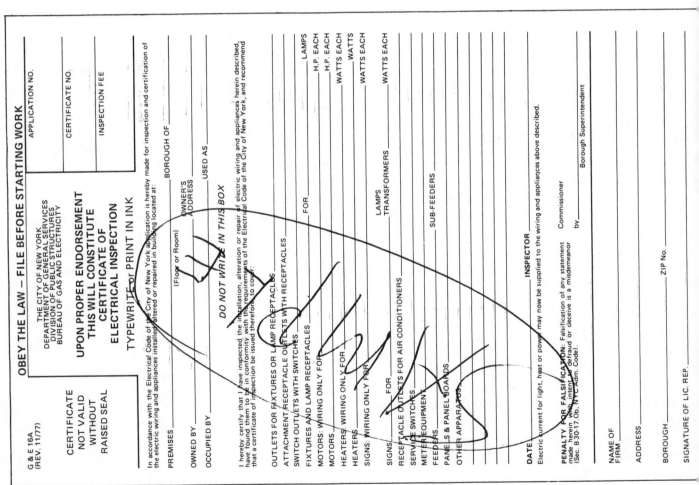

additional filing fee must be paid before a Certificate of Electrical Inspection is validated by an inspector. After the work is completed an inspector will come by to check out the work and issue an inspection certificate which you will be required to keep on file.

If the electrical work being done is to remove a written violation, the process is the same, but the filing fees are doubled.

LOCATION	Number of Outlets				No. Fixtures & Lamps Receptacles		Motors			Heaters			Air Conditioners			Branch Circuits		Lamps	
	Ceiling	Side Wall	Attached Recept.	Switch	Ceiling	Side Wall	No.	Type	H.P. Each	No.	Watts Each	No.	Type	H.P. Each	No.	B&S Gauge	No.	Watts
Sub-Basement																		
Basement																		
1st Floor																		
2nd Floor																		
3rd Floor																		
4th Floor																		

When feeders are installed a diagram must accompany this application (Sec. B-30-157.0b)

Size of Wire, Feeders	Sub Feeders	SIGNS: No of CKTS.	Total Watts
Service Equipment(s) No.	Size	No. of Lamps Transformers	
Meter Equipment(s) No.	Type	Maker of Sign	
Work to be started		Date of Completion	

Each outlet, each fixture, each horsepower or fraction thereof of a motor, each kilowatt or fraction thereof of a heater, each horsepower or fraction thereof of an air conditioner, installed, altered or repaired shall be assigned the value ONE UNIT.

LICENSEE MUST COMPLETE FEE CALCULATIONS

	Number	Units	Number		Fee
1. Outlets		1 to 5			00.0
2. Fixtures		6 to 5000		@	.15
3. Sum of Motor HP		in excess of 5000		@	.10
4. Sum of Heater KW					
5. Sum of Air Cond. HP					
Total of Units					
6. Service Switches					
a. up to 100 amps.				@	2.00
b. 101 to 200 amps.				@	5.00
c. 201 to 600 amps.				@	25.00
d. in excess of 600 amps.				@	100.00
7. Feeders				@	5.00
8. Sub-Feeders				@	2.00
9. Application Fee					2.00
(Application + Inspection)			Total Fee		

OFFERING BRIBES OR GRATUITIES MAY RESULT IN REVOCATION OF LICENSE AND CRIMINAL PROSECUTION.

REMOVAL OF VIOLATION for Work done by unlicensed persons. (DOUBLE the above INSPECTION FEE)

INSTRUCTIONS: See back of yellow contractor's copy of this application.

permits to install or alter plumbing

If any plumbing work needs to be done, an application for this permit must be filed by a licensed plumber. It must state that he is either doing the work himself or that he is supervising the work being done. This application should be filed at the Department of Buildings before the work is begun; and a plumbing inspector must sign-off the work before a final approval is issued by the Department. Schematic plans must also be filed.

The fees involved will be based upon the same schedule that applies to the Altered Building Application, except where the alterations are under $1,000 and involve neither structural changes nor a change in occupancy. In this case the fee is $11 for the first $500 and $22 for costs over $500 but under $1,000.

Department of Consumer Affairs license

In order to legally operate a theatre in the City of New York, a license must be obtained from the Department of Consumer Affairs (DCA). This license is required for all theatres, regardless of size.

Before this license is issued all of the various City agencies will be notified, including the Department of Buildings, the Fire Department, and the Department of Gas and Electricity, to make certain that the space is in compliance with the Codes. And DCA must receive inspection approvals from these departments before the license is issued.

This license must be renewed every two years. Again inspection approvals from all the departments listed above are required for license renewal.

DCA does not require a financial statement from not-for-profit theatres. It does require a copy of the letter granting not-for-profit status and an affidavit from the applicant affirming that it is a not-for-profit corporation. Since you have not-for-profit status, DCA is not interested in checking out your financial status.

Form 1-30M-923054(77) 346

City of New York
Department of
Consumer Affairs

Application
For A License

Items 1 to 14 apply to all applicants

(If insufficient space on this form for answers, attach rider)

Record No. ....

Type of License } ....

Date Received } ....

(1) Name (Print) .... Business Tel. No. ....
(INDIVIDUAL, CORPORATE OR PARTNERSHIP (NAME(S). IF PARTNERSHIP OR CORPORATION, ALSO ANSWER ITEM 16.)

(2) Address of premises to be licensed } ....
(STREET AND P.O.)
Zip Code .... Floor or Room No. ....

(3) Mailing address ....
(STREET AND P.O.)
Zip Code ....

(4) Trade, Assumed or Display Name } ....
(IF A TRADE NAME IS USED, CERTIFIED COPY OF SAME FROM COUNTY CLERK MUST BE FILED WITH THIS APPLICATION.)

(5) Residence (if individual) } ....
(STREET ADDRESS)
Apt. .... P.O. & Zip Code .... Residence Tel. No. ....

(6) Citizenship (Insert Code "Letter") (a) Native born (b) Naturalized (c) Declared Intention (d) Husband's Papers (e) Father's Papers }
Date .... (Produce proof of citizenship if not native born)
Where .... Date of Birth ....

(7) If business previously licensed, in whose name? } ....

(8) Who besides applicant will share in profits? To what extent? } ....

(9) Other licenses held (Past or Present) ....

(10) Any License ever been denied, cancelled, suspended or revoked? .... If so, when, where and disposition ....

(11) Have you ever been convicted of any offense ....

(12) Workmen's Compensation Insurance: Name of Company .... Policy No. .... Date of Expiration ....

(13) Liability Insurance: (Wherever required or requested) Name of Company .... Policy No. .... Date of Expiration ....

(14) New York State Sales Tax Identification No. ....

(15) Seating Capacity: (a) Orchestra .... ; (b) Balcony .... ; (c) 2nd Balcony ....
(d) 3rd Balcony .... ; (e) Boxes and loges .... ; (f) Mezzanine. ....

(16) PARTNERSHIP: List names and residences of all partners. (Submit certified copy from County Clerk.)
CORPORATION: (a) List names and residences of all Officers, Directors and any Stockholders owning 10% or more of the stock. (b) If New York Corporation submit photocopy of receipt of Secretary of State of proof of filing Certificate of Incorporation; (c) If other than New York State Corporation, submit receipt of New York Secretary of State of Certificate of Authority to do business in New York.
IF ANY CHANGE, NOTIFY DEPARTMENT IN WRITING WITHIN 7 DAYS OF EACH CHANGE OF OFFICERS, DIRECTORS OR STOCKHOLDERS OWNING 10% OR MORE OF THE STOCK.

Names	Residence Addresses	Partner, Officer (Title) Director or Stockholder	Citizenship of Partners as outlined at item 6

State if any of the above has (a) Held a license previously; (b) Had a license denied, cancelled, suspended or revoked; if so, when, where and disposition:

....

....

(17) Has any Officer, Director or stockholder ever been connected with an individual, firm or corporation currently or previously licensed by this Department? ....

If so, give particulars ....

(18) I acknowledge receipt of a copy of the Laws and Regulations relating to the license for which application is being made.

In consideration of being granted the license hereby applied for, it is agreed that the applicant will comply with the rules and regulations of the Department of Consumer Affairs that are now in force or that may in the future be promulgated. PENALTY FOR FALSIFICATION: Falsification of any statement made herein is an offense punishable by a fine or imprisonment or both. (N.Y.C. Administrative Code Section 1151-9.0)

Examined By ....
                                                                SIGNATURE AND TITLE

ADDITIONAL INFORMATION

AMUSEMENT. (See Theatrical.)

BILLIARD AND POCKET BILLIARD. Number of tables ....

BOCCI BALL ALLEY. (Common Show) Number of alleys ....

BOWLING ALLEY. Number of alleys ....

CHECKING FACILITY. (a) How many checkers employed .... (b) Are they licensed? ....

COMMON SHOW. Kind of show or Manufacturer's name of game .... No. of games ....

COMMON SHOW RIDES. Complete Item No. 13.

CONCERT. (See Theatrical.)

EMPLOYMENT AGENCY. (a) Number of Placement Employees .... (b) Do you intend to conduct a lodging house? ....

EXPRESS WAGON. (a) How many wagons .... (b) Are all drivers licensed? ....

GARAGE. Complete Item No. 13.

HORSE DRAWN CAB DRIVER. Complete Item No. 13.

JUNK BOAT. (a) How many boats .... (b) Coast Guard Registration Nos. ....

(c) Locations where boats are moored ....

JUNK CART. How many carts? Push .... Horse .... Motor ....

Give names and addresses of dealers with whom you conduct or intend to conduct business.

JUNK SHOP. Kind of Junk handled ....

MINIATURE GOLF COURSE. Number of holes in course ....

MOTION PICTURE THEATRE (INDOOR OR OPEN AIR). Answer item No. 15.

PARKING LOT. Complete Item No. 13.

PING PONG TABLE (Common Show). Number of tables ....

PUBLIC CART. Number of vehicles to be licensed .... Motor .... Horse Drawn ....

Owner of vehicles (Name and address) .... If so, Certificate of Public Convenience issued by the

Number of employees .... Do you transport household goods .... New York State Registration Nos. ....

Public Service Commission: Number .... Expiration Date ....

SHOOTING GALLERY. (a) Type of arms and ammunition used ....

SKEE BALL GAME (Common Show). (a) Number of games .... (b) Name of games ....

SIDE SHOW. Character of show .... ; reply also to item No. 15.

STAND (STOOP LINE OR SMALL) Articles to be sold...........................

    BOOTBLACK. Number of chairs ....

    CURB, EL or SUBWAY STAIRS. (a) Married? .... (b) Dependents .... (c) How long in city? ....

    (d) Physical incapacity..................... (e) Disabled Veteran .... (f) Veteran ....

THEATRICAL. Answer item No. 15 and give name and address of owner ....

    Character of performances ....

OFFICE REPORT

Applicant's previous department record ....

....

Hold any other }   Other licenses at }
License?   these premises

Departmental Reports, Letters, etc.

To	Sent		Received		Action
	Date		Date		
Dept. of Buildings					
Fire Dept.					
Dept. of WSG&E					
Health Dept.					
Police Dept. (F.P.)					
Insp. Div.					
Dept. of Highways					

Pre-Filing Fees: Amount .... Date Received .... Recommended for APPROVAL / DISAPPROVAL

Fee Balance: Amount .... Date Received ....

                                                          Application Clerk

COMMISSIONER'S ACTION

Based on Statements in Application, Reports, Office Report, and any other relevant matter.

.... Date.................. 19 ......

.... Approved   Denied

Applicant Notified: Date .... 19 ....   Director, License Issuance

License Issued: Date .... 19 .... Document No. ....   License Clerk.

City of New York
DEPARTMENT OF CONSUMER AFFAIRS
80 Lafayette Street
New York, N.Y. 10013
566-5599

GENERAL INSTRUCTIONS FOR
FILING APPLICATION FOR LICENSES

CAUTION	The filing of an application does not constitute permission to operate.
FILING	The application must be filed in person.
FALSE INFORMATION	A false answer in the application or a misstatement of fact in any paper submitted in support of the application may result in the denial of an application for an original or renewal license, or may result in cancellation, revocation or suspension of the license after issuance.
CITIZENSHIP	If foreign born, citizenship or declaration of intention to become a citizen is required of all applicants for license as prescribed by Chapter 32, Article A of the Administrative Code. The Naturalization Certificate or permanent Board of Elections personal registration card may be used as proof of citizenship. A declarant for citizenship must exhibit duly authenticated proof of his application for naturalization or the proper certificate of declaration of intention.
AGE	Ordinarily, the applicants must be a least eighteen years of age, but the minimum age varies for certain licenses and permits. The specific license or permit instructions should be consulted. The minimum age requirements are applicable to officers of a corporation.
WORKMEN'S COMPENSATION	Proof of Workmen's Compensation as well as Disability Benefits are required for all employees.
LEASE	Change of ownership applicants must submit a photostatic copy of a lease, bill of sale, contract or other document showing proof of tenancy. In such cases, the previous owner must surrender a current license. Caution: All such leases should be contingent on the granting of the license applied for.
CONVICTION RECORD	You will be required to state convictions for offenses against the law and if you are now under charges for any offenses against the law. You may omit (1) parking and other minor traffic offenses, and (2) any offense which resulted in a finding of juvenile delinquency, youthful offender, wayward minor or person in need of supervision.
INDIVIDUAL APPLICANT	Individuals operating under a trade name must present a certified copy of the trade name certificate filed in the County Clerk's office. Three (3) passport type photos are required of the individual. Fingerprints are required of the individual applicant.
PARTNERSHIP	A partnership conducting business whether or not under a trade name, must submit a certified copy of the partnership certificate filed in the County Clerk's office. Three (3) passport type photos are required of each partner. Fingerprints are required of all partners.
CORPORATIONS	A corporation must furnish a photostatic copy of the filing receipt for the Certificate of Incorporation from the New York State Secretary of State. A corporation from outside New York State must furnish a photostatic copy of its application for authority to do business in New York State from the New York State Secretary of State. Some applications require proof of the election of the corporate officers, and in such cases, there must be filed a copy of the minutes of the corporate meeting electing directors and officers. Photographs are not required of corporate applicants. All officers must be fingerprinted and also any stockholder of ten percent or more of the stock.

Facsimile of:
FORM #LID-2 (10/1/75)

THE CITY OF NEW YORK
DEPARTMENT OF CONSUMER AFFAIRS
80 LAFAYETTE STREET
NEW YORK, N.Y. 10013

SPECIAL NOTICE TO APPLICANTS FOR LICENSES FOR PREMISES
REQUIRING A PLACE OF ASSEMBLY PERMIT
OR CERTIFICATE OF OCCUPANCY

I.   Please be advised that no license will be issued until the
      premises which are the subject of your application have been
      approved by various city agencies.

II.   Requests for certification of approval are transmitted by the
      Department of Consumer Affairs to those agencies involved.

III. In any event, requests will not be transmitted unless you
      present, with your application, either one of the following:

      1. If capacity of premises is 75 or more persons:

          (a) Photostatic copy of current Place of Assembly Permit
               showing that premises may be used for purpose for which
               license is sought, or

          (b) Evidence that Application for Amendment of Place of
               Assembly Permit has been filed for use for which license
               is sought and that required plans have been approved.

      2. If capacity of premises is less than 75 persons:

          (a) Photostatic copy of current Certificate of Occupancy
               showing that premises may be used for purpose for
               which license is sought, or

          (b) Evidence that Application for Amendment of Certificate
               of Occupancy has been filed for use for which license
               is sought and that required plans have been approved.

IV.   Two (2) scale drawings of premises which will indicate general
      size of dance floor, if any; location of bar, tables and other
      facilities and all points of access and/or egress (indicate
      dimensions to the nearest foot). Drawings need not be of
      professional quality.

V.   Your failure to furnish the foregoing may result in serious
      delay in processing your application.

Facsimile of:
Form No. 0I 64 (10/78)

                              Bruce C. Ratner
                              Commissioner

THE CITY OF NEW YORK
DEPARTMENT OF CONSUMER AFFAIRS
80 LAFAYETTE STREET
NEW YORK, N.Y. 10013

IMPORTANT NOTICE TO ALL APPLICANTS FOR CABARET
PUBLIC DANCE HALL, CATERING ESTABLISHMENT
& THEATRE LICENSES

THE FIRE DEPARTMENT of the city of New York has directed that all
applicants submit the following documents with application.

   1. COPY OF FLOOR PLAN WHICH HAS BEEN APPROVED BY THE
       N.Y. CITY DEPT. OF BUILDINGS.

   2. COPY OF PLACE OF ASSEMBLY PERMIT OR CERTIFICATE
       OF OCCUPANCY (ISSUED BY THE BUILDINGS DEPT.)
       WHICH PROVIDES FOR THE USE FOR WHICH THE APPLICATION
       IS INTENDED, i.e. CABARET, DANCE HALL, CATERING
       ESTABLISHMENT OR THEATRE

   3. AFFIDAVIT TO CERTIFY NON-FLAMEABILITY OF DRAPES USED
       ON PREMISES. IF NO DRAPES ARE USED, AFFIDAVIT MUST
       SO STATE.

It is absolutely essential that the above items be included with
application when filed. THE FIRE DEPT. WILL NOT APPROVE ANY APPLI-
CATION WITHOUT THESE ITEMS. Failure to submit the above will result in the undue delay or denial of Application.

                              Bruce C. Ratner
                              Commissioner

Form No.
Rev. 6/78   01A 75

violations

If you are inspected by any of the departments and as a result violations are found, they must be presented to you in writing. Generally you are given anywhere from 24 hours to 30 days in which to comply; only if a gross violation has occurred will you be threatened with immediate shut-down. Compliance really means that you will need to hire the correct licensed professional to remove the violation within that specified period of time. If the inspectors return to check on the violations, you must have proof in writing that you have hired a licensed professional to do the work. It is possible to hire the licensed professional only to file and sign the proper applications for inspection and to supervise the work, with your theatre providing the actual labor.

If the inspectors only tell you what your violations are, then you are not required by law to correct them; but it is wise to do so since they may come back and issue a written violation the next time around.

If there are violations, the Department of Consumer Affairs will also receive information about the violations. When a violation is reported, the theatre should immediately send DCA a letter stating its intention to correct it and then another letter to DCA that it has been corrected. This is done in order to keep the theatre's license application or renewal application from being denied for violations.

These letters should be addressed to:

License Issuance Division
Department of Consumer Affairs
80 Lafayette Street
New York, N. Y. 10013

If you are in need of professional help or advice in correcting a violation, or dealing with the agencies, call the OOBA office for information.

agencies

name and address	phone	services
DEPARTMENT OF BUILDINGS Municipal Building 1 Centre Street (Centre & Chambers) NYC, NY 10007	566-2384	Location of all offices listed under Dept. of Bldg.
Borough Superintendent for Manhattan	566-2387	Questions for Manhattan only. Call Exec. Off. for other boroughs.
Plan Examiner's Office	566-2392	To check eligibility for Place of Assembly Permit. Will help answer questions re: requirements of public assembly space.
Index Room #2012	566-2484	To find out if C of O exists.
Certificate of Occupancy Room #2024	566-2488	Will help with location of C of O. Will give you info. to be used at Plan Desk.
Plan Desk Room #2017	566-2383	Folder on building—classification, last legal use, info. on bldg., violations, drawings, etc. Application for Place of Assembly Permit.
Application for C of O Room #2015	———	To obtain application forms for new C of O.
Executive Office, 120 Wall Street NYC, NY 10007	482-7750	Will channel your call to proper office. General information.
DEPARTMENT OF CITY PLANNING 2 Lafayette Street NYC, NY 10007	566-7600	General information.
Maps and Publications Room #1616	566-7595 566-7596	Questions regarding zoning classifications. Zoning Area Maps for all boroughs. Zoning Handbook. Community District Maps. Community District Fact Books.

DEPARTMENT OF CONSUMER AFFAIRS 80 Lafayette Street, NYC, NY 10007	566-5599	General information.
Licensing	566-5360	Obtain form for license to do business in NYC. Questions answered re: theatres.
DEPARTMENT OF FINANCE Municipal Building 1 Centre Street NYC, NY 10007	566-4451	Location of all offices listed under Dept. of Finance.
Office of Public Information Room #500	566-4984	General information for all boroughs.
Bureau of Real Property Assessment Room #946	566-3532	Information re: assessment for all boroughs.
Manhattan Borough Office	566-3400	Assessor's office for Manhattan. Obtain assessed value of buildings located in Manhattan.
Department of Tax Collection Room #100	566-2467	Information for Manhattan. "In Rem" listing for Manhattan.
DEPARTMENT OF HIGHWAYS 40 Worth Street NYC, NY 10013	566-3683	Information re: permits for awnings, signs and canopies.
Permit Section 51 Chambers Street Room #415	566-4000	Obtain applications for permits here.
DEPARTMENT OF PUBLIC WORKS Bureau of Gas and Electricity Electrical Division Room #2322 Municipal Building 1 Centre Street NYC, NY 10007	———	———
Superintendent of Public Structures	566-3481	General information
Superintendent of Private Structures	566-3387	General information
NEW YORK CITY BOARD OF STANDARDS AND APPEALS 80 Lafayette Street NYC, NY 10013	566-5174	Information on obtaining zoning variances and modifications on zoning requirements.
CITY RECORD SALES OFFICE Municipal Building Room #2213 1 Centre Street NYC, NY 10007	566-2616	Purchase copy of: NYC Electrical Code, NYC Building Code, NYC Fire Prevention Code, NYC Official Directory (listings of all agencies with phone numbers, names, and addresses).

196

publications of interest

The American Theatre Planning Board, Inc. *Theatre Check List*. Middletown: Wesleyan University Press, 1969.

Association of British Theatre Technicians. Roderick Ham, ed. *Theatre Planning*. Toronto: University of Toronto Press, 1972.

Brockett, Oscar G. *The Theatre: An Introduction*. New York: Holt, Rinehart and Winston, Inc., 1974.

Burris-Meyer, Harold, and Cole, Edward C. *Theatres and Auditoriums*. 2nd ed. New York: Reinhold Publishing Corp., 1964.

Burris-Meyer, Harold; Mallory, Vincent; and Goodfriend, Lewis S. *Sound in The Theatre*. 2nd ed. New York: Radio Magazines, Inc., 1964. Distributed by Theatre Arts Books.

Farber, Donald C. *From Option to Opening*. Rev. ed. New York: Drama Book Specialists, 1977.

FEDAPT. *Investigation Guidelines for Setting Up a Not-For-Profit Tax-Exempt Theatre*. New York: Foundation for the Extension and Development of American Professional Theatres, 1978.

Joseph, Stephen. *New Theatre Forms*. New York: Theatre Arts Books, 1968.

Langley, Stephen. *Theatre Management in America: Principle and Practice*. New York: Drama Book Specialists, 1974.

McNamara, Brooks; Rojo, Terry; and Schechner, Richard. *Theatres, Spaces, Environments: 18 Projects*. New York: Drama Book Specialists, 1975.

Mielziner, Jo. *The Shapes of Our Theatre*. New York: Clarkson N. Potter, Inc., 1970.

NYC Dept. of City Planning. *Zoning Handbook*. 3rd ed. New York: NYC Dept. of City Planning, 1976.

Pilbrow, Richard. *Stage Lighting*. New York: Van Nostrand Reinhold Company, 1970.

Ramsey, C. G., A.I.A., and Sleeper, H. R., F.A.I.A. *Architectural Graphic Standards*. New York: John Wiley & Sons, Inc., 1970.

periodicals

TABS. Rank Strand Electric, 32 King Street, Covent Garden, London, WC 2E 8JD, England.

Theatre Crafts. Rodale Press, Inc., 33 East Minor Street, Emmaus, Pa. 18049.

Theatre Design and Technology. United States Institute for Theatre Technology, Inc., 1501 Broadway, New York, N.Y. 10036.

Lighting Dimensions. Lighting Dimensions Magazine, 3900 South Wadsworth, Suite 560, Denver, Colo. 80235.

acknowledgments

Leslie Armstrong, Armstrong Childs Lang Associates
Mike Bailkin and Patricia Zedalis, Stadtmauer & Bailkin
Stanley J. Barth, Barth-Gross Electric Co.
Jay Broad, Performing Arts Foundation of Long Island
    (PAF Playhouse)
Richard Bruno, Department of Cultural Affairs, NYC
Victor Caliandro, Architect; Columbia University; New
    York Landmarks Conservancy
Paula Caplan, City Planning Commission, NYC
Mac Carr, Theatre Technology, Inc.
Nancy Castleman, Fund for the City of New York
Giorgio Cavaglieri, Architect, F.A.I.A.
Donald Checki, Office of Economic Development, NYC
John C. Cimarosa, Association for Recreation
    Management, Inc.
Carol Clark, New York Landmarks Conservancy
Paul Cooper, Department of Consumer Affairs, NYC
Eileen Daly, 42nd Street Local Development
    Corporation
Robert Davis, Jules Fisher Associates, Inc.
Jim Duncan and Hugh Southern, Theatre Development
    Fund
Coco Eiseman, New York State Council on the Arts,
    Architecture and Environmental Arts Program.
Peter M. Forward, Production Arts Lighting, Inc.

Sarah Garretson, Cultural Council Foundation
The Reverend Leland E. Gartrell, Council of Churches
    of NYC
Moe Glickman, Department of Development, NYC
Robert I. Harris, NYC Public Development Corporation
Malcolm Holzman; Hardy, Holzman, Pfeiffer Associates
Herbert Leger, Variety Scenic Studio
Robert Mayers, Mayers & Schiff, Architects Planners
Michael Mehlman, Cultural Assistance Center
Carolyn Meinhardt, Community Board #4, Housing,
    Land-Use and Neighborhood Development, NYC
Nancy Moore, National Endowment for the Arts,
    Planning and Design Program
Jim Morgan, Community Board #15, NYC
Roger Morgan, Roger Morgan Studios, Inc.
Kenneth Morris, Office of Economic Development,
    NYC
Jeremy Nussbaum (OOBA Board Member) and Ivan
    Shapiro; Greenbaum, Wolff & Ernst
Steven Robinson, Steven Robinson Associates
Steven Rossi, Office of Economic Development, NYC
Stephen Somogy
Frederic Vogel, FEDAPT
Volunteer Lawyers For The Arts
Peter Wexler, Designer

theatres

Amas Repertory Theatre—Rosetta LeNoire
Bond Street Theatre Coalition—Patrick Sciarratta
Circle Repertory Company
Colonnades Theatre Lab—Steven Simon
Counterpoint Theatre Company—Howard Green
Drama Committee Repertory Theatre
Ensemble Studio Theatre—Curt Dempster
Hudson Guild Theatre—Craig Anderson
Impossible Ragtime Theatre—Ted Story
Intar (International Arts Relations)
Interart Theatre—Margot Lewitin
Jean Cocteau Repertory—Eve Adamson (OOBA Board
    Member)
Joseph Jefferson Theatre Company—Cathy Roskam
    (OOBA Board Member)
Judson Poets Theatre
Lion Theatre Company—Larry Carpenter
Manhattan Theatre Club—Barry Grove (OOBA Board
    Member) and Robert Buckler
Meat and Potatoes Co.
New York Shakespeare Festival—Bernard Gersten
New York Stageworks—Craig La Plount (OOBA Board
    Member)
The Performance Group—Jim Clayburgh
Playwrights Horizons—Robert Moss (OOBA Board
    Member)
The Proposition Workshop
Roundabout Theatre Company
Shelter West Company
Soho Rep—Marlene Swartz
Theatre for the New City—Crystal Field and George
    Bartenieff
Theatre Off Park
Theatre of the Riverside Church

Special thanks for help with the Profiles to Impossible Ragtime Theatre—Ted Story, Colin O'Leary; Manhattan Theatre Club—Diane de Mailly, Robert Buckler, Barry Grove; Theatre Row—Patricia Zedalis of Stadtmauer & Bailkin.

And to Thomas Kalsky, P.C., consultant on the Codes section of the book; the OOBA staff and associates: Executive Director, Ellen B. Rudolph, and Kimberly S. Myers, Christine Wright, Maggie Schmidt, Wendy Goldman, Mitchell Ivers, Thomas Murphy, Enoch Brady, Carole Cook; Editor, Judy Sagarin, and Graphic Designer, Bob Fitzpatrick; for their concern, and commitment to this project.

199

index

205